Individual Freedom *Selected Works of William H. Hutt*

Edited by SVETOZAR PEJOVICH
and DAVID KLINGAMAN

 Contributions in Economics and Economic History, Number 14

GREENWOOD PRESS
WESTPORT, CONNECTICUT • LONDON, ENGLAND

Library of Congress Cataloging in Publication Data

Hutt, William Harold, 1899-
    Individual freedom.

    (Contributions in economics and economic history ;
no. 14)
    "Bibliography of William Hutt's writings" · p.
    Includes index.
    CONTENTS: Civil rights and young "conserva-
tives."—Unanimity versus non-discrimination (as
criteria for constitutional validity).—Illustration
of Keynesianism. [etc.]
    1. Laissez-faire—Collected works. 2. Keynesian
economics—Collected works. 3. Economic policy—
Collected works. I. Title.
HB95.H85   330.15.'6   75-16965
ISBN 0-8371-8283-2

Library of Congress Catalog Card Number: 75-16965
ISBN: 0-8371-8283-2

First published in 1975

Greenwood Press, a division of Williamhouse-Regency Inc.
51 Riverside Avenue, Westport, Connecticut 06880

Printed in the United States of America

Contents

iii

Introduction

Professor Hutt has spent most of his academic life writing on the ageless problem of power and individual liberty. While his writings should have long been admired by the general scholarly community, they have received less attention from the economics profession than they deserve. One reason is the unfortunate convention which requires that an economist must distinguish himself for some obscure technical specialty before he is "entitled" to the profession's attention for his work in the interstices of economics and philosophy. We hope that this book will help to put Hutt's writings in the proper perspective.

We believe that the selected papers capture the essence of Hutt's contribution to a better understanding of the effects of economic and political power on the allocation of resources, the distribution of income, and the quality of life in general. The selected papers are also highly relevant to the problems of the day. A great advantage of the volume lies in its readability. Professor Hutt uses nontechnical language to present a well-reasoned analysis of the consequences of political coercion and economic power on individual freedom. Thus an intelligent layman should easily and readily follow Hutt's reasoning.

Professor W. H. Hutt was born in London in August 1899. He served in the RFC and the RAF between August 1917 and March 1919, after which he studied at the London School of Economics, University of London. After graduation, he entered the publishing business in 1924 as "personal assistant" to the late Sir Ernest Benn, whom he helped in establishing the British Individualist Movement, initially through The Individualist Bookshop Ltd. He continued to study economics at the London School of Economics as an "occasional student." One product of this period was an article entitled "The Factory System of the Early Nineteenth Century," which was published in *Economica* in 1926 and is still in print in F. A.

Hayek's symposium, *Capitalism and the Historians* (University of Chicago Press).

In March 1928 he left business for academic life at the University of Cape Town. Three years later, he was appointed professor and dean of the Faculty of Commerce, succeeding Professor (now Sir) Arnold Plant, who had been invited to fill the Chair of Commerce at the London School of Economics. During his thirty-seven years at the University of Cape Town, Hutt lectured on the economics of business administration ("commerce"), public administration, and the philosophy of business. After World War II, conforming to trends elsewhere in the world, he guided the development of graduate work (then called postgraduate work) in business administration and the establishment of a Postgraduate School of Business Administration, of which he was the first director.

He went to the United States in December 1965 to accept an invitation to serve as visiting professor of economics at the University of Virginia for the year 1966. Since then he has served in the same capacity at Rockford College, Illinois; Wabash College, Indiana; and Texas A&M University. In addition, he has served as distinguished visiting professor at California State University (Hayward) and at the University of Dallas, Irving, where he is teaching at present. From 1969 to 1971, he was visiting research fellow at the Hoover Institution at Stanford.

ACKNOWLEDGMENTS

The editors are grateful to the *Economic Journal, Economica, Modern Age, South African Journal of Economics*, Institute for Economic Affairs, Macmillan Publishing Co., and Van Nostrand Co. for permissions to reprint William Hutt's works published in this volume, and to the Institute for Humane Studies for financial assistance and moral encouragement.

part I ● *THE CONSEQUENCES OF INDIVIDUAL LIBERTY*

1 • Civil Rights and Young "Conservatives"

I recently addressed a large private conference under the auspices of a student group of "conservative" or "libertarian" persuasion. Students from many universities and leading academic economists, sociologists, jurists, and historians attended. The topic discussed was "Civil Rights." Possibly because of the privacy of the occasion, the exchange of arguments and opinions occurred with the utmost frankness.

The general impression I formed, as a temporary sojourner in the United States, was that these young "conservatives" were burningly sincere, realistic in their approach, independent-minded and intellectually courageous. Although no simple consensus emerged from the discussion, it was demonstrated beyond doubt that the great majority of those present were unequivocally sympathetic to Negro aspirations. This impression clashes radically with what I had gathered from the press. But the fact seems to be that most of those in the academic world who find it necessary to call themselves "conservatives" or "libertarians"[1] appear convinced that the Negro's claim to full civil rights has the highest moral substance.

Admittedly, all present on this occasion were contemptuous of the current official civil rights policy which was held to be defective because its primary motivation has been immediate electoral advantage. They deplored also the methods commonly adopted by demonstrators under the civil rights banner, and the strategy of some so-called "liberal" organizations which cash in on every genuine protest movement or expression of grievances. Some of the

Reprinted with permission from *Modern Age* 10 (1966).

civil rights leaders were alleged to be cynically sacrificing the Negroes' interests for ulterior political or careerist purposes. And as an outside observer, I can testify that when "leftist" initiatives infiltrate in the field of color relations, the objective all too often seems to be the spreading of hatred and suspicion, not the achievement of understanding between races.[2]

My own contribution to the gathering was a comparison of the not altogether dissimilar situation in my own country (the Republic of South Africa). I explained the origins of injustices to which the non-whites of South Africa have for long been subject; and general discussion suggested that, in several respects, the real disabilities of the American Negro population can be traced to the identical ultimate causes. Yet these causes (recognized, I believe, in the light of the debate in which I shared, by most social scientists or economists of "conservative" leanings) are virtually never *mentioned*, let alone freely discussed in the press.

Before developing my thesis, it is necessary to refer to four differences between the color problems of my country and those of the United States. (1) In South Africa about four-fifths of the population are non-whites. In the United States only about one-twelfth are non-whites. (2) In South Africa the Africans (who make up about 11 million of a total population of about 16 million) have mostly not yet freed themselves from all tribal influences, whereas in the United States, Negro culture—although possessing some distinct sociological attributes—is essentially part of a unified American social heritage. (3) The non-whites of South Africa (as a group) must be described as very poor by modern world standards (although not badly off if the material standards of the whole African continent are the criterion), whereas the *average* real income of the Negroes of the United States is impressively high by world standards (although still very much below the average for white Americans).[3] (4) The Negroes appear to be treated with courtesy and consideration by the majority of white Americans. A similar claim cannot yet be made for the attitude of the majority of white South Africans toward the Coloureds and Indians, still less toward the Africans.

These and other differences do not prevent us, however, from recognizing that in both countries, and for not very different reasons, non-whites are condemned to inferiority of productive opportunities, income, status, and respect. The reasons are rooted deeply in history. Yet many of the whites of this generation must share responsibility for perpetuation of the inferiority; for there are *deliberately imposed man-made barriers to equality of economic opportunity—barriers which are, I suggest, by all odds the most important ultimate cause of inequality of civil rights.*

In my country, the survival of economic injustices to non-whites has been due to governmental appeasement of a white proletariat. Because this proletariat has been no more enlightened nor generous than most others, governments have found it politically expedient to demonstrate to the enfranchised masses—by conspicuous action—that the non-whites are being kept down and the privileges of the whites preserved.

The *spirit* of this repression in South Africa is disclosed in two acts which are popularly known as the "color bar acts" (officially, the *Mines and Works Acts* of 1911 and 1926). Under these acts, no African may be employed in (or trained for) skilled or responsible work in mining and connected industries. They were passed in order to secure good industrial relations among the white miners following a number of violent strikes which had involved sabotage and the shedding of blood. The two "color bar acts" may be regarded as the greatest triumph in the life of the labor union leader who had been most prominent in the strikes, one W. H. Andrews. It is not without significance that he was to become, shortly afterwards, Secretary of the Communist Party of South Africa and later its President.

The "color bar acts" embody the principle which has become known as "job reservation." Of recent years, its application has been conspicuously extended. There is now quite a list of simple jobs which, in specified districts, only non-whites are permitted to perform. In the Cape, for instance, only whites may work as elevator attendants or as traffic police. And there are other ways of imposing racial discriminations in order to placate the white proletariat. For instance, residential segregation (under the "Group Areas" legislation) may force non-white employees to live further from their work places, or non-white traders to move their stores away from the districts which their customers frequent. And again, "influx control" can be used to keep Africans from certain urban employments.

Now blatant discriminations of this type do not, I think, exist in the United States. But open color bars are important only as indicators of *the spirit* which tends to dominate race relations when the apparatus of government can be used for sectional advantage. *As restraints on equality of opportunity—job reservations and the like—they are of almost negligible importance.*

The serious color bars are imcomparably more subtle. In South Africa, they were introduced through what was known as the "civilized labor policy," following a coalition (in 1924) between a Labour Party (doctrinally allied to the British Labour Party of the early 'twenties') and a Nationalist Party imbued with the maxim which had been enshrined in the Constitutions of the old Transvaal and Free State Republics that there was to be no equality in Church or State between white and black. Under the "civilized-labor" regime, the chief method relied upon to keep the non-whites in economic inferiority was simply exclusion of competition in the labor market, through insistence upon "the rate for the job," i.e., what is sometimes called the principle of "the standard rate" or "equal pay for equal work."

Chiefly through the Industrial Conciliation Act, 1924 (which enhanced labor union power), and the Wage Act (1925), non-whites were prevented from discounting their initial inefficiency for industrial employments. As employees, they were inferior in respect of (a) nutrition, (b) social background, (c) education (general and technical), (d) the prejudices of the whites against working side by side with them, and (e) the additional costs incurred when they were employed (for it was part of the "civilized labor policy" to require separate entrances to work-places, separate cloakrooms, etc.).

The simple insistence upon "equal pay for equal work" has throughout maintained an obstacle to racial equality of opportunity which has been immeasurably more oppressive than all the other color bars, including unfair use of the apprenticeship system. And one of the reasons why this method of repression has been so effective has been the fact that well-meaning "liberal" idealists everywhere have welcomed it. Occasionally, shrewd leaders of the "Coloureds"[4] have perceived the harm which "the rate for the job" has wrought on their people. For example, the greatest leader the "Coloureds" ever had was the late Dr. Abdurahman who, in the Minority Report of the Cape Coloured Commission of 1937, pleaded for the right of the non-whites to under-cut established wage-rates. Until this could be done, he said, the advancement of the group of which he was a member[5] would be held back permanently.

What confuses so many idealists is the indisputable truth that, under any defensible wage system, there is a powerful tendency to establish equality of remuneration for output of equal quantity and quality, irrespective of the race or color of the supplier. But economic justice so ensured is *the consequence of* economic freedom. *Imposition of* "the standard rate," like any other suppression of the right to compete, defeats the purpose of those who seek justice in distribution.

The truth is, as I have spent almost my whole academic life in reiterating, the free market is color blind and race blind. When we buy a product, we do not ask "What was the color of the person who made this?" We ask, "Is this good value for money?" Hence there is a strong profit incentive to search out and, as far as possible, offer more productive and better-paid employment opportunities to members of any races which have been excluded from them by custom or prejudice. There is an equally strong motive to break down color bars imposed by labor unions or government wage-fixations. In short, what is known as "competitive capitalism" gives rise to powerful pressures against economic injustices of racial origin (as, indeed, against *all* forms of social injustice). On the other hand, "socialism" (in the sense of the centralization of economic power) or what Americans have come to call "liberalism," is the chief channel through which color injustices appear to be perpetuated.

For instance, to take the case of the United States, not only does minimum wage legislation seem to me to have been effective in preventing a more rapid development of the industrial South, but successive governments, confronted with the fact that the labor unions are extremely powerful in elections, appear to carefully refrain from taking any *effective* steps to secure the right to a larger proportion of the jobs in the highly paid artisan trades for the Negro population generally.[6] That capitalism has not yet succeeded in eradicating all color injustices is due to ultimate power residing in governments, while the so-called "public sector" has been growing.

Today the free market has been shackled in most countries because governments can intimidate managements, particularly those of the big corporations. Indeed, in my own country many leading business men have become deplorably subservient toward the powers that be—almost grovelling, as one confessed not long ago in my presence (after a particularly obsequious speech of welcome to a minister at an association meeting). To serve the interests of their stockholders best, managements must today think more about what the politicians would like, and less about their customers' needs. And in all countries where governmental agencies may legally bestow favors and impose penalties, this power can be used and is often used to weaken effective political opposition.

Because the Negroes seem to have suffered most under these trends, it has puzzled me a great deal to explain to myself why their leaders have not allied themselves wholly with the "conservative" minorities in the Democratic and Republican Parties. I am inclined to believe that this is due almost entirely to skillful exploitation by the "liberal" politicians of the Negroes' resentment at their inferiority of status. It is easier to arouse anger at contempt for color than to explain the causes of economic repression, out of which that contempt originates.

During many years of thought and observation of race relations in South Africa, I have become convinced that inequality of status and respect between races is derived from inequality of economic rights. To some extent, of course, it has appeared as a vicious circle. But in spite of the fact that the immediate effect of any weakening of barriers to the acquisition of industrial skills by non-whites has usually meant an intensification of prejudice on the part of those who have felt their privileges to be threatened, nearly all of us tend to respect those who can display, in a manner which does not unduly offend custom, the outward symbols of material success.

Whatever the origins of equality of respect between races, all have to recognize that the achievement of this mutual respect is vital if people of any multi-racial community are to live together amicably. In South Africa the hope of the present Government has been to find some sort of solution in segregation, i.e., "apartheid" or "separate development." If we are tempted to think that *compulsory* segregation is a way out, however, we must remind ourselves that members of races with inferior status most often *wish* to associate with races of higher status, and will quietly do so where possible. When whites say, as they are all too apt to do, "the non-whites no more wish to associate with us than do we with them," it is wishful thinking. Of course, if the consequences of one race attempting to associate with another are made unpleasant, it will not happen. But I am now concerned with a psychological factor that no realistic reformer dares ignore.

Everyone would surely admit that, if the different races *could* be accorded their own territories, with natural resources and man-made capital allocated according to some acceptable principle of justice, a superficial solution would have been found. Segregation and discrimination are, it has been justly claimed, separate concepts. The latter implies injustice while the former does not. But even if separate development in a formerly integrated country had been sought with some attempt at a just division of that country's resources (and this cannot be claimed in the case of South Africa), the feeling would have remained with the presently under-privileged races that the wish to segregate was itself an insult—a suggestion that darkness of skin has to be regarded like an infectious disease.

The non-white peoples of my country are smoldering at the continued slur which, they think, attaches to their color. It is useless for the whites to deny that there is any stigma when their actions suggest the opposite. And sheer white arrogance sometimes aggravates the position, an arrogance which tends (in South Africa at any rate) to be greater the lower the intelligence or economic status of the whites, while resentment at the slur tends to be greatest in those non-whites who have risen most above the rest in income and education. The mere wish to segregate may, not unnaturally, strike the cultured non-whites as inherently insulting.

Such feelings similarly complicate the problem of free association. It is true (and this truth cannot be over-stressed) that the right of *free* association implies the right *not to associate* as well as to *associate*. In any free society, a club should have the right to restrict its membership to, say, women, tee-totallers, veterans, Negroes, Baptists, Jews, or whites. Equally, clubs which wish to admit both whites and Negroes should, under the same rule, have the *effective* right to do so, and be protected from private coercion of the Ku Klux Klan type.

Judging from what I have observed (in the admittedly very different conditions of my own country), however, it is almost certain that more Negroes would like to join white clubs than whites would like to join Negro clubs. And will that not remain the position until equality of status has somehow been established? In view of past indignities, and antipathies based on color prejudice, the gesture of admitting acceptable Negroes, conspicuously and *voluntarily* adopted by at least *some* leading white clubs, could do much to dispel racial bitterness. Might not "conservatives" encourage this? Compulsion, even if *called* "persuasion," would defeat the whole purpose. There may perhaps be other, even better, ways of proving equality of respect by those who feel that respect. But can we rationally expect Negroes to accept the right of freedom of association in its fullest sense (with its implication of the right *not* to associate) unless the whites can offer them unchallengeable evidence that they are not regarded as social lepers?[7]

There remains one other point of importance. While segregation does not necessarily mean *discrimination* (which was well defined at the conference as "the use of criteria for the treatment of people which are not relevant to the purpose or task"), in practice it all too often *does* mean discrimination.

Thus, in South Africa, because the Coloureds, the Indians, and the Africans have long been confined to segregated schools, they have, on the whole, had to be contented with unquestionably inferior education. The almost insoluble difficulty of achieving "separate but equal" facilities may well make assurances that segregation does not mean inferior treatment appear to the non-whites as hypocrisy.

In stressing the reasonableness of resentments which the Negro (particularly in the middle class) may harbor, I must not belittle the really remarkable American achievement in race relations in this century. That achievement strikes any South African as impressive, in spite of the probability that fomentation of racial violence will continue for some years.[8] For instance, an African from my country would be astonished at the courtesy and respect with which the whites would address him. And even in a "southern" state like Virginia, Negroes of both sexes work side by side with whites in obvious harmony, mutual respect, and friendship (especially in occupations in which labor unions are weak or absent). That is proof of the spirit which *could* prevail in all human relations.

It seems to me that most young "conservatives" support the Negro in so far as his demands for full civil rights are concerned; they sympathize with his attitudes toward surviving denials of respect for race; they realize that any hopes of a dissolution of racial resentments depend on conservative initiatives; and that to succeed they—the conservatives—will have to be imaginative, realistic, and less casuistic than most contemporary politicians. I accordingly now put to the young conservatives the following proposition. *Whenever the Negro has been allowed to compete on terms of equality in sports, he has, through his achievements, commanded the respect of all. I suggest therefore that the human side of the color problem will be solved if the Negro can be secured a similar right to compete in the economic sphere.* I forecast that, within two decades of the repeal of all minimum wage-rates and the outlawing of all acts of enforcement of the "rate for the job" by labor unions, not only will the aggregate flow of wages have been greatly increased and full employment secured without inflation, but the Negro will have experienced incomparably more rapid economic progress (relatively and absolutely) than at any time in the past.[9] Remember, the free market is color blind.

My advice to the young American conservatives is, then, that they should face objectively the issues to which I have referred, but concentrate first and foremost on exposing the origins of the Negro's most serious injustice, namely factors which restrain his ability to compete—to acquire marketable skills and develop the qualities needed for leadership in business and industry. And here "the rate for the job" is the crucial restraint. As I have already insisted, all other perpetuations of historically-determined racial injustices are negligible in comparison.[10] If the conservatives really understood this and could communicate their understanding, they would find every intelligent and disinterested Negro drawn to their ranks.

United States' "liberals" are unanimous in their condemnation of South Africa; yet they can be shown to be approving for the United States what are basically the same economic policies and the same labor union practices. Of course, American "liberals" cherish ideals of the common rights of man— ideals which the white proletarians of South Africa reject. Both those ideals are equally cherished—and held with greater consistency—by most of the American "conservatives" I have met.

Suppose, then, the "conservatives" were prepared boldly to announce a program of effective steps toward the gradual achievement of complete racial equality of opportunity in the economic sphere. They could then sincerely charge the "liberals" with tolerating the prolongation of Negro inferiority. For how many "liberals" would really be prepared to reform the system which at present denies the Negro the full right to discount the historical, sociological, and psychological impediments to more skilled and responsible forms of employment?

The enemies of this policy I am suggesting will be firstly the labor-union bosses, the total effect of whose activities has so far been to slow down the rate at which technological and managerial achievements have been raising the real earnings of their members. Secondly, hostility may be expected from those politicians who have a powerful vested interest in the continuance of actual or apparent racial injustice. As an economist of world repute remarked at the conference, "if it had not been for the civil rights issue, the Left (in the United States) would have been bankrupt." Thirdly, resistance will come from reds in pink clothing, extremist liberals dedicated to the exacerbation of mistrust and the fostering of racial strife. As the barriers to Negro competition are broken down, they can be expected to turn on greater and greater pressure to frustrate the process. Through smear campaigns, misrepresentation of motives, and similar tactics (which they often *seem* to perform as an allotted task in the cold war) they will try desperately to sabotage any such program.

There are those who believe that it was *because* Welensky was actually showing the world (in his words) "a splendid concept in multi-racial living and nation building" in the short-lived Federation of Rhodesia and Nyasaland, and the fact that his policy had "galvanised into dynamic life the economic possibilities of this area and raised the standard of living of all its inhabitants,"[11] that enormous hostility was aroused from the British reds and their sentimental followers. But certainly a pusillanimous British "conservative" Government then thought it expedient to bring to an end Welensky's program of deliberately sharing the heritage of the West with the Africans. In doing so, the British destroyed what appears superficially to have been the most remarkable experiment that mankind has yet witnessed in the achievement of good relations in a racially complex country.

But "liberals" are a mixed lot. Some of the most active are genuine, dedicated, and naive. The young conservative must aim, with pertinacious patience, at converting the sincere. He will often be exasperated at the rigidity of their stereotypes and maddened by the insincerity, casuistry, and unscrupulousness of many of their leaders. That is his challenge.

Notes

1. Because the word "liberal" has been stolen by those who are hostile to what used to be known as "liberalism."

2. Demonstrations in the form of processions may have a defensible purpose, but they may be used to incite violent retaliations and to create emotional barriers to intergroup sympathy.

3. Because Negroes mostly find employment in work of relatively low productivity and remuneration. Negroes are, however, rapidly entering better paid trades where labor unions have been unable to bar the way, e.g., in white-collar pursuits.

4. The "Coloureds" of South Africa are half-castes. They number about $1\frac{1}{2}$ million out of a total population of 16 million. "Asians," mostly Indians, number about $\frac{1}{2}$ million.

5. Actually, Dr. Abdurahman was a member of a subgroup of the "Coloureds," namely, the Malays (Moslems). But he was regarded as a leader of the "Coloureds" generally. The cortege at his funeral was the largest in South African history.

6. It has been suggested to me that piecemeal action against racial exclusiveness in labor unions will be taken only when there is considerable propaganda advantage to be gained therefrom.

7. In case this sentence should be quoted out of context in my country, I can usefully refer to an experience which will put my strong words into due perspective. I

recently attended a basketball game at Charlottesville, Virginia (where the Negro problem could be supposed to be acute) between a champion Negro team and a mixed team. An enormous crowd, mainly white, not only applauded the skill of the players but cheered heartily each of the famous Negro players as they were introduced at the beginning of the game. White Americans seem proud of their Negro sportsmen. I do not think that political campaigns have done much, if anything at all, to encourage the emergence of this admirable spirit. In my country, the power of the State has been used to prohibit the mixing of whites and nonwhites on sportsfields.

8. Some present at the conference placed chief responsibility for continued violence on inflammatory speeches, for electoral purposes, by top rulers and officials (harping on the ''guilt'' of the whites generally and the ''oppression'' of the blacks generally).

9. Unless (as I personally do not believe) he should have been held back by inborn defects of intelligence and character.

10. Some present at the conference referred to unemployment pay and public assistance as causes of the demoralization of large members of the poorest Negroes (manifested in exceptionally high unemployment, welfare dependency, desertion, and crime rates). Most disinterested sociologists recognize that ''doles'' in various forms have been a primary cause of the demoralization of laboring classes in this century. The condition is relevant to the present context because it militates against the more early emergence of equality of respect. But in the great majority of cases, the ''rate for the job'' is mainly responsible, as it closes openings through which the less fortunate can strive to qualify themselves for more remunerative kinds of work.

11. The leftists succeeded in leaving the impression that all the benefits were going to the whites, which was far from true. Certainly, there were surviving privileges—chiefly conferred through labor unions of the traditional type. But when the experiment was suppressed, the ''supremacist'' elements were losing to those who saw the inevitable need to share economic and political power on a nonracial foundation.

2 • *Unanimity Versus Non-Discrimination (As Criteria For Constitutional Validity)*

The doctrinal evolution which led, early in this century, to the gradual substitution of the term 'economics' for 'political economy' can by no means be thought of as a wholly beneficial specialisation. Indeed, among the problems which arise in the study of issues in which economic science and political science overlap are some of the most difficult as well as the most vital in the era which appears to be emerging. During the last decade, several works of importance have been published devoted to analysis of these issues. They are all broadly concerned with alternative yet complementary ways in which man's objectives may be sought, namely, *via* centralised, governmental decision-making (whether democratically controlled or undemocratic) and *via* democratic consumers' sovereignty (i.e., *via* 'free' markets). These studies have, in other words, concentrated attention upon two distinct and very different methods of exercising social discipline upon those who determine resource use—through governments (possibly disciplined by the ballot box) or through business entrepreneurs (disciplined by the loss-avoidance, profit-seeking sanctions).

Reprinted with permission from *South African Journal of Economics* 34 (1966).

The Calculus of Consent[1] (from now on to be called 'the *C of C*), by James M. Buchanan and Gordon Tullock (from now on to be called 'the authors') is the latest major study in this field. It has shown the market and the ballot box (that is, individual action and collective action) to be alternative machinery for responding to the economic preferences of individuals. In doing so, it has directed attention to the conditions under which governments may be wisely entrusted with the powers their function requires—that is, to the formulation of 'rules for making rules.'

These developments may be regarded as re-creating 'political economy' or what might be called, to avoid misunderstanding, 'politico-economics.' In the words of a recent contributor in the field, W. H. Riker, they have been 'remaking the field of political theory.'[2] So-called political scientists have usually been, suggests Riker, either historians of ideas or literary critics lacking the power of rigorous analysis, with the consequence that "most contemporary political theory has been produced by politicians and journalists."[3] In spite of an element of exaggeration in so sweeping a generalisation, it is true that the problems most urgently needing solution in the intellectual discipline Riker disparages, are those located where the two territories (economics and political science) meet on common ground. And these problems demand consideration of factors in the handling of which the political scientist who lacks a rigorous training in economics *is* ill-equipped.

Of the recent contributions in which the two disciplines find contact, it is the *C of C* which has had the greatest impact.[4] Published early in 1962, it has been reviewed with respect, and its importance recognised, by economists and political scientists of standing, some of whom seem to shrink from its implications, whilst others welcome these implications. The appearance of a paper-backed edition has prompted the present writer to attempt an assessment—a consideration of some of the criticisms to which the book has so far been subjected and a development of its principal thesis.

The scope of the *C of C* led the authors originally to contemplate the title, *An Economic Theory of Political Constitutions* (p. 13). This would have been a more informative description. It was rejected on semantic grounds, Marxist usage having clouded the usual connotation of 'economic' in this context. The aim has been to analyze the rationale of voting rules in the choice of voting rules to find an answer to the question, "What set of rules *should* the fully rational individual . . . seek to achieve if he recognizes that the approval of such rules must embody actual agreement among his fellows?" (p. 312).

The authors' approach to the task they assumed has been strikingly detached and original. In order to discern what is crucial, they have resorted, with rare intellectual tenacity for the field studied, to limited but explicit assumptions about the nature of the State and the nature of the individuals who employ it. Largely because of the independence of its methods, the present writer has found the *C of C* a rewarding but rather difficult book. As it is concerned with the formulation of rules for making rules, it had necessarily to be individualistic in approach. The whole *raison d'être* of a constitution is to prevent officials, or elected rulers, or certain sections of the electorate who have exceptional voting strength, from using the machinery of the State to obtain some privilege—some differential advantage; and when we fix our attention on the problem of what a constitution *ought* to be, we are, as the authors themselves put it, viewing the State as 'an artifact,' something which can be fashioned to fulfil desired purposes, or refashioned to fulfil its intended purposes better. Is it not self-evident that these purposes can only be those of the individuals who, if the constitution functions well, are thereby protected against possible discrimination?

Yet in an appreciative discussion of the *C of C*, Anthony Downs, who is one of the pioneers in the recent movement to bring the economic and political (voting) aspects of human action into perspective, objects to the individualistic approach. He describes the authors' recognition of the impossibility of conceiving of utility functions for the community as a whole (or for groups of persons) as a 'restrictive axiom.'[5] But it is, we suggest, no *axiom*. Certainly the authors' handling of the issue may well leave the impression that they regard it as such, or as a simplifying (but otherwise arbitrary) assumption; for they describe themselves at the outset as rejecting *without argument* the idealist notion (developed mainly by German philosophers) of an organic State with its own valuation schedules and motivations, as part of which the individual is alone capable of self-realisation.[6]

The individualistic method of the *C of C* is, however, neither restrictive nor truly axiomatic. The authors have not adopted their 'methodologically individualistic' (p. 3) approach through mere whim or prejudice.[7] The boot is on the other foot. In the modern world we are all conditioned by innumerable influences towards thinking of some vaguely conceived, mystical common good, some 'national interest' which is in no way compounded of the benefits of the private individuals who make up the community or nation. Unusual insights alone allow us to perceive that notions of the collective advantage which are not derived from concepts of individual advantage have no meaning. Of course, we know that in practice when 'the national benefit' is appealed to in justification of policy, all too frequently what is really meant is the good of a ruling government, or the good of an electorally powerful group. Without explicitly making this point (and the failure to do so may have been a tactic of inspired exposition), the authors have simply shown the meaninglessness of social utility notions which do not reflect individual utilities.

Supported by this understanding, the authors conceive of the objectives of individuals being sought not only through their own efforts and property, and through intermediaries (markets), but through the State, collectively. Viewing the process of human action in this way clarifies their purpose, namely, to determine the conditions under which the decision-makers who act in the name of the State may truly seek the ends preferred by the individuals they represent.

Curiously enough, Downs himself shows that the acceptable concept of social advantage is indeed *clarified* by analysis built on the so-called axiom that he has questioned. Thus he recognizes that the authors have constructed "an impressive structure of useful analysis" upon the thesis that universal consent alone can be accepted as the "true measure of 'betterness' for any social action",[8] and he describes their demonstration that cooperation to determine the distribution of the benefits of co-ordinative action decided collectively can win the required consent, as "a refreshing shift from the common view that A's political gain is necessarily B's loss."[9] But it seems to the present writer that, when questions of compensation and taxation of betterment arise (and it is really such questions which are concerning Downs), it is solely through a rigorous individualistic approach that a policy of central planning (e.g., town planning) for the 'common good' can be thought out with any measure of self-consistency.

Let us consider the position when the development of communications demands expropriation of sites and buildings. The problem of compensation is then inescapable. Moreover, if fundamental institutional changes appear to be the general advantage, the payment of compensation to those whose 'established expectations' are adversely affected may be wisely treated as part of the costs of progress.[10] Such an insight is the fruit of reasoning *developed from* the 'individualistic' approach: it is not an insight which that approach hinders or prevents.

The *C of C* is *submitted* as what might be called a 'theoretical' model, although the questions on which it can help us to think with consistency are those which can be recognised in actual contemporary political controversies. Now the assumptions of such a model need not be realistic. The immediate purpose of purely theoretical constructions is not to give us a final answer to any of the questions we are investigating but to assist us in obtaining conceptual clarity. Reality has still to be observed or reobserved. A 'theoretical model' cannot be used as a practical tool, i.e., for dealing with the problems of the actual world, unless a careful assessment of observable or undisputed relevant facts as a whole establishes its adequacy. Such an assessment is itself model-making on a *different plane* rather than of a *different kind*. It is all a question of degree of simplification through abstraction. In 'realistic models' we must still conceive of the data in those simplified terms in which the infinitely complex, heterogeneous actuality of things has been reduced to a form in which it is intelligible. But the summarised facts, prédictions and relationships so envisaged (which constitute 'realistic models') can include no *unrealistic* assumptions except those due to the limitations of the human mind or made necessary by the time factor—the need for prompt understanding (in thought as well as action).

Turning now to the *C of C*, we do not feel sure that *all* the simplifying assumptions which it has been thought desirable to make (in the 'theoretical model') actually do facilitate thought. We refer particularly to the postulate that the individuals envisaged in the model are motivated by self-interest and are rationally seeking to maximise their utility. The authors recognise that this is 'the most controversial part' of their analysis (p. 312). But is it a *necessary* part? We suggest that exposition would have been improved and that none of the tentative conclusions reached would have had to be changed in any important respect if the authors had built on unchallengeable realistic assumptions about the nature of men, i.e., if (in their basic thinking) they had viewed individual decision-makers as we know them to be—affected by whim, fashion, greed, concern for the welfare of others, and usually not thinking it worth the effort to calculate carefully whether one aim, or line of action taken to achieve it, is perfectly consistent with other aims and the means taken to achieve them. The only simplifying assumption about individual motivation which is really essential for the 'methodological individualism' of the authors' approach is that people are continually expressing preference about ends (altruistic or egoistic) for the achievement of which the means are scarce and hence cost-bearing, and choosing among different ways of employing their efforts, skills, knowledge, and material resources (individually or collectively owned) to fulfil their preferred ends.

Viewing the individual in this way requires no ethical judgment about whether any particular conduct is egoistic or altruistic.[11] Nor is any assumption about the individual's rationality necessary (as H. G. Manne, quoting Alchian and Becker in support, has also contended).[12] We repeat that in our opinion the unnecessary assumptions adopted do not in any way weaken the force of the general theses enunciated; but they play into the hands of carping critics and they do hinder the student, especially as the authors do not rely on their stated assumptions with complete consistency (partly because they switch often from 'theoretical' to 'realistic' models).

For instance several reviewers regard—understandably but wrongly—the basic assumption of the *C of C* to be that, in Meade's words, "the individual citizen is wholly selfish in his behaviour in the voting booth and in the market place."[13] Yet the authors claim, almost at the outset, that "the representative individual in our model may be egoist or altruist or any combination thereof." Their basic assumption at this stage is simply that "individuals are likely to have different aims and purposes . . .", i.e., that their interests may be expected to "differ for reasons other than those of ignorance" (p. 4).

If the authors had strictly adhered to this simple behavioural assumption alone, they would certainly have eased the study burden for some at least of their readers. But they turn early to more unrealistic postulates, even to the extent of holding that a relationship is not purely economic when one party to a transaction takes into account the interests of the other. We see no justification whatsoever for such a conception of 'economic.' Thus, the possibility that a doctor may decide to work in the slums or as a missionary in a primitive land—at a much lower income than he could obtain elsewhere—because of his concern for the material well-being of the poor or for the spiritual well-being of the heathen, no more restricts the individualistic method than does the fact that an entertainer may choose his profession partly because of the pleasure he obtains from giving pleasure. When a person achieves the happiness of the other party to a transaction as one of his objectives, he is contributing to the 'utility' he wins from the deal. Individuals expressing their preferences and exercising choice in respect of means may, if we wish, be *described* as 'maximising their utility,' provided we recognise that, in successfully seeking the good of others, when that is what they prefer to do, they are equally 'maximising their own utility.'

The *observed* selfishness of groups to which the authors refer (p. 300), could be used to justify assumptions *chosen for their realism.* The authors could say, that is, "We do not assume that most persons and groups are egoistic in order to simplify the argument or facilitate exposition, but because this is an indisputable fact and must be accepted as part of any *realistic* model." But they do not *need* this assumption to prove their thesis against critics who might argue that the obvious altruism of many other persons and groups invalidates the whole case of the *C of C.* The evidence of undeniable egoism they present merely constitutes powerful support for the proposition that human institutions (whether controlled socially through the market or through the ballot) cannot be wisely fashioned on an assumption of universal altruism. This *is*, of course, exactly what the authors have shown.[14]

R. S. Milne criticises both the theoretical and the realistic models in saying, "The authors are not convincing when they attempt to justify their 'behavioural assumptions' by suggesting that they can be refuted only if we should observe 'single groups deciding unilaterally to give up special privilege legislation' and similar odd behaviour."[15] Milne would like quite different assumptions because he sees (he thinks) the facts differently. He holds that the real problem arises rather because "less well organised groups, or individuals, may not act whole-heartedly *in favour* of their interests, in the sense of being fully informed, rational and seeking to maximise utility."[16] His meaning is, if our interpretation is correct, that were individuals or unorganised groups rational, they would organise themselves for some form of collective action to serve their private interests. If organised, they might, through political pressures or the private use of coercive power, remove the privileges which had been militating against their interests. But the possibility so envisaged in no way conflicts with the argument of the *C of C.* The authors' thesis is rather, we suggest, that if under-privileged groups *were* "fully informed, rational and seeking the maximisation of their utility," they would be *more likely* to succeed in their efforts to reduce, through political activity, the burden on them of the privilege of others.

The authors claim that they have at times "referred to certain institutional facts that seemed to lend support to the theoretical model" (p. 299). We should say that they are actually thinking with realistic models throughout. Consider, for example, the shrewd observation which has prompted their assertion that whilst ethical principles have found expression in the stress laid on "the importance of generality in the distribution of the tax burden. . . , no such principles have guided the distribution of expenditure among the several possible uses'' (p. 164). This is an empirically based and highly relevant generalisation about the nature of governments under contemporary constitutional arrangements.

When appropriate, they warn that their theoretical constructions are probably inapplicable, in phrases such as: ''There seems to be decisive empirical evidence that individuals do not behave as the above argument would indicate'' (p. 192). More frequently, however, the conclusions drawn from their intendedly abstract models will be recognised—by the detached or sympathetic reader—to be directly relevant to the world we know. This can be illustrated by their demonstration of how, in the light of a game theory model, there are no effective limits to resource wastage under majority rule, because ''any project yielding general benefits, quite independently of cost considerations, will be supported by the dominating majority if they are successful in imposing the full tax financing of the project on the shoulders of the minority'' (p. 165).[17] In spite of the abstractness of the construction which leads to this inexorable conclusion, it brings home forcibly to students whose attention is fixed on the functioning of contemporary political institutions, the dangers inherent in unrestrained majority decision. Moreover, the game theory model establishes, in the phrase just quoted, a general principle for interpretation of the modern trend (an observable trend) away from 'general,' i.e., non-discriminatory legislation, and towards 'special,' i.e., privilege-conferring legislation.

Nevertheless it is in respect of the simple *applicability* of the conclusions reached that the greatest risk of misunderstandings arise. For example, in considering what the situation would be if individuals *could* be assumed to be perfectly rational beings, each endeavouring, by careful calculation, to optimise the benefits flowing from the combination of his energies, knowledge, skills and property, the authors are not asking the reader to suppose that people *are* indeed as rational as that. Similarly, in showing that consitutional rules based upon unanimous *prior* consent confer a certain validity upon collective action taken in accordance with them, whilst in practice the costs of securing unanimity may force a compromise in the form of acceptance of a majority decision (see p. 27 below), the authors do not assume that no constitutional decision which is defensible in the light of their principle can in fact be brought into being except by *prior* consent (with or without unanimity).[18] But they may leave that impression.

In the *C of C*, the State is regarded as a set of processes or as a piece of machinery. Certainly the institutions may be so regarded. But when we think of the State, should we not rather envisage realistically a number of individuals—a small group of private people—who may be servants of the community or themselves sovereign (laws unto themselves) in a greater or less degree? For even when we regard them as our servants, is it not realistic to remind ourselves that, although entrusted with great powers, they cannot be unconditionally entrusted with them?

A relevant comparison is with the sanctions for *laissez-faire* in the market economy.[19] The virtues of planning and co-ordination under *laissez-faire* institutions (i.e., by private entrepreneurs *via* contract) are dependent on the axiom that market institutions cannot be rationally designed upon the assumption of a universal or even greater altruism (see above, p. 20). *But political institutions also must be considered in the light of this axiom.* This is (for the present writer) the most important principle that the *C of C* establishes. It is a principle which is brought out even more clearly in an article by one of the authors, published about the same time as the book.[20] In this article, Buchanan questions the Pigovian assumption that "individuals respond to different motives when they participate in market and in political activity." Man is assumed, says Buchanan, "to shift his psychological and moral gears when he moves from the realm of organized market activity and vice-versa."[21] He admits that, "in his voting behaviour, the individual probably tends to choose among alternatives on the basis of a somewhat broader and more inclusive value scale than that which will direct his behaviour in the making of market choices." But, he adds, this does not justify acceptance of "the idea that the motivation for individual action is wholly transformed as between two separate structures."[22]

As the present writer's own ideas have developed (before and since the publication of the *C of C*), the issue has come to be viewed as involving the different social disciplines which individuals can exert upon others whose decisions influence their lives.[23] Although a powerful, active State is the pillar of any *laissez-faire* system, it is very much more difficult to subject the politicians and officials who act for the State to a discipline as effective as that which the free market can impose upon business intermediaries. And an effective form of such a discipline is, we suggest, what the authors of the *C of C* are seeking.

The grounds for choosing the State in preference to markets in the pursuit of individual ends, in any particular case, can be phrased thus. Owing to, say, the frequent small scale of private operations, certain inefficiencies arise which a planning authority, blessed with a wider vision (and *assumed* to be acting disinterestedly), can eliminate. That is, external economies may be realised (or external diseconomies avoided) *via* corrective 'central controls.' But, the authors argue, we must begin by recognising that there is an incentive for *voluntary*, co-ordinative action to avoid such diseconomies and achieve such economies. As we have always preferred to phrase it, the motive to avoid 'losses' (output yields valued below input costs *plus* interest) or to gain 'profits' (output yields valued above input costs *plus* interest) leads to a constant search for the least-cost method of making any product or achieving any objective; and *if co-operation with others appears to offer that method, it will be adopted*—unless, of course, some obstacle is placed in the way by the State or the private exercise of coercive power.

To this sort of argument, Mancur Olson (in a review which again is appreciative of the book as a whole) has objected that, "when large numbers of people are involved, there is no incentive for any one of them voluntarily to support an organisation dealing with the problems posed by externalities. If a voluntary organisation were formed to alleviate the problem . . . , those who did not participate or pay their share would benefit as much as those who did. Accordingly no one would have an incentive voluntarily to support the organisation."[24] He goes on to illustrate the point by familiar text-book examples. But we find nothing in the *C of C* to suggest that the authors would deny, or that they have overlooked, the principle that Olson has repeated. All of us, however liberal our bias, still insist (a) that there are situations in which *some* form of collective action can (subject to the degree of disinterestedness which can be assumed in the sort of decision required) alone optimise the yield to direct effort or maximise the profits of intermediaries; and (b) that when such action is called for, taxation of *all* the apparent beneficiaries (when this is practicable), and not merely of those who may have pressed for the State initiative, *may* be justifiable. Would Olson expect the authors to plead for the right of certain ships to refuse to pay 'light dues' (devoted to the upkeep of lighthouses) on the grounds that their captains are so skilled in navigation that they do not need such assistance?

One wonders whether the implications of this part of the analysis could not be summarised as follows: "There is in general no case for calling upon the State *to force* individuals to act, singly or through contract, so as to optimise the yield to their energies and their employment of valuable factors, or, when they are intermediaries, to maximise their profits or minimise their losses. But *some* collective action may well tend to optimise or maximise the prospective yields of all and, on the assumption of rationality, be unanimously acceptable, especially if those who may happen to suffer some disadvantage from the collective decisions required may either (i) expect to be compensated (*via* taxation and transfers) by those who happen to gain; or (ii) have the right to bargain for some countervailing concession.'' (We shall return to this last possibility.)

A sharp distinction is made in the *C of C* between 'constitutional decisions' on the one hand, and legislating within the constitutional framework—'operational decisions'—on the other hand. But the concept of 'constitutional' is very wide. It covers all decisions about whether an end is to be sought individually or collectively and, if collectively, under what voting rules. At the 'constitutional' stage, it is argued, general agreement is much more likely than at the 'operational' stage. Thus, ''a potential thief, recognising the need for protecting his own person and property, will support laws against theft'' (p. 251).

One of the factors determining whether certain ends can be best sought through market institutions or collective action is obviously the efficiency or otherwise of the ballot box as a means of expressing the ends people wish to pursue. On this point, in a masterly analysis, the authors demonstrate certain inherent defects in decisions dependent upon majority voting—defects which have so far been ignored, we feel, by all too many political theorists. The authors draw attention to the significance of the fact that not only do the chosen objectives of different individuals diverge, but that they stand at different points on their schedules of preference—that is, their preferences have different degrees of intensity. One vote in a ballot for a certain objective may express intense desire whilst another, although 'for,' may be motivated by near indifference. Thus, a majority of votes expressed for a particular measure may record an almost casual approval on the part of the majority, yet take no account of passionate disapproval on the part of a large (or small) minority.

This reality alone limits the tolerable sphere of governmental activity and makes some constitutional checks desirable. But the authors show that 'log-rolling'—the trading of votes—can in some measure assist the achievement of unanimity or near unanimity, thereby rendering constitutional checks less essential. For not only is 'political exchange' viewed as a form of 'economic exchange,' but the principle that there are mutual gains from trade—all parties gain—is shown to hold in the voting sphere as in the market (p. 250).

In our judgement, the most revolutionary achievement of the book lies just here, in its demolition of a certain axiom, quite fairly stated by the authors as follows: "If the interests of two or more individuals conflict, unanimity is impossible. Some interest must prevail over others if action is not to be wholly stifled" (p. 252). The *C of C* has demonstrated (a) the relevance to political science of the truth—familiar in economics—that, although the interests of the parties conflict in every exchange, bargains can be struck *without coercion;* and (b) that the "notion of mutuality of gain may be carried over to the political relationship" (p. 252). "Political exchange at all levels is basically equivalent to economic exchange" (p. 250);[25] and "collective activity, like market activity, is genuinely *cooperative* activity in which *all* parties, conceptually, stand to gain" (p. 266). In this demonstration the authors have turned a powerful light on issues which the traditional liberal would wish to be brought into consideration in the process of constitution-making.

This part of the *C of C* is so stimulating that it sets the mind off on explorations into possibilities that will seem fantastic or outrageous to those who have not grasped the implications. For instance, why should we not make the heroic mental adjustment necessary and consider whether there may not be conditions under which it would be desirable to abolish the secret ballot and allow every voter openly to sell his vote if he values it at less than he is offered? For as soon as side-payments or log-rolling are possible and seen to be mitigating the 'social wastage' inherent in majority rule, the vote becomes a legitimate 'marketable property right' (p. 186), a 'scarce commodity' (p. 270).

A factor which, for certain critics, obscures a realisation that a choice as rational as other economic choices is possible between market and collective activity is the current political phenomenon of the State being employed as a means of transferring capital and income from some to others—under universal suffrage, from the minority to the majority. For instance, S. S. Ulmer certainly appears unaware that this is the crucial distinction when he compares the purchase of a can of beans (where the purchaser knows what he is going to receive through the transaction) and voting for a national health service. He says of the latter decision: "I may prefer the private sector if my medical bills are going to be negligible, the public sector otherwise."[26] But a voter will only prefer the public sector if he does not expect to pay, through taxation or a special levy, the full cost of the service, but assumes that it will be borne by someone else.[27] In short, people may vote for 'free' medical or other 'social' services because they think that they themselves are going to contribute a relatively small proportion of the total cost, rather than because they believe that a State service can be better (i.e., more economically) run.[28] And as we have seen, the authors have shown that the resource wastage due to such decisions constitutes a major objection to unqualified majority rule.

We can at this stage re-phrase what we believe to be one of the most important propositions of the *C of C* about the role of the State. Collective decisions which are not activated by the intention to facilitate more rational action on the part of *individuals* (including more effective loss-avoidance, profit-seeking decisions on the part of *intermediaries*), cannot be expected "to exhibit any sense of order" (p. 32). Now this proposition does not, as Downs assumes, ignore "the extremely important problem of co-ordinating various governmental actions so that they do not cancel out each other's effectiveness."[29] It is common cause that certain economic ends, e.g., street lighting, can only be achieved with the minimum sacrifice of other ends if the State (in some form) accepts the entrepreneurial role (see above, p. 23). But self-consistent action in this role demands a recognition that the capital and income devoted to the provision and upkeep of the lighting may be too large or too small, i.e., such amenities compete with privately-sought ends as well as with other collectively-sought ends; and rational determination of the volume of resources to be devoted to the different objectives in that class is possible only after a careful weighing of all the alternatives. Any 'sense of order,' therefore, demands interpretation of consumer preference just as much as the budget plan of a manufacturing firm, in which sales forecasts are the determining factor.

The argument against the attempted achievement of order *via* vote-selling may well be that, owing to the ignorance of the average voter, wealthy vested interests could buy the right to line their pockets, against the interests of those whom they could dupe into selling their protection. But if so, does it not raise the question of whether such voters could be assumed to be any wiser in 'buying' (as Downs sees the process) the programmes, promises, etc., which the various parties offer for sale?

Now we may all be regarded as continuously, although passively, voting for the continuance (by not pressing for the discontinuance)[30] of those forms of State activity of which we all (virtually unanimously) approve, because we believe we *perceive* that they are working for our benefit. And there may be other activities of the same kind which we might command the State to carry out for us, again virtually unanimously, if every one of us could be educated on the issue, or if the necessary vote-trading could be arranged. But this process of persuasion, education, defensible long-rolling, etc., to win the consent of the voters may be exorbitantly expensive. Hence the *authors construct their case for accepting majority (as distinct from unanimous) decisions on the avoidance of the costs of obtaining consent.*

But what about that kind of proposed collective action the desire for which is far from unanimous? The authors put forward convincingly the proposition that the greater the fear that collective decisions may work against the interests of those who would oppose them (because, in the *C of C* terminology, the opponents expect 'external costs' to be imposed on them), the stronger is the case for the authorisation of such decisions only by a large percentage majority.

The discussion of these issues has, however, left the writer far from certain about all the implications. Admittedly the conferring on a minority of the right to block change may be a legitimate means of protecting a minority against the majority. In the special form of a weighted franchise for voting on constitutional questions, it may be intended to re-assure a particular minority—those of a specified colour, creed, language or district—against possible discrimination or other injustice from a dominating group. But there are dangers in according a minority the right to block or obstruct change—dangers which should be frankly faced, even by those who are convinced that this power is essential to deter undue haste or prevent injustice in amendments of basic law. The fact is that a minority—sometimes a very small minority—may be in a position to demand extortionate rewards (*via* the log-rolling process) for permitting reforms which are obviously for the good of all.

A parallel from public utility economics may illuminate the problem. It is universally recognised that the State must be in a position to expropriate sites in order that new roads or railways (whether privately or publicly owned) can be constructed without exploitation by one or a few land-owners. Similarly, it is essential that minorities shall not be accorded the right to obstruct constitution-making when those minorities are merely demanding privileges for themselves, as distinct from blocking attempts to seize privilege by others.

We are led to a conclusion to which the *C of C* appears again and again to be pointing, although without any explicit statement of the principle, namely, that the constitutional protection of minorities should be sought *via* rules for making rules which invalidate all discriminatory law rather than by continuous minority concurrence. Amendment of the non-discrimination principle alone, we suggest, should be subject to approval by large percentage majorities or the explicit approval of defined minority groups which have been granted special constitutional safeguards. Only in this respect does there appear to be an irrefutable case (from the ethical standpoint of a classic liberal) for permitting a minority to block or obstruct (if those words are appropriate in the situation discussed).

It is at the 'operational' level, however (in the process of legislating within the limits of the constitution), that it may be most important to prevent blocking by minorities. But if the constitution (a) forbids discrimination *except after some form of unanimous consent* (a qualification to which we shall return) and (b) enshrines the principle of compensation (when legislation—assumed to be for the common gain—harms the few in favouring the many),[31] there seems to be no other surviving purpose for the unanimity principle at the 'operational' level. Given the entrenchment of these two qualifying rules, it seems to us that simple majority decisions would be acceptable. Legislative changes urgently demanded by the community could not then be indefinitely held back, subjected to a kind of blackmail by small groups of organised voters (threatening to withhold the required proportion of votes). For in the light of the non-discrimination rule, the consent of all would have been obtainable, and the unanimity principle honoured, if no power existed for a minority to hold up the community to ransom.

We suggest, then, that a constitution incorporating the principle of non-discrimination *except by unanimous consent* (with open log-rolling being permitted to secure that consent)[32] *would* rule out the legitimacy of other forms of vote-trading. Side payments or benefits would then again become, in the authors' words, "clearly immoral since the receipt of a money payment provides definite proof that the individual is receiving 'private' gains from his power to participate in political action" (p. 275). Our suggestion seems to conform to the authors' ultimate condemnation of *"vote-trading under rules for collective choice requiring less than full agreement* among all members of the group" (p. 279) (the authors' italics). But they do not stress non-discrimination as unequivocally as we have done.

It is pertinent to mention a recent short but highly relevant reference by Phillip Areeda to the process of vote-trading "among groups each striving for its place in the sun or at the trough . . ." in which "each interest achieves satisfaction of its most acute desires at the expense of issues it considers less important." Areeda warns us that "the political market, like the economic one, is distorted by ignorance, monopoly and combination.

. . . It would be hard to justify granting Green benefits denied Brown where the only difference between them is that Brown lives in a state certain to vote for you while Green lives in a swing state.''[33] Is not the problem to be faced, then, one of finding some principle corresponding to anti-trust applicable to the political sphere? And here, we suggest, the non-discrimination rule (with the qualifications recommended above) provides the most obvious remedy. F. A. Fetter once remarked of market operations, ''Monopoly and discrimination are like Siamese twins. Cut one away and the other necessarily dies.'' Is this not just as true in the field of political bargaining? If legislation which specially favours a particular province or state is 'unconstitutional,' for example, will not that form of injustice mentioned by Areeda be simply excluded?

Recognition of the democratic sanction for State action which is provided by bargained voting unanimity seems therefore to lead directly to the acceptance of the non-discrimination rule. And if this suggestion is acceptable, the authors have succeeded in clarifying the ultimate rationale of classic liberalism. We must, as was suggested above, develop the habit of viewing the State realistically as a small group of private people, necessarily entrusted with great powers, who can be subjected to social discipline partly through the ballot but mainly through rules for making rules, *the paramount rule being that of non-discrimination.*

The authors are emphatic in disclaiming the classic liberal view of the purpose of constitutional restraint, namely, that of preserving inalienable human rights, although they admit that ''something akin to that doctrine can easily be reconciled with'' their construction (p. 252). Yet almost every conclusion they draw appears to us to justify constitutional restraint to exclude the use of the State for the achievement of differential advantages. And that enshrines, we suggest, the most basic of all human rights and what classic liberalism has above all stood for.

Those who accept the logical content of the *C of C* may well differ widely in their forecasts of the exact sphere in which, under the unanimity they envisage, legislative edict or the discretion of officialdom should be allowed to decide either ends or means. But all who *really* understand the argument must, we feel, accept the principle that collective decisions should be non-discriminatory, except with the prior consent of those discriminated against. Unless this condition is fulfilled, laws of any kind which, directly or indirectly, discriminate in favour of or against any particular group (whether on the grounds of race, colour, ancestry, creed, sex, occupation, district, property or income) *should* be ruled unconstitutional and void.

The entrenchment of the non-discriminatory principle would undoubtedly precipitate an enormous disinvestment of the capital invested in what the authors call ''organization aimed at securing differential gains by political means.'' This form of investment, which has emerged with the growth of the importance of the public sector, ''has taken the form of an increasingly differential or discriminatory impact on the separate and identifiable groups of the population'' (pp.286-7). It is a development which seems to have involved a formidable aggregate cost. But the remedy is surely obvious. Would not the qualified non-discriminatory rule we have suggested bring about a reversion to the system, for which the authors claim ''considerable historical validity,'' in which ''a government . . . undertakes only those activities which provide *general* benefits to all individuals and groups and which are financed from *general* tax revenues'' (p. 287). In such a regime, they point out, the incentive for investment to secure privileges from governments would be dissolved.

The task of the *C of C* has been to serve as an intellectual catalyst. It has certainly disturbed profoundly the present writer's thinking, to his advantage. It ought to inspire, over the next few decades, several studies—critical and realistic—of constitutions, governments, parties and programmes (and under 'governments' we include the private elected governments of business corporations, where the issues raised are distinctly relevant). But the ideas put into circulation must not be confined to academic treatises and students' note books. They bear on the liveliest political issues of the age. They need a fresh exposition in language and concepts which the ordinary well-read man in the street and the typical politician will be able easily to grasp. Popularisation is called for.

Notes

1. J. Buchanan and G. Tullock, *The Calculus of Consent* (Ann Arbor: The University of Michigan Press, 1962).

2. W. Riker, ''The Calculus of Consent'' (review), *Midwest Journal of Political Science* 6 (February 1962), p. 408.

3. Ibid., p. 408.

4. Page references to Buchanan and Tullock, *The Calculus of Consent*, will be given in brackets in the text.

5. A. Downs, ''The Calculus of Consent'' (review), *Journal of Political Economy* 72 (February 1964), p. 87.

6. They write on the issue, "We shall not pause to argue the case with those who might disagree" (p. 3).

7. In a note to Appendix I (p. 358) Buchanan refers to Mises' discussion of methodological individualism on pp. 44-47 of *Human Action*. This passage is directly relevant to our own argument which follows.

8. Downs, p. 87.

9. Ibid., p. 87.

10. The present writer has constantly stressed this consideration. See W. Hutt, *Economists and the Public* (London: Jonathan Cape, 1936), Chapter 23; *Plan for Reconstruction* (London: Kegan Paul, 1943); and "South Africa's Salvation in Classic Liberalism," published in this volume.

11. At times, the authors appear to agree here. See Buchanan and Tullock, *The Calculus of Consent*, p. 265.

12. H. Manne, *George Washington Law Review*, 1963, p. 1066. Realistic assumptions about rationality would not hinder the aim of considering what rules for making rules a fully rational individual *would* seek to achieve.

13. J. Meade, "Welfare Criteria: An Exchange of Notes," *Economic Journal* 72 (March 1962), p. 102.

14. And the authors recognise this point exactly as we see it when, in a slightly different context, they say: "The market order is founded on the empirical reality that not all men renounce self-interest" (p. 304). The point is, we think, made more clearly and with greater generality in Buchanan's article in *Economica*, cited below.

15. R. Milne, "The Calculus of Consent" (review), *The Political Quarterly* (October 1962).

16. Ibid.

17. This is particularly important, it should be noticed, when the voter's inspiration is collective altruism, i.e., not philanthropy at his own expense, but the use of public funds, contributed by others, for the benefit of those for whom he feels disinterested compassion.

18. The point can be illustrated by consideration of the situation in the Republic of South Africa where, the present writer has recently argued, a peaceful and just solution of the race problem can be won only by the adoption of rigidly entrenched provisions which protect racial minorities like the Whites, the Indians, and the Coloureds, by declaring unconstitutional legislation or administrative decisions which discriminate on grounds of race, colour, ancestry, property, income, or district. But owing to the bitterness aroused among the Africans by decades of pandering to a white proletariat, and owing to British and American encouragement of African nationalism, there is now hardly any chance of free general acceptance of such a constitution at a national convention at which the Africans were represented. Indeed, the Africans are beginning to perceive the consequences of their being in a majority. The Afrikaner Nationalists have taught them the lesson, and they now wish

to turn the tables and themselves dominate. But this should not prevent a sufficient number of white leaders in South Africa from seeing the writing on the wall and leading the Whites to a gradual unilateral renunciation of privilege in the not absurd hope of winning the *ultimate* (as distinct from the *prior*) consent of all. (See Chapter 4 of this book.)

19. By laissez-faire, we mean a system which, as far as is practicable, subjects the decision-makers who determine resource use to social discipline *via* the power of substitution possessed by consumers and intermediaries (specialized entrepreneurs).

20. Buchanan, "Politics, Policy and the Pigovian Margins," *Economica* 29 (February 1962).

21. Ibid., p. 23.

22. Ibid., p. 24.

23. We think it unfortunate that the authors have accepted the tendentious current convention of using the term *social* as a synonym for *collective*. Both the market and the ballot are means of social control, whatever their respective fields and merits.

24. M. Olson, "The Calculus of Consent" (review), *American Economic Review* 52 (December 1962), pp. 1217-8.

25. We should have preferred the words "a form of" instead of "equivalent to."

26. S. Ulmer, " The Calculus of Consent" (review), *Journal of Conflict Resolution* 7, No. 2, (1963), p. 171.

27. Ulmer's point cannot be that the voter expects the State service to be *cheaper*, in the sense of more efficient, even if he had expected his medical bills to be small; for otherwise the voter would equally have preferred the cheaper service.

28. The fact that one cannot always estimate with great accuracy one's future medical needs, which is the consideration Ulmer stresses, is irrelevant; for exactly the same uncertainty, covered by the insurance principle, confronts all those who voluntarily enter upon private, self-financing schemes for meeting future medical expenses.

29. Downs, p. 87.

30. We ignore here that passivity which is due to a feeling that, being in a minority, our opposition would be useless.

31. The case for compensation of those who would otherwise be materially prejudiced by desirable legislation is, of course, important also at the "constitutional" stage, even when amendments merely dissolve former privileges. Compensation appears then to be expedient, provided it is temporary, ceasing with the death of the beneficiary, or perhaps with his retraining. The present writer has discussed this type of compensation in his *Plan for Reconstruction.* The case for it is *not* that it justifies the dissolution of privilege, but that it is the most humane method of doing so and may be expected to lessen opposition.

32. The case for permitting discrimination in legislation when it is based on the consent of the parties discriminated against resembles the case for discriminatory

charging for goods and services. Such charging is legitimate when it is to the advantage of those who are forced to pay the higher charges (because they thereby get a product or service which would otherwise not be available at all, or only available at a higher price than the discriminatory price they have to pay).

33. P. Areeds, "Decision Making in the White House" (review), *Harvard Law Review* 77 (March 1964), p. 991.

3 • *Illustration of Keynesianism*

The harm wrought through the failure of economists to bring political economy and vote-gaining imperatives realistically into the study of economic problems can be further illustrated by the Keynesian phenomenon. The clash between Keynes and those he called 'classical' economists arose utlimately out of issues clouded by vague tacit assumptions on both sides about the 'politically possible'.

The classical analysis and prescription

The 'classical' economists can be said, broadly speaking, to have diagnosed economic depression as caused by repression of aggregate purchasing power (the flow of wages and other income). The income constriction was caused, they held, through input prices (costs) and output prices having been forced higher than the people (as investors or consumers) were able (or willing in the light of price expectations) to pay out of uninflated income for the full flow of productive services and products. In simpler terms, goods and services (including labour) were being priced at levels which people found beyond their pockets, so that unsold stocks piled up in the shops and warehouses, workers were laid off, factories had to work below capacity, and equipment had to stand idle. While this condition persisted, the flow of profits and wages was held down. Because prices were too high, people

Reprinted with permission from *Politically Impossible* by William H. Hutt. © 1971 by The Institute of Economic Affairs, 2 Lord North Street, Westminster SW 1, London, England.

simply found themselves with insufficient income to make normal purchases in the absence of inflation. Then as now, high prices meant low 'real income', and that meant in turn low money incomes as long as (to take Britain) the pound sterling was to continue to be convertible into gold and allowed to retain its purchasing power.

The 'classical' prescription for the cure of such a condition was, firstly, prevention of its emergence, through avoidance of an inflationary boom (in which the price structure of a community became distorted), and, secondly, if a depressed economy had inadvertently come about, to rely on 'economic pressures' to force the required value re-adjustments. It was thought that the unwillingness of people to remain unemployed, and the unwillingness of the owners of assets to see their resources idle or idling, would gradually force a downward shift of costs (wage-rates and interest on capital) and product prices. This would in turn restore both the ability and the willingness of people to absorb the full flow of inputs (whether of labour or capital) into the replacement of stocks consumed, or into replacement and accumulation of fixed or longer-life assets. That is, reduced money costs would enable manufacturers to use their assets more intensively and bring back laid-off workers into their jobs; for the manufacturers could then charge prices at which their customers could and would make their normal purchases. And 'customers' here meant not only final consumers but also other manufacturers buying outputs of capital goods to replace or add to their stock of assets and outputs of materials to add to 'work in progress', and merchants buying goods of all kinds to replace or add to their stocks.

Moreover, the 'classical' economists recognized that governments had some responsibility for the defence of, or the facilitation of, this co-ordinative process of costs and prices and hence for the downward cost and price adjustments needed. But they tended to rely heavily upon the assumption that those who were *mainly* responsible for unemployment and depression, namely, trade unions that forced the price of labour in some important sectors of industry too high, were most severely punished by their members' privation, worry and shame of being without jobs. The pre-Keynesian economists thus relied in part upon 'individual' incentives which, they believed, would tend to bring about recovery. Some of the economists whom Keynes would have termed 'classical', such as Edwin Cannan, recognized also and spoke out strongly against political aggravation of depression via 'unemployment benefit'. In Britain in the 1920s and 1930s it had taken a form which was alleged to be 'subsidizing the occupation of being unemployed', as Cannan once put it.

Economic adjustments thought politically impossible

Nevertheless, pre-Keynesian economists seemed loath to draw attention, with adequate explicitness, to the neglected role of government in suppressing anti-social monopoly pricing practices, whether by trade unions or the price rings of businessmen. That was understandable enough in Britain where nothing resembling anti-trust laws existed save mere remnants of the old common law against restraint of trade, and where a long tradition (which began back in 1824) of non-interference with trade union activities stood in the way. But the harm caused by the chaos due to strike-threat power was clear enough to all dispassionate observers. And if British economists had been able to speak with some unanimity in the late 1920s and early 1930s, more or less in the following terms, subsequent history would, I suggest, have been quite different.

> The present hardships of the unemployed are inevitable in view of a situation which ties the hands of all political parties. The temper of the unions today is such that collective action to restore the flow of wages through wage-rate adjustments in competitive markets would arouse so much indignation in trade union circles, and so many opportunities of political misrepresentation, that no government could survive the attempt. Hence the transition to prosperity, instead of being rapid and planned, will have to be haphazard, long drawn out and painful. Contemporary institutions—the practice and tolerance of monopoly by labour and capital—destroy any hope of a rapid and orderly rehabilitation of the economy. Political realities (due to governments' conviction that the true position cannot be explained to the nation or their unwillingness to risk the unpopularity accompanying an attempt to explain) force the community to be resigned to a long and arduous path to recovery.

One reason why economists did not speak out in this way was that, as the difficulties of the 1930s were looming ahead and encountered, the idea was growing that there might be a *politically* easier economic solution, which would not imply that it was government's duty to risk sacrificing votes. The notion began to catch on that, if aggregate purchasing power was deficient because aggregate supply was deficient (owing to input prices and output prices having been forced—by trade union or other monopolistic pressures—above full employment levels), this deficiency might be remedied in some manner by the stimulation of aggregate demand.

In Britain the writings of A C Pigou, Hubert Henderson, Dennis Robertson, Henry Clay and others contained passages in which the responsibility of unduly high wage-rates (in some industries) for recession, and hence for an unduly low flow of income and wages, was clearly stated.[1] But these economists appeared to speak with two voices. They all significantly fought shy of explicitly recommending the market-selected price and wage-rate adjustments needed to restore the income flow in an economy suffering from value discoordination, or some cruder method of mitigating it along 'incomes policy' lines.

For instance, Pigou alleged in 1927 that the current wage policy was 'responsible for adding some 5 per cent to the volume of unemployment', a 'post-war development' which he regarded as 'an extremely serious matter.'[2] At that time he did recommend reducing labour costs, although with supplementation of wage-rates by income transfers. But later, having dropped his wage-subsidies proposal,[3] he still conspicuously refrained from recommending the only remaining non-inflationary solution, that of pricing labour's inputs lower so that they would be within reach of final consumers' pockets. Before the Macmillan Committee of 1931, in spite of agreeing that at reduced real wage-rates 'you would employ more people', he insisted that he did not suggest, 'as any form of remedy, lower real wages in the depressed industries'. Instead, he suggested, unemployment would be diminished 'if the conditions of demand could be so altered that there should be a higher demand'.[4]

'Practical difficulties and frictions'

Now demands for outputs in general (and hence for inputs) can be raised under the conditions Pigou was postulating only through the reduction of input prices or via inflation. Yet he insisted that he was 'not advocating a reduction of real wages'.[5] And in 1933 he embraced the opinion that 'for prosperity to be restored either money costs must fall or money prices must rise'. But, he contended, 'the practical difficulties in the way of the former solution have proved so serious and the friction to be overcome so great that the main body of instructed opinion has turned towards the latter.'[6]

Here we run into the crux of the matter. What 'practical difficulties,' what 'frictions' were met with in attempts to increase the wages flow via market-selected wage-rate and price adjustments? When and where was such a policy tried out? Certainly there were union resistances to market pressures. But Pigou was discussing the role of government in recession. I suggest that no 'difficulties' or 'frictions' were encountered by the Government because no attempts were made; that the prospective 'difficulties' which discouraged such attempts were all concerned with vote-acquisition, and that the prospective 'difficulties' were magnified *precisely because the majority of economists were talking with two voices.*[7]

Professor Hutchison scathingly criticizes Professors R Lekachman, E A G Robinson, L R Klein and Mr M Stewart for having unfairly charged Pigou (and others) with having advocated wage-cuts and non-inflationary policies.[8] But they always stopped short of doing so. The trend of the analyses criticized suggested again and again that Pigou and the rest were about to grasp the nettle and advocate reforms conducive to price and wage flexibility, but they did not go further and do it. There is thus something to be said in defence of Professor Lekachman and the others, because they were misled through glaring inconsistencies between the analytical findings and the policy recommendations of the pre-Keynesian economists whom they attacked.

Far from questioning Professor Hutchison's contention, however, I am giving it a special emphasis. Keynesian ways of thinking were quite widespread in Britain (and, indeed, in the United States) before the publication of Keynes' *General Theory.* What has caused misunderstanding is that in 1936 Keynes turned on many of his former supporters precisely because they had, directly or indirectly, argued that wage-rate reductions could restore the flow of wages and income, although they had always been careful to insist that such a solution was 'unrealistic' (for unexplained reasons), and to make it unchallengeably plain that they were not advocating unsophisticated remedies. Keynes and his young advisers felt uncomfortable at having to rely upon the argument that (my wording) 'a little inflation would be much better'. It was this that inspired Keynes (or his young advisers) to invent the 'unemployment equilibrium theory'.

We ought to be careful not to attribute Keynesian-type ideas to the economists who, just after the British devaluation of 1931, were prepared frankly to recommend 'inflation' in the United States as an *emergency* measure, and to *call* it 'inflation'.[9] The distinguishing attribute of what I have called 'Keynesian-type' thinking before *The General Theory* was the impression that cheap money is not inherently inflationary. That impression was left so successfully in Keynes' *Treatise on Money* in 1930 that Roosevelt's monetary policy in 1933, reflecting the policy implications of that book, could claim that the aim was to 'maintain a dollar which would not change its purchasing power during the succeeding generation'. Keynes' policy prescriptions were always clearly intended as *generally* applicable for incipient recession.

Keynesian error provoked by political anxiety

The economists who (before 1936) supported Keynes in rejecting the policy of working for more efficiency in the co-ordinative mechanism of the pricing system (by eliminating the arbitrariness due to restrictive practices, including strike-threat influences) did not explicitly say: 'The virtue of a "cheap money" stimulus rests primarily in its *political* practicability. It will not lose votes for a government which adopts it.'

In most cases, economists who inclined to a cheap money solution seemed oblivious of any bias towards 'the politically acceptable'. On the face of it, they were simply believing, in increasing numbers, that a deficiency in aggregate demand meant something different from a deficiency in aggregate supply. Nevertheless, the root cause of such thinking in 'the new economists' (the Keynesians') inhibitions is to be found in vote-procuring considerations. Groping for some means of getting the economy's wheels turning again, without being so 'unrealistic' as to refer to a supposedly 'politically impossible' solution (market-selected price and wage-rate adjustments), they came to abandon the view of *production* (to replace consumption or to add to the stock of assets) as the source of demands (for the services of men and of assets). They fell instead into the serious error of thinking of *consumption* (often conceived of as 'spending')[10] as in some sense the origin of the ability to demand. Confused by their recognition that the *form* of consumption determines the *form* in which production may be expected to replace (or add to) what is consumed, they were led into the fallacy that the *volume* of consumption is the source of the *volume* of demand for production. Instead of thinking in micro-economic concepts and relationships they thought in macro-economic totals.

The thesis that underconsumption is the origin of recession is, of course, tailor-made for political acceptability. It meant an enormous advantage for the popularity of 'the new economics' against the old. It implies that income transfers to 'the poor' will restore a declining economy because 'the poor' are less thrifty than 'the rich', and so will 'spend' not 'save' the income diverted to them. And this notion having once been accepted, it was easy for the venerable but naïve idea of the 'monetary cranks' (such as Silvio Gesell and J A Hobson) to become respectable, namely, that men and assets were idle because insufficient was being spent on them. The 'old-fashioned' pre-Keynesian economists (such as Edwin Cannan, L von Mises, Lionel Robbins, Theodore Gregory, and F Lavington and Benjamin Anderson) had regarded as platitudinous the notion that in depression there was insufficient uninflated money income to ensure the purchase of normal outputs; they held that the whole point at issue was the reason why *outputs* in general were insufficient to generate the required uninflated money income. The new ideas implied that a fiscal or monetary policy which, superficially viewed, could seem inflationary, might prove non-inflationary by drawing forth larger outputs via enhanced entrepreneurial optimism due in turn to boosted prospective spending. If so, it could bring about the restoration of aggregate output—the very reaction on which the 'classical' theory itself relied for recovery.

This was the type of thinking which was tending to win growing sympathy in British official circles during the late 1920s and early 1930s although (possibly because of opposition from the Treasury and old-fashioned bankers) deliberate inflation had not yet become a 'politically possible' policy. It became respectable only when the sophistication of Keynes' *General Theory* (published in 1936) conferred stronger apparent authority on such notions. There was, of course, no controversy whatsoever among economists about the ability of 'a little' inflation to induce a restoration of output. (But so could 'a little' wage-rate reduction—a corollary which no Keynesian ever thought it expedient to mention.)

It was the *other* consequences feared which gave rise to non-Keynesian resistance. The 'old-fashioned' pre-Keynesian economists doubted, firstly, the ability of any country adopting a policy of spending itself into prosperity to fulfil its obligations to convert deposits or currency into gold (and failure to do so was regarded as national dishonesty or akin to the incompetence which caused private insolvencies); and, secondly, the possibility of avoiding inflation under any 'cheap money' system. But the economists who became influential and gained coveted reputations (Keynes and his early disciples in Britain and the 'New Deal' economists in the United States) were those who could encourage governments to think there *was* a politically easier way of maintaining sufficient popularity for re-election than that of eradicating by governmental action the privately contrived obstacles to the restoration of the wages-flow—not least monopolistic trade unions and industrial associations.

'Political' presentation of inflation

The 'new economists' were careful not to advocate inflation openly. Indeed they showed exceptional ingenuity in presenting their proposal in such phrases that its inflationary foundations were hidden. Even in the 1930s, open advocacy of 'mild inflation' in Britain and America would have gravely weakened the vote-winning virtues of the policy. Voters and, even more important, opinion-makers (including bankers) had become obsessed in their bias against any breach of monetary obligations with the world. The sheer prejudice of the intelligentsia, and especially of 'old-fashioned' bankers, against purposefully engineered 'debasements' (as they regarded deliberate depreciations of currencies), however innocuous or gentle the 'debasements' envisaged, was the obstacle to the only 'politically possible' means to recovery. 'Inflation' was politically suicidal. But an inspired insight enabled the Keynesians to perceive that, if called something else, 'the maintenance of effective demand' for instance, it can become respectable and even respected, like 'family planning' for 'birth control'.

In wisely obscuring the inflationary essence of their proposals, 'the new economists' recognized also, although less clearly, that any openly declared inflationary policy would be largely self-defeating. The co-ordinative merits of a depreciating money unit depend upon the maintenance of 'the correct climate of opinion', i.e., upon misleading the public about the planned speed or duration of any inflation deemed expedient (in the light of developing circumstances) from time to time. For otherwise costs would rise in anticipation of increased product prices, and interest rates would rise so as to frustrate the intended exploitation (Keynes said 'euthanasia') of the *rentier*.

To view the course of events in perspective, it is important to repeat that

Keynesian ways of thinking had been powerful in Britain and the United States long before the publication of Keynes' *General Theory*. The so-called 'monetary cranks' like C H Douglas and J A Hobson do not seem to have commanded much respect in influential circles in Britain, although the arguments of Foster and Catchings had a real impact in the highest circles in the United States.[11] Nevertheless, the notion that 'cheap money' could bring prosperity and mitigate unemployment without serious contra-effects was growing in industrial and business circles in both continents. And all this time ideas such as Keynes had expressed in his *Tract on Monetary Reform*, 1923, in his *Economic Consequences of Mr Churchill*, 1925, in numerous articles and speeches, and in his *Treatise on Money*, 1930, were making the 'cheap money' way of trying to cure recession seem plausible. Keynes could not be dismissed as a crank. Either his ideas or similar ideas had kept in circulation the hope that there might be an easy way out of recession. These ideas had encouraged government passivity or procrastination in the economically fundamental but (supposedly) politically dangerous steps required to mitigate the depressive effects on the wages-flow of the private use of coercive power in strike-threat form. Through this influence, Keynesian notions may have been more responsible than any other factor for Britiain dishonouring the gold standard in September 1931, and indirectly for the prolongation of the depression. Keynes' personal influence during the late 1920s and early 1930s is difficult to assess. Perhaps the extraordinary publicity he then received was due to his swimming with the tide. But what his *General Theory* did was to give explicit academic status to ideas which had already been rapidly gaining general approval in influential, governmental and business circles. Immediately after its publication I was moved to comment on its 'alluring and politically easy suggestions' and to refer to Keynes having 'for years believed and preached . . . what many persons of influence in finance and politics have found it easy to believe', and that it could 'prove to be the source of the most serious blow that the authority of orthodox economics has yet suffered'.[12]

It did indeed have that consequence. And yet, if Keynesian criticisms of governmental policy in Britain had been couched in terms which placed adequate explicit emphasis on 'the political factor', the ultimate consequences of otherwise identical policy recommendations would have differed radically. Suppose Keynes, in 1930 or 1931, had said more or less something like the following. Would not the response in the press and parliamentary debates have been radically different?

The position in Britain has become desperate. Year by year the economy operates at well below its full capacity and the Government is unable to do anything effective about it. We all know that the unions have forced real wage-rates in several crucial industries too high to permit the good living standards and employment security which would otherwise be within our reach. But the union hierarchies control too many votes for any government to do anything about them. They act as "pigs", "sabotaging British industry,"[13] yet nothing can be done. In forcing up wage-rates and labour costs, strike-threats and strikes cause outputs that can be paid for to decline and compel thereby the lay-off of many workers. The result is that high wage-rates bring about a reduction in the wages-flow. Therefore I advocate a little inflation to make up the deficiency in the wages-flow that unions have created, and hence restore general prosperity. It need not be much inflation—just sufficient to reduce *real* wage-rates to nearer their free market level. That is all that is necessary. But it will do the trick by reducing real wage-rates.

Such a reform is politically possible: it will entail no loss of votes because its effects will be concealed. But "classical economics" stands in the way. Its exponents *hint* at union responsibility for unemployment and low average wages but dare not recommend, any more than their critics dare, action to curb strike-threat power. And so our economy limps along, crippled by spanners in the pricing system, and solely because we have not had the courage to resort to the only *politically* possible way out— mild inflation. The inflationary solution will satisfy not only the political parties but the union officials also, because they will be able to claim the credit for continuous increases in *money* wage-rates which the market will enforce as long as inflation continues. "Classical economics" has failed to give the answer because it has overlooked the vital factor, namely, that any acceptable policy has to be compatible with the business of acquiring votes.

An attack on the 'classical economists' along such lines would have been justified, at least in part. Pigou's great book, *The Theory of Unemployment* (1933), hinted at but did not explicitly declare union responsibility for unemployment. And other economists (as we have seen) failed to speak out. They all felt that governments could not then be expected to legislate against the will of so powerful a vote-controlling institution. In 1971, as this is written, the present Government appears likely to do so in Britain.

Unemployment equilibrium

But Keynes' tactics were to destroy the whole authority of 'classical economics',[14] with no reference to the avoidance by its expositors of explicit reference to the basic vote-gaining issue.

The central prong of his attack was the wholly fallacious 'unemployment equilibrium' thesis—the idea that price reductions to restore full (or optimal) employment are somehow self-frustrating. Cutting costs means cutting aggregate demand, his theory implied. This fallacy, now almost universally recognized,[15] is the crucial originality of *General Theory*. Schumpeter felt that Keynes would have liked to rely wholly upon it but that he kept wage-rate rigidity 'in reserve', i.e., that Keynes regarded the method of pricing labour as a second line of defence. But Keynes himself did not consciously rely upon wage-rate rigidity or 'wage-push' in any passage in *General Theory*. It was critics like Professors Franco Modigliani, Gottfried Haberler and Don Patinkin who demonstrated that wage-rate rigidity was an assumption implied by the argument, although Keynes himself had been unaware of it. And it was his disciples who bolstered the rigidity assumption by reliance on the wage-earners' 'money illusion'.[16] My explanation is that Keynes was using all his ingenuity to escape having to base his thesis as a whole on a frank and categorical assumption about the 'political impossibility' of persuading any government to protect or facilitate a labour-pricing process subject to the co-ordinative discipline of the market. This is what two British Governments, Labour and Conservative, have now accepted in principle must be done to tackle the curse of inflation, after 40 years of stop-gap policies ending with the discredited 'incomes policies'. I return to the significance of the apparent change in British policy.

Professor Samuelson, referring to the unemployment equilibrium notion as '. . . the most shocking view in the *General Theory*,' comments that

> what is most shocking in a book is not necessarily most important and lasting. Had Keynes begun his first few chapters with the simple statement that he found it realistic to assume that money wage-rates were sticky and resistant to downward price movements, most of his insights would have remained just as valid.[17]

The truth is, of course, as Professor Haberler has pointed out, that 'as soon as we assume wage rigidity and wage push . . . the main difference between

Keynes and the classics disappears', while without that assumption 'the Keynesian system simply breaks down'.[18] That is, it was the 'classical economists' (the pre-Keynesians) who had pin-pointed the source of a constricted wages flow and income in 'wage push' (i.e., collective bargaining pressures) and resistance to wage-rate adjustment, although they failed specifically to recommend the policies needed to remove the constraint they diagnosed because they thought them 'politically impossible'. But Keynes, perceiving that it would be politically suicidal to mention the unmentionable, saw a way out through the most successful conjuring trick in history which, deceiving an audience that wished to be deceived, led to its being hailed as a great discovery, as revolutionary and important as Einstein's theory of relativity. I am not accusing Keynes of intellectual dishonesty. He deceived himself with his 'conjuring trick'. That is how I have come to regard his 'unemployment equilibrium' notion, together with the subsidiary theories with which it was bolstered. Professor Harry Johnson says that classical economics stood in the way of a 'sensible' solution in the 1930s.[19] Certainly it hindered the policy which in the event proved to be 'politically possible'. But the 'classical economists' were to blame only for their reluctance to *explain* why acceptably rapid co-ordination through price adjustment was 'politically impossible'. They would never have resisted on *theoretical* grounds any policy recommendations put forward by others based on an assumption that, because trade union influences on money wage-rates were reducing the wages flow and causing depression, the only 'politically possible' way out was 'inflation', which could mitigate the situation by reducing real wage-rates, thereby crudely restoring co-ordination in the economy.

Keynesian macro-economics unhelpful for political decisions

Although other fallacies confuse the *General Theory*, the remainder of it is primarily devoted to an examination of the mechanisms through which money expenditures are believed to bring about reduced real wage-rates (in terms of 'wage-goods'), higher prospective yields to investment, and hence fuller employment. And much of what has become modern economics consists in the elaboration or development of this part of Keynes' contribution. It seems almost as though most economists who write on what we now call 'macro-economics' have been trying to devise an apparatus which can be used by fiscal and monetary authorities to judge the optimal rate of depreciation of the money unit. The concept of 'optimal rate' here really means a speed of inflation so adjusted to emerging circumstances as to maintain a delicate balance between the prospect of loss of votes through unemployment (or recession) and loss of votes through inflation.

The econometric and macro-economic developments of the Keynesian apparatus may help us in understanding how different ways of changing the number of money units in relation to changes in output (and in relation to the other causes of change in demand for monetary services) are likely to have different consequences. But they do not help one iota in the sort of practical decision-making by, say, the Governor of the Bank of England or the economic adviser to the British Treasury, or Professor A F Burns of the Federal Reserve Board or Professor Paul McCracken of the Council of Economic Advisers. Had the new methods which Keynes and his successors have put at the world's disposal assisted a solution of the basically *political* problems of monetary policy, some consensus or unanimity would have crystallized about what steps ought to be taken in a given situation. But obviously there is not. For instance, Professor Samuelson seems to differ so fundamentally from these noted American economists that, in commenting on the award to himself of the Nobel prize for economics, he thought it appropriate to make clear (without mentioning names) that he regarded their recent decisions and advice as disastrous. He obviously felt that the inflation they have been able to bring about is too mild, and he charged them by implication with having created 'cruel unemployment'.

The phrases he used could not be better devised for electioneering purposes. 'You do not kill the patient to get at the tapeworm', he said. 'There must be a better way than this cruel trade-off between unemployment and prices'.[20] '*A better way*'. This is what Keynes was telling the politicians in the 1920s and the 1930s. Keynes meant (my words) 'better than not inflating a little', or 'better than permitting deflation'. But when Professor Samuelson thinks of 'a better way' today, he means 'better than inflating too mildly'. What else can his strictures imply? In the 1930s mild inflation was enough. With the expectations which have been generated during the last decade and a half, *mild* inflation is no longer sufficient to prevent unemployment. The monetary experience of 1958 to 1970 amply confirms this inference. The expansionists are in time driven to advocating not merely more than *mild* inflation but *rising rates* of inflation, not only *high* but *accelerating* inflation.

Futility of inflation

Successive editions of Professor Samuelson's best-selling textbook seem to reflect his gradual perception of the ultimate futility of the inflationary nostrum. In the 1948 edition of his *Economics* he told his young readers that 'a mild steady inflation of, say, 5 per cent per year . . . need not cause too great concern'. In the 1955 edition he reduced it to 3 per cent; in the 1958 edition he came down to 2 per cent[21] and in the 1961 edition to below 2 per cent. In subsequent editions (the seventh and eighth), he specified no percentages at all.[22] Yet now, relying on the full authority of a Nobel prize-winner, he tells the world, by implication, that the heartless Nixon regime is inflating too mildly for the circumstances which its other policies have created. But in common with the rest of the neo-Keynesians, he avoids any explicit reference to the origins of those circumstances. The origins are to be discerned, as he knows well enough, in the political unpopularity of reforms calculated to arouse the opposition of a privileged sector of society—the highly organized labour unions—believed to wield decisive voting strength. This is the position in the USA and Britain today, just as it was in the early 1930s.

When challenged by Frank D Graham, Keynes himself eluded the issue of the political unpopularity of policy with characteristic finesse. Professor Graham had suggested[23] it was appropriate to refer to the labour unions as 'rackets', because Keynes himself had implied that they would always be responsible for unemployment (under any international monetary regime which required a common money unit of defined value—the topic of debate). But if unions acted anti-socially, Graham suggested, they constituted the problem which had to be tackled. Keynes was silent on the point.

Cruelty of inflation

In truth, the notion of 'a better way' ought not to be envisaged as 'a play-off' between unemployment and higher prices. The evil to be eradicated is the disease of discoordination in the pricing system, of which unemployment and inflation are *alternative* symptoms. More of the one may mean less of the other. But since the quiet abandonment of Keynes' 'unemployment equilibrium' thesis, every economist again knows that, if the disease is incurable, that is simply because of a supposedly irremediable defect in the institutions of representative government—the assumed 'political impossibility' of reform to establish a framework of law under which the disruptive price consequences of strike-threat power are curtailed or eliminated. It is the responsibility of economists always to assert this disturbing truth in every relevant context.

Professor Samuelson refers to 'cruel unemployment.' Inflation is equally cruel. The Nobel prize-winner's failure to mention also the cruelties caused by a depreciating currency reflects the contrast that people harmed by it are regarded as politically weak, whereas trade union leaders who fear that unemployment is likely to generate pressures to wage-rate adjustments disadvantageous to their private interests are politically strong.

Is the 'politically impossible' becoming possible in Britain?

It is indeed a new awareness of these very cruelties which seems to be forcing a revolutionary change of outlook and policy in Britain. Recognition of the injustices suffered for so long by the politically weak—the old people and many of the lower-income groups—reinforced an awareness of the inefficiencies of an inflationary system. The misgivings aroused led to a full-scale investigation of the phenomenon by a Royal Commission.[24] The Commission's report was followed by a general welcome by the public of its proposals—*inter alia* for reform of the unions. Of course the Labour Government's Bill to curb the worst abuses of union power encountered bitter opposition and it was abandoned in 1969. But the Conservative Government's more far-reaching Bill appears likely to pass in 1971. Such legislation would reverse so long a tradition that undue optimism about the early achievement of more justice in the labour market could lead to acute disappointment and discouragement for those who have fought for it. But the point now at issue is that it was the 'cruelties' of inflation which eventually forced a reluctant Labour Government to take unpopular action and a Conservative Government to follow with more chance of success.

But suppose Professor Samuelson had stated his political assumptions openly, would he not then have been forced to say something like this?

Although it is politically quite out of the question, there is an incomparably better method of achieving prosperity—one which could eliminate cruel unemployment without inflation. It would involve increasing the uninflated wages flow,[25] partly by raising the employment level but partly by absorbing a larger proportion of workers into higher paid kinds of work. This would be the consequence of downward market-selected wage-rate and price adjustments. But to allow such a solution would arouse the antagonism of the AFL-CIO and that would involve too many lost votes to any party advocating or adopting it. For that reason it is not worthy of further consideration.

If Professor Samuelson had spoken in this kind of way, bringing thereby the relevant—indeed vital—political factor of vote-acquisition into the picture, and if a sufficient number of his economist colleagues had supported him, such reactions as his authority commanded would have been diametrically different. A tendency for the vote factor to change would have been the consequence. People would begin asking, 'Why is the dismissed alternative "not worthy of consideration"? If the obstacle to what is desirable is simply the opposition of an identifiable group which is acting anti-socially, why should we put up with it?' The number of votes likely to be lost through advocacy of a policy aimed at boosting an uninflated wages-flow (and raising profits and prospects of profits also) would have been reduced. In other words, a return to what Keynes, shortly before his death, called (unexpectedly but respectfully) 'the old classical medicine' would have become less 'politically impossible'.

Keynes encouraged neglect of the cause

Keynes' dissatisfaction with the Cambridge economics of the 1920s is certainly understandable.[26] The economists' typical attitude to the continued appearance of depression apparently convinced him that they were encouraging mere passivity on the part of governments towards chronic idleness of men and assets. That his own kind of thinking had been far more responsible for that passivity would never have struck him or his young advisers. Yet governmental failure to take legislative steps to stop the strike-threat depletion of the wages-flow was certainly due mainly to a conviction which the Keynesian type of thinking was encouraging, namely, that there was a relatively painless remedy—'a better method'—the reduction of real wage-rates via 'cheap money'.

My judgment of Keynes is that he himself would never have risked offending the unions, even in the 1920s. He was held in respect in political parties, and he knew that the remarkable influence attaching to his pronouncements would evaporate at once if he were so unsophisticated as to refer to politically unthinkable possibilities. In 1930 he had expressed 'grave doubts whether an indiscriminate public opinion, reinforced by the votes of the wage-earners, in favour of raising wages, whenever possible, is really the best means . . . for attaining . . . the betterment of the material conditions of the working classes.' It was 'inexpedient', he said, to attempt to achieve this aim 'by the method which reduces the rewards of capital below what is obtainable in other countries. . . . It never pays to render the entrepreneur poor and seedy.'[27] If justice and charity required that the working classes should be better off, income transfers, not high wage-rates, were called for.

But Keynes refrained from translating this philosophy into unequivocal policy recommendations (such as appear now—February 1971—to be contemplated by the British Government). I do not suggest that any political party would have been likely to give any support to such proposals at that time. But both Keynes and the economists he later criticized were to blame in the 1920s and 1930s for having inhibited more candid references to the political obstacle to recovery.

And so back to the central argumant of this essay. The steps needed to recoordinate a depressed economy have throughout been 'politically impossible' largely because the economists did not frankly describe them before tacitly dismissing them on the grounds of currently adverse public opinion or the voters' collective ignorance or short-sightedness.

Notes

1. Several pertinent passages are conveniently quoted in Hutchison, *Economics and Public Policy*, Appendix, pp. 277-301.

2. Ibid., p. 278.

3. Pigou continued to advocate a disguised wage subsidy in his recommendations of public works of a "boondoggling" nature, i.e., provided for other reasons than that of collective entrepreneurship exploiting the least-cost time for investment in public goods—when labour for such purposes appeared to be exceptionally cheap.

4. Ibid., p. 283.

5. Ibid., p. 283.

6. Ibid., p. 288.

7. Of the leading British economists of the 1920s and 1930s, E. Cannan, L. C. Robbins, F. A. Hayek, T. Gregory, F. Lavington, and A. Plant were among the minority pleading unequivocally for price flexibility.

8. Ibid., pp. 285-95.

9. This was recommended by a group of eminent Chicago economists—F. H. Knight, Henry Simons, Jacob Viner, Aaron Director, L. W. Mints—together with the suggestion that the harmful drug should be dosed in the least dangerous form, through public works. J. R. Davis, "Chicago Economists, Deficit Budgets, and the Early 1930s," *American Economic Review* 58 (June 1968), pp. 76-82.

10. This confusion survives. We still often see references to "saving instead of spending." W. H. Hutt, *Keynesianism, Retrospect and Prospect* (Chicago: Regnery, 1963), pp. 104, 184-5, 218, 252-4, 257-60, 436.

11. M. Rothbard, *America's Great Depression* (Los Angeles: Nash Publishers, 1963), pp. 177.

12. W. Hutt, *Economists and the Public* (London: Jonathan Cape, 1936), pp. 245-7. These passages were inserted in the text in page-proof.

13. These words were used *privately* to one another in February 1931 by Sidney and Beatrice Webb. See M. Cole, *Beatrice Webb's Diaries* (London: Longman, 1956), 2, pp. 283-4. As a cabinet minister, Sidney Webb (Lord Passfield) would have been expected to act against the "saboteurs." He did not.

14. W. Hutt, *Keynesianism, Retrospect and Prospect*, pp. 19, 36.

15. W. Hutt, "Keynesian Revisions," *South African Journal of Economics* 23 (June 1965), pp. 101-13.

16. In *Keynesianism*, I was myself led, just as Schumpeter had been, into inferring that Keynes relied (as a second line of defence) upon wage-rate rigidity, because only such an assumption appeared to make any sense of his theory; and I even gave him credit for recognition of what other economists have called "the money illusion" (p. 161). Professor Leijonhufvud has pointed out that the inference is insupportable: *On Keynesian Economics and the Economics of Keynes* (Oxford: Oxford University Press, 1968); *Keynes and the Classics*, Occasional Paper 30 (London: Institute for Economic Affairs, 1969).

17. P. Samuelson, in Lekachman, *Keynes' General Theory—Reports of Three Decades* (New York: St. Martin's Press, 1964), p. 332.

18. G. Haberler, ibid., p. 291.

19. H. Johnson, "The General Theory After Twenty-five Years," *American Economic Review* 51 (May 1961), p. 26. Professor Johnson maintains that Keynes' "polemical instinct was surely right . . .," for "neo-classical ways of thinking were then a major obstacle to sensible anti-depression policy."

20. *Business Week*, October 21, 1970, p. 90.

21. In 1959, Dr. E. C. Harwood emphasized that Professor Samuelson offered no explanation for the change from 5 to 2 percent, as it was in the fourth edition, 1958 (American Institute for Economic Research, Book Review Supplement, 1959).

22. It is amusing to notice that, just about the time that Professor Samuelson had, in gradual stages, reduced what he regarded as a tolerable annual rate of inflation to "below two percent," the actual annual rate of inflation in the United States began rising (from 1962 to 1970 inclusive, according to the price index for gross national product, which covers both private and government outputs) at the following annual percentage rates: 1.1, 1.3, 1.6, 1.8, 2.8, 3.2, 4.0, 4.7, 5.2.

23. The debate is in the *Economic Journal*, 1943, pp. 185-7, and 1944, pp. 429-30.

24. Royal Commission on Trade Unions and Employers' Associations, 1968.

25. By "uninflated wages flow" is meant the aggregate value of the flow of wages measured in pounds or dollars (or other money units) of unchanging purchasing power.

26. But if Keynes had really absorbed F. Lavington's teachings (he was editor of the series in which Lavington's major work, *The Trade Cycle*, 1922, appeared), the *General Theory* might never have been written.

27. Hutchison, *Economics and Economic Policy*, p. 279.

4 • *South Africa's Salvation in Classic Liberalism*

The purpose of this essay is to show that superficially intractable problems of colour and race in the Republic of South Africa are capable of peaceful solution if certain crucial political principles, recently termed 'classic' or 'right' liberalism,[1] are recognised. We do not assert dogmatically that a peaceful solution is unobtainable without the adoption of the particular proposals (mainly of a constitutional nature) which are to be developed here. But the author, after nearly six years' experience of the disaster which has resulted from attempts to solve not wholly dissimilar problems along different lines in the United States, now feels—even more strongly than he did previously—that non-violent progress towards a free, just, stable regime in South Africa, whatever detailed form that progress may take, demands recognition of the political and economic principles which are about to be enunciated.

The term 'classic liberalism' (which we shall use) describes a political philosophy traceable through the writings of Locke, Montesquieu, Hume, Kant, Constant, von Humboldt, J. S. Mill, Tocqueville, Spencer, Acton and Hayek.[2] In the works of these thinkers there are two common threads of agreement: firstly, that the primary function of the State is to ensure the freedom of men in thought, communication and action; and secondly, that the State consists of a small group of private people, necessarily entrusted

Reprinted from *Studies in Economics and Economic History*, edited by M. Kooy with permission of Macmillan London and Blasingstoke.

(as legislature or as executive) with great powers, whom it is essential to subject to some form of social discipline.

Three broad methods of exerting the required social discipline exist: (i) representative government, under which governments may be changed without violence; (ii) an entrenched consititution providing 'rules for making rules', that is, rules to which all valid legislation must conform; and (iii) some form of *effectively entrenched* 'separation of powers', the Courts being accorded the function of declaring unconstitutional any legislation or administrative act which breaks the constitutional rules, but strictly denied any right to change or add to those rules.

Because the prime function of the State is to ensure the freedom of men, 'classic liberalism' assigns it the duty of suppressing all private use of coercive power. The exclusive right to command the use of force is accorded to (i) the Courts and (ii) an Executive which, *subject to the Courts*, must accept responsibility for the enforcement of constitutionally valid laws. In a society in which the State is failing in this duty, a person may be forced to carry and even use a pistol, or to participate in strikes, lock-outs or boycotts, as a defence against the aggression of others.[3] But in a fight there can be no presumption or even probability that right will triumph. Victory is to those with the strongest weapons. That is why the State should be prepared to act immediately against the instigators or perpetrators of internal physical or economic violence as readily as it is prepared to defend the community against external aggression.

Strikes, lock-outs and boycotts are not the only forms in which coercive power of economic origin may be privately used. All collusive agreements to fix prices, or to limit output, or in any way to restrict production are coercive. For competition being simply the process of substituting what any person or group of persons believes to be the least-cost method of producing and marketing outputs or of achieving other economic objectives,[4] restraints on it are as much a curtailment of freedom as is theft with violence. Hence the enactment and enforcement of laws to prevent agreements to limit competition are an important governmental function.

Almost universally, however, laws to forbid the suppression of competition are applied only against the politically weak.[5] We suggest, therefore, the constitutional entrenchment of the principles (i) that private economic coercion be outlawed,[6] and (ii) that all legislation shall be non-discriminatory and all private economic contracts void and non-enforceable if they can be shown to be discriminatory. Such an entrenchment must, we suggest, be accepted as *the key to peaceful co-existence in racially complex communities.* But that principle is also the pillar of *any* society in which freedom is effectively enshrined.

There is no *detailed* agreement among 'classic liberals' about the appropriate sphere or range of the State's 'planning' functions;[7] but there *is* complete agreement on one point, namely, that objectives sought should be non-discriminatory (i.e. affect all members of the community in the same sort of way). Moreover, since some form of collective bargaining is inevitable,[8] and since it may seem impossible to exclude the possibility of *all* use of private coercive power in such negotiations, it is equally important to provide that private agreements shall at least be void and unenforceable (if not illegal) when they are discriminatory.

The concept of non-discrimination is admittedly far from simple. It is not *necessarily* discrimination, for instance, to treat persons with different relevant attributes differently. Thus, in some European towns, legal enactment confers privileges in public transport on the crippled. But as every person who might have the misfortune to become crippled may benefit from this humane enactment, it is not discriminatory. Similarly, there is no discrimination in an electoral law which limits the franchise to persons who have attained educational or responsibility qualifications, provided either that there is genuine equality of opportunity to acquire such qualifications, or that genuine steps are being taken to create opportunities for that equality (and provided, of course, that any test is justly applied). Nor would it be discrimination against the unfortunate if voting laws incorporated the principle, put forward by J. S. Mill,[9] that recipients of State assistance, while retaining other citizen rights, should be denied the right to vote (a point to which we shall return).

Now among the discriminations imposed by or tolerated by the State, those which appear to conflict most seriously with the principles of freedom are based on race, colour or creed. For a host of psycho-sociological reasons, races (or other groups) possessing political power tend to exploit any race or class which lacks that power. But had the State in South Africa been restrained from discriminating on the grounds of race or colour, and had it prevented such discriminations as have been enforced through the private use of coercive power, problems for which many think it is now hopeless to expect a peaceful settlement could, we suggest, have solved themselves gradually—as they arose.

This does not mean that the abandonment of long-accepted discriminations at any time would not have aroused bitter emotions. It is platitudinous to say that there would have been resistance among races or classes whose privileges were reduced. *But even more bitterness would have been released among those who benefited from the dissolution of past injustices.* If there is any apparently indisputable proposition about the removal of barriers to equality of opportunity and consideration, it is that races or classes rescued from former inequities may be expected to demand privileges for themselves and be easy prey to incitements to vengeance. This is particularly important in the case of those minorities who, previously denied the franchise, suddenly become 'swing voters'. Within such a group feelings of envy will combine with long-repressed, now awakened resentment. This has, for instance, been the history of the achievement of political equality for the Negro in the United States.

For these reasons, any planned trend towards the eradication of race discrimination in South Africa will require the most stringent legislation for the enforcement of law and order during a long transitional period. In a society as complex as that of the Republic, the peaceful extension of political power to all racial groups will need, as a top priority, machinery to ensure vigilance and stern discipline in the suppression of deliberately fostered unrest. But the restraint of subversion, the difficulty of which will be magnified the more rapidly past injustices are dissolved, can occur in a tolerable manner only if it is subject to *the rule of law* and a drastic elimination of 'the law's delays'. Ministerial and administrative jurisdiction in this sphere must be gradually abandoned and the necessary decisions transferred to politically neutral Courts. The timing of the different stages in the withdrawal of economic privileges will need careful calculation to ensure orderliness and coordinative adjustments, and to avoid extreme disturbance of established expectations in the labour field. For this to be achieved, wide discretion will have to be delegated to a responsible authority. But appeal to the Courts against its actions and decisions will be essential for the preservation of the confidence that is basic to the policy I am suggesting. And even so, the scope for mischief-making will be prodigious.

Following the 1970 General Election, the South African Prime Minister described the Government's policy as that of *creating* 'prospects and opportunities' for every racial group, 'without fear that the one will deprive the other of that which is his own as a result of the prospects and opportunities which it has been afforded'. Except that the reference to '*creating* opportunities' should be to '*releasing* opportunities,' the principle stated seems to be exactly that which we are here enunciating. At any rate, we can claim that it *is* the same principle if it means acceptance of the principle of dissolution of privilege by legislation as distinct from seizure of property by legislation. The distinction between privilege[10] and property is vital.

Conservative sceptics will ask whether, people being as we know them to be, the achievement of non-discriminatory freedom in a multi-racial society can ever be made sociologically tolerable when racial privilege has coincided initially with class privilege. They will fear that the eradication of colour barriers must precipitate even worse injustices. Freeing the labour market and conceding the right to vote to all races may release a flood of destructive envy to burst the fabric of ordered social relationships and mock the ideals of those who had fought for equality of opportunity. *But such a fear overlooks the stabilising role of the institution of property when the Constitution is deliberately fashioned to prevent spoliation and exploitation via the government itself or in other ways.*

Race discriminations in South Africa had their *origins* in history. Their *perpetuation* has been due to the quite natural use of State power and trade union collusion (especially since 1910) to preserve the *status quo* in the interests of the enfranchised proletariat. The growth of equality of opportunity among the races has been prevented thereby, and the policies of all parties have prevented the gradual emergence of equality of respect and consideration. The 'Civilised Labour Policy', on which the Labour Party members of the 1924 Coalition Government insisted, had the superficially defensible aim of mitigating an unduly rapid dissolution of racial barriers. A sudden withdrawal of the privileges of the Whites could have caused a cruel disturbance of expectations. The wage-rates of white workers, as they were in 1924, had been determined in ways of which very few had disapproved. Typical trade union methods had been virtually without criticism by religious teachers or moralists generally.[11] If, therefore, the purpose of the 'Civilised Labour Policy' had been simply to ensure a levelling up rather than a levelling down, there would have been much to be said for it.[12] It could have been regarded as the most humane and sociologically acceptable method of eradicating historically created injustices. But the aim of the Labour Party was to maintain the *relative* standards of Whites.[13] This was achieved mainly through colour bars in forms which satisfied the consciences of the politicians responsible, won the support of many well-meaning friends of the exploited races and seldom led to protest or opposition from the victims.[14]

Incomparably the most powerful and unjust of all the discriminations against the non-Whites has been a simple insistence upon 'the rate for the job' or 'equal pay for equal work'. The races which, in the middle 1920s, would have been able to enter relatively skilled employments in increasing numbers, through the pressures of the free competitive market, were denied the right to discount their *initial* inferiority by the 'standard-rate' provisions of the *Industrial Conciliation Act* (1924) and the *Wage Act* (1925). The authors of this legislation knew full well (i) that educational facilities for the Coloureds and Indians (and still more for the Bantu) were hopelessly inferior; (ii) that the home background and traditions of the non-Whites constituted a formidable competitive handicap; (iii) that proletarian prejudice against employing non-Whites in occupations traditionally associated with the Whites would be a further obstacle to competition; (iv) that the discriminatory consequences of inferiorities of education, upbringing and sociological environment could be enhanced by the requirement, under the Factories Act, of separate entrances, separate cloakrooms, etc. for non-Whites; (v) that many of the trade unions were already enforcing the 'closed shop'; (vi) that 'employers', faced with the reality of the strike weapon, would be anxious to appease the unions; and (vii) that the apprenticeship system would, given the educational qualifications laid down and the composition of the boards of selection, make it virtually impossible for non-Whites to obtain entry to most kinds of skilled artisan work.[15] In the light of all these circumstances, it was shrewdly foreseen that the superficially just principle of 'equal pay for equal work' could act as an impregnable barrier to racial equality.[16]

Since the official adoption of the 'apartheid' or 'separate development' policy in 1948, more honest, if not more effective, methods of discriminating against the non-Whites have been adopted. To satisfy the white electorate, it became opportune to impose *conspicuous* colour bars. Indeed, the real purpose of most of the discriminatory legislation since 1948 seems to have been that of perpetuating the inferior social status of non-Whites rather than the erection of new *economic* barriers.[17] The most deplorable effects are to be seen in the deliberate and often almost sadistic affront to the dignity and self-respect of the non-white races. This must, one feels, have left sullen, smouldering resentments in the hearts of many of the better-educated (usually the more enterprising and able) Coloureds, Indians and Bantu. In so doing, it has presented potential trouble-makers with a moral justification for the stirring up of discord and disunity.

We reach now the crucial conclusion of this essay. The colour bars which have perpetuated the historically determined material inferiority of the non-Whites, engendering virulent animosities (due even more, we believe, to the the wounded self-esteem of races than to economic injustices), can be traced to the power of the State to discriminate; and the colour discriminations in the economic sphere have all been effected through restraints imposed on the competitive market. The free market is manifestly colour blind. When one buys a product one does not ask, 'What was the colour of those who made this?' One asks simply, 'Is this product good value for money?'[18]

Only a few years ago, officialdom appeared to be engaged in a tug-of-war within itself. On the one hand, the political necessity for continued prosperity made it expedient to permit creeping economic integration. On the other hand, conspicuous restraints on the competition of non-Whites were maintained. At one time the Bantu were being discouraged from becoming part of the private enterprise system, ostensibly for their protection against the evils of 'capitalism.' When the present Prime Minister (as Minister of Bantu Administration) was introducing legislation to establish the African 'homelands', he defended the policy of forbidding private investment in these areas on the grounds that 'we will not let the wolves in, those people who simply seek where they can make money in order to fill their own pockets.'[19] Since then, however, there has been what at present appears to have been a fundamental shift of position. Private investment in the 'homelands' from outside is now being actively encouraged, although investors in the 'homelands' are committed (wisely, we think) to selling out to Bantu investors within fifteen to twenty-five years. Moreover, the Government is using its power to allocate African labour, relying on the carrot of indirect subsidy rather than on the whip, so as to attract industrial expansion to areas where employment will be available for the Bantu, both in the 'border areas' and in the 'homelands'.

The 'separate development' policy has thus turned out to be much less rigidly doctrinaire than early Government pronouncements had led detached observers to fear. Nevertheless, the situation in the Republic remains politically unstable. By this we do not mean that the present Government seems likely to lose its formidable majority in the foreseeable future, or that there are prospects of successful subversion inside the country. But the threat of ultimate military aggression from outside is likely to increase *as the world seems now to be going*, unless 'separate development' can be amended to allow an *acceptable* participation for all races in the democratic process, and the abandonment of the humiliating features of *apartheid*—those sometimes cruel features of South African policy which cannot be hidden from the world. But the concession of what I have vaguely termed 'acceptable' participation in representative government could itself force the gradual relinquishment of such separateness as necessarily implies an insult to the non-white intelligentsia.

A large majority of the Whites in South Africa believe that, were greater equality of social status to be permitted, it would inevitably lead to a demand for universal suffrage or a common roll—'one man one vote'—while that would mean disaster. Such a fear, although quite natural, would prove unfounded under the constitutional arrangements here suggested.

It would be equally understandable if sophisticated critics objected that nothing less than universal adult suffrage would silence South African critics abroad. Certainly the attitude of the world generally towards Rhodesia under the amended Whitehead Constitution seems to confirm this conviction.[20] *On paper*, that Consititution had created the nearest example to a pure 'J. S. Mill democracy' that has existed anywhere since the 1870s. The application of sanctions against the Government which was administering it, on the grounds that it did not confer the right to vote on *all* adult Africans, hardly suggests that the world would be less misinformed about any sharing of political power in South Africa.

Yet this tragic piece of history does *not* constitute a tenable objection. If the sanctions imposed on Rhodesia had not crushed the pure non-racial democracy there, the regime could have survived outside mis-representations. In spite of untruthful reporting, the facts would gradually have filtered out. Similarly, if changes in the required direction within South Africa or even serious preparations for such changes (in the form of official multi-party studies of the issues) are initiated *sufficiently soon*, that is before a hostile and often hypocritical world causes them to appear merely as a reluctant retreat in the face of threatened military aggression, the Republic will surely receive at least some credit and some sympathy for the difficult task it will be tackling.

But any progress along the lines suggested requires a clear recognition that the fears of the presently dominant Whites in the Republic are reasonable, realistic and genuine. A system of 'one man one vote', without an unchallengeable limitation of State power, *could* mean—and in the light of the anger aroused against the present regime, almost certainly *would* mean—spoliation and revenge. But a planned transition to an era in which the right to change rulers by voting is gradually shared with all races, under the constitutional safeguards of 'classic liberalism', could open the path to a more acceptable, more just and incomparably more prosperous regime.

The chief practical obstacle to the acceptance of any such solution is, of course, the utter lack of faith which the minorities are likely to have in the entrenchment of the recommended Constitution. The failure of the attempt to entrench certain clauses of the South African Act of Union (which clauses, after a number of manoeuvres, were eventually overridden by the stratagem of packing the Senate) is only too well rememberd. Moreover, in the great working example of an effective constitution, which at one time might have been regarded as a model, that of the United States, the Supreme Court has been allowed to develop (as one critic has described it) into 'a constitutional convention in permanent session'. For such reasons, the technical task of providing machinery for iron-clad constitutional entrenchment becomes the primary issue.

We suggest (i) that an acceptably rigid entrenchment of the non-discrimination principle *is* practicable, but (ii) that an important transitional requirement will be a weighted franchise to reassure the minorities (Whites, Coloureds and Indians) who could not be expected to perceive the protection inherent in an irrovocable separation of powers. There might well be special amendment provisions, however, under which the minorities (recognising later that adequate guarantees *are* provided by the non-discrimination principle) could renounce the initial weighting at some future time.

A further requirement will be a high educational or responsibility franchise qualification. The enormous complexity of the racial and sociological set-up and the scope for the trouble-maker so created seems to make it essential that, while all citizens should have *an equal right to qualify* for the vote, the qualification should be based upon other factors than age. We suggest that (i) *during the transition*, all presently qualified voters shall be allowed to remain on the roll for the purpose of electing the Lower House, all additions to that roll being subject to an appropriate, *non-discriminatory* test of education and responsibility; and (ii) *special qualifications* (educational or indicating responsibility[21]) shall be demanded *at the outset* for the election of an Upper House, which should possess the right of veto. The *eventual* membership of the Upper House should be designed to bring about gradual equality of representation for each of the four racial groups *as such*.[22] A further requirement for electors of the Lower House which, we believe, would be conducive to the success of the scheme would make qualification optional for otherwise qualified citizens with an income below a certain level. Those in this income class could be allowed to achieve full citizenship, which would include the right to vote, if they accepted the obligation to pay income taxes over and above the rather low poll taxes such as exist at present. Taxation generally would be based on the 'proportional' and not the 'progressive' principle (except for a countervailing progression to offset the regressiveness of indirect taxation). Citizens with an income below a level to be determined could, however, if they so wished, contract out of the right to vote.

The purpose of such a condition can be more clearly envisaged in respect to another desirable qualification for the franchise, namely, that the voter shall not, during any electoral period ending, have benefited from any 'handout' or any 'welfare' benefit from the State other than any insurance, pension or other benefit which his contributions (including the absurdly named 'employers' contributions') fully finance under an actuarially sound scheme. For in a democratic society perhaps the most vital non-discrimination principle which has to be entrenched is that majorities shall have no power to enrich themselves through government at the expense of minorities.

In order to guard against a *coup d' état* and create faith in the permanence of the entrenchments, the police and the armed forces must be made responsible to a President, chosen initially by the Judiciary according to their appraisement of his political independence and ability to win the trust of all racial groups. It is possible that a person of the required attributes could be found in the Public Service, but it is more likely that he would be found in the Judiciary itself. In any case, we recommend constitutional provision for *all subsequent Presidents to be elected, or otherwise chosen, from the Judiciary*—preferably *by* the Judiciary.

Because of the vital role of the Bench, the method by which judges are appointed is of major interest. To achieve a complete divorce of the Bench from politics, we suggest that advocates, on being raised to senior status, shall be called upon to decide whether or not they wish to be *eligible* for ultimate elevation to the Bench. If they so elect, they will be expected to cut themselves off from membership or association, direct or indirect, with any political party.[23] The purpose of these suggestions will be obvious to anyone who has followed the history of the United States Supreme Court, especially since the 1930s.

Finally, the Courts must themselves be bound by the Constitution which it will be their duty to interpret. They must not be allowed to drift from interpretation to constitution-making. That similar provisions were not explicitly written into the United States Constitution has proved its chief weakness. Clarity of wording could probably provide a sufficient safeguard. Nevertheless, procedures must be designed not merely to permit constitutional changes desired by a majority of all races but, in the unlikely event of the Courts being generally believed to have exceeded their powers, to allow reasonably easy responsible appeal by persons or corporations (not by political parties) to a carefully constituted Committee of Senate, *acting as a Court of Constitutional Appeal*. This Committee could then adjudicate solely on the allegation that, in a specific decision, the Judiciary had gone beyond its purely interpretative functions. The crucial difficulty of course is to devise machinery to enable the white minority (or some other minority) to protect itself against a possible judicial tyranny without weakening the guarantees needed to win consent. But if every race is to have faith in the entrenchment being impartially enforced, special safeguards will certainly be needed. The problem is not beyond solution.

We return now to the constitutional provisions intended to guarantee the *survial* of full civil rights for the Whites, and the *achievement* of these rights for the other races. These provisions must declare unconstitutional all legislation which discriminates on the grounds of race, colour, creed, ancestry, sex, language, income and property,[24] and render void or unenforceable all private economic agreements which similarly discriminate.

The elimination of discrimination through private agreements will facilitate the task of the Legislature and the Executive in gradually eradicating the private use of coercive power. When this has been done, private economic discriminations will have disappeared; for as we have seen, the free market is inherently non-discriminatory.

It will be especially important, however, in a country as complex as South Africa that there shall be no misapprehension about the purpose. In no way should the right of every person to choose his associates be questioned. Because discrimination on grounds of sex, religion, race or colour is forbidden, that does not mean that the Courts must force every women's club to admit men, every Catholic club to admit non-Catholics, every Jewish club to admit Gentiles, or every white university to admit non-Whites. But to the extent to which the free choice of associates has the indirect effect of excluding those of a particular group from economic opportunities, then persons who feel themselves materially prejudiced thereby should have the right to seek admission (if they are qualified on other grounds).[25] The existence of material prejudice would be a question of fact. For instance, at one time the universities of Oxford and Cambridge excluded Catholics and women. This was clearly an abuse because there were no other institutions of learning which could offer opportunities of a roughly equivalent nature. But there *may* be no discrimination involved if some universities and colleges restrict admission to students of a particular religion or sex or colour. Of course if institutions of learning are State subsidised the duty to ensure that there is an equal right for all to enjoy the subsidised services is enhanced.

It goes without saying that entrenchment of the right to free choice of associates ensures protection against private coercion for people whose preferences do not happen to conform to those of the mass. Thus persons in South Africa who might wish to form or join a multi-racial club or university must have the right to effective protection not only against physical violence (of the Ku-Klux-Klan type) but against any form of boycott or retaliation. There might be no means of protection against the expression of disapproval; but an individual harmed should have the power to claim damages against any who *organised* disapproval.

Some might feel that to respect the right of a person to choose his friends and associates in the light of whatever attributes he happens to value must imply a humiliating insult for those he does not choose. If that viewpoint is accepted, the achievement of racial harmony in a free society will be regarded as impossible unless people are *forced*, not *taught*, to see what they lose in the richness of life and experience when skin colour, race or ancestry rule out friendships and acceptance. The 'classic liberal' will not dogmatically reject this viewpoint, although J. S. Mill regarded as vital the principle that it is never justified to compel a person to act *for his own good* in a manner in which he would not otherwise have preferred to act but only to prevent him from harming others. Nevertheless, as the present writer argued in 1936,[26] Mill's principle does not necessarily hold when the purpose of the restraint is *educative*. For instance, the forcing of schools and universities in the United States to open their doors to Negroes and other minority groups could have been bringing about the required educative consequences had other circumstances been favourable. The balance of opinion among

American observers whom the writer has consulted on this point is that *the compulsion might well have had this effect*, but that it has in fact created a milieu for the deliberate perpetuation of racial resentments and hatreds.

In the case of the Republic, however, any attempt at general compulsory social integration would constitute so sudden a disturbance of tradition[27] that it would prevent, not assist, the attainment of the objective. On the other hand, *compulsory* social segregation would have to be courageously abandoned under the proposals here put forward, and that would provide a compensating educative factor.[28] Moreover, persons of all races would have to be conceded the right of election to Parliament. In the lobbies, in the House of Assembly restaurant, in the traditional governmental and provincial receptions, 'garden parties' and like social events, all colours would have to be welcomed (as they already are in the Republic's embassies and consulates abroad). Moreover, the formerly 'open' universities would almost certainly decide again to admit students on academic merit alone. And under the new Constitution non-Whites would, we believe, be allowed to return to these universities under conditions of greater genuine social equality than had ever before existed. For one of the unchallengeable lessons of integration experience in the American universities is that, in student societies, in social activities like dances, in sport, and so forth, there have been virtually no *spontaneous* difficulties at all. Where trouble *has* occurred, it seems always to have been skilfully instigated by professional infiltrators from the 'Left.' But wise policy could prevent this; and the 'togetherness' of students of all races would provide an important part of the education of the classes from which non-white Members of Parliament and Senators would be drawn. Hence the 'educative' principle might be held to be relevant here.

The means of eradicating private economic coercion is simply the enforcement of legislative provisions similar to those of the Anti-Trust Acts of the United States applied in all spheres (i.e., with agriculture[29] and labour included). But the laws needed would have to be based upon the clearest recognition (*a*) that competition (the substitution, for the consumers' advantage, of the least-cost method of producing and marketing any product or securing any economic objective) can never be 'unfair' or 'wasteful;'[30] (*b*) that restraints on economic freedom (restraints of competition) can *never* be a means of securing 'full employment', or of fostering a foreign trade which is more productive than internal trade, or of facilitating the maintenance of the trade balance, or of permitting the consumer to enjoy any freely preferred advantages which he could not otherwise have enjoyed;[31] and (c) that the essence of the conduct to be outlawed is not the achievement of 'monopoly' as such but *the contrivance of scarcity*, i.e., the forcing up of the price of any commodity or service (via collusion or otherwise) above its 'natural scarcity' value.

But big practical difficulties would be met in planning a gradual transition to the new non-discriminatory economic order. Great powers would have to be delegated to a *Restraint Eradication Board* which would have the task of organising a *slow but sure* relaxation of economic restrictions, with a view rather to a *levelling up* than a *levelling down* of economic standards. They would need the authority to call for the abandonment or successive modifications of any restrictive labour practice or any other privately or legally imposed restraint which had been excluding any group or person from the wage bargaining table, but no power to impose any new restraint. A certain minimum speed at which they would be committed to take the steps required could well be specified, but otherwise the process would be best entrusted to their untrammelled discretion. For instance, the reduction of any wage-rate previously fixed under any strike-threat influence (whether or not through the procedures of the Industrial Conciliation Act) or any minimum wage-rate previously fixed under the Wage Act, might well be at least 10% *per annum* for the first year, $7^1/_2$% (of the reduced minimum) for the second, 5% for the third, etc. (These percentages are, of course, completely arbitrary.) It would *not* be an offence for any management to continue to pay more than the falling minima, but it would be an offence to resist, by the threat of or resort to the strike (or other violence), any use that managements might make of their power to expand outputs by cutting wage costs within the limits enacted. For when managements do this, they add to the source of demands for non-competing outputs and set in operation the wages-multiplying process. The *average* real wage-rate would soon begin to rise, and the new minima fixed would cease to have any relevance. Severe labour scarcity, caused by the rapidly increasing wages-flow, would have brought about, in nearly all fields, free market values of labour well above the corresponding minima for all degrees of skill or competence.

Another, quite separate authority, the *Compensation Board*, would have to be entrusted with the task of authorising compensation for the very small minority of workers in formerly privileged groups whose established expectations were drastically harmed, the compensation being dependent upon the willingness of any individual helped to undertake alternative employments offered and/or training. *Ceteris paribus,* any compensation would vary according to the age of the recipient and the estimated versatility of his skills. The funds for compensation could be obtained from a very small percentage levy on the greatly increased general wages flow. We judge that a period of two decades would be sufficient to allow the formerly privileged races to have adjusted themselves to emerging equality of opportunity. Thereafter, a small minority *might* still need special protection or subsidy.[32] But on principle the beneficiaries of such *continued* protection should, while the assistance continued, be deprived of the franchise.

At the end of the transitional period, no colour bars or race discriminations *imposed by law or by clearly discernible private collusion* would survive. Admittedly, large differences in the average income of the various racial groups might well continue for many decades still to come, protected by the sociological cushion of human inertia. But surviving customary restraints would all the time be subject to steady erosion *where the beneficiaries of the new opportunites were prepared to fight* against inertia (*a*) through deliberately pricing themselves into higher remunerated and more productive work and (*b*) through investing in themselves, not only in skill acquisition but in building up a reputation for reliability, co-operativeness and loyalty ('loyalty' not to managements or investors or corporations but to the great society which the workers, as well as managements, investors and corporations, are serving).

Nevertheless, the understandable resentments aroused by the *apartheid* era, the external threat of black nationalism and the realities of the cold war seem to make very remote any hope of initial formal and voluntary acceptance by the non-Whites of any new order of the kind we have tried to show would be practicable. If efforts were made to win approval via a National Convention at which the different races were represented by elected delegates it would, we feel, be doomed to failure. However sincere the proclaimed objectives, the dismal truth is that the easiest path to prestige, influence or elected office in a racially complex community is via the exacerbation of the prejudices, hatreds, envies and general unreasonableness to which proletariats are subject.

Moreover, as we have already stressed, the greatest danger with which any purely democratic society is faced, and especially a society which is in process of eradicating historically determined racial discriminations, is subversion. Hence, frankly recognising the fact that good constitutions are based *on the absence of faith,* that is *on mistrust,* we envisage a voluntary, *unilateral renunciation of dominating political power and economic privilege* on the part of the Whites *on their own terms,* but on terms which will be so obviously just and enlightened that disinterested non-white sceptics at home and abroad will gradually learn to be satisfied *as they perceive the new era in operation.* For the regime will certainly not endure unless it *is* based on equality of opportunity, *conspicuous* equality of respect for persons of all races and colours and the absence of surviving discrimination through subterfuge.

The sanctions for a Constitution framed in the manner suggested would be that each individual acquiring the qualificatons for the vote would specifically contract in and thereby pledge himself to uphold the Constitution and any provisions for its amendment. Under the kind of qualifications envisaged, it would mean that, for a long time to come, the aggregate number of votes cast by Whites for the different parties would exceed those cast by non-Whites. But this would not mean 'domination' or 'oppression' by the Whites (although we must expect that charge to be made). Discrimination through new legislation and official administration of that legislation would be forbidden; discrimination through existing legislation would have been eradicated by the end of the 'transitional period'; private contracts which discriminated in the spheres of trade, production and employment would then be void and unenforceable; and the most burdensome kinds of economic injustice based on race would have been eliminated through the proscription of any private use of coercive power.

For the enforcement of the non-discrimination principle and therefore protection of *the rights of the unenfranchised,* arrangements similar to those which were operative under the *Declaration of Rights* of the former Rhodesian (Whitehead) Constitution would seem to be appropriate. A *Human Rights Advisory Council* consisting of a certain number of nominated ex-judges willing to serve *plus* one nominated representative each from the Whites, the Coloureds, the Indians and the Bantu should be set up.[33] This Council should have the duty to examine Bills introduced in Parliament and draw the attention of the legislators to any clauses which might involve racial discrimination. If clauses on which they commented adversely remained unamended when the Bills were passed, the legislators would know that they faced the virtual certainty that the clauses in question would be held unconstitutional and void by the Courts, before which the Council's advisory opinion could be placed in the event of any challenge.

It is absurd to suggest that a person is 'oppressed' or 'unfree' because he does not possess the franchise. The writer has lived continuously as an alien in the United States for nearly six years and he has enjoyed every bit as much 'freedom' as any United States citizen. Nor would any representation of different races in proportion to their numbers be likely to bring about greater 'freedom' to majorities (unless 'freedom' were interpreted to mean 'freedom to exploit minorities'). We cannot insist too strongly that the suggestions here put forward would have no chance of voluntary acceptance by minorities in the absence of a weighted franchise.

Under the proposals here submitted, the Bantu 'homelands' policy would not have to be discarded. One possibility is that the chief Bantu areas would be conceded complete independence so that they were constitutionally in the same position as, say, Lesotho, Botswanna, Swaziland and Malawi. Recent official pronouncements in the Republic seem to have implied that this possibility has indeed received consideration. Areas that are sufficiently homogeneous from the racial standpoint, like the Transkei, might well be left as autonomous as the former 'Protectorates'. But 'homelands' like Ovamboland would have to retain something resembling their existing political status until a numerous enfranchised class had emerged and attained a comparable degree of sophistication. The many small Bantu areas also would require some specially devised form of representation. However, 'homelands' of all constitutional types could, we feel, form part of a Federal Union with the Republic, possibly with provisions for the franchise in such areas gradually being adjusted to accord with parallel constitutional limitations under the Republic's Constitution.

An alternative, which the present writer would strongly favour, is that all the 'homelands' be in due course conceded the *present* status of the Transkei, which is somewhat similar to that of the Provinces. Their inhabitants should then have the right to qualify for votes in the Republic. At the outset, of course, only a small minority would be eligible. But the Bantu *would* have direct representation in the Parliament of the Republic in both Houses.

Our purpose in thus outlining a 'classic liberal' solution for the problems which arise when political power, initially monopolised by one race in a multi-racial society, begins to be shared with the other races, has been designed simply to show the inherent practicability of a peaceful and morally acceptable way out. *The same objectives could perhaps be secured in quite different ways.* But we can claim for the 'classic liberal' suggestions as here put forward that the objective is clearcut and unequivocal. In 1934, the present author charged that writers about race policy in South Africa seemed typically to refer to 'an orderly march' of the Bantu, yet were 'reluctant to state the destination except with intentional obscurity'.[34] The 'destination' we have envisaged is that of full equality of opportunity, consideration, respect and status for every racial group. Moreover, our suggestions cover protection of the objective from subversive attempts to prevent the destination from being reached. Political incentives for subversion will certainly *tend to* increase as growing affluence in any group creates the unrest which seems to be its inevitable concomitant when mischief-makers cannot be restrained.

Opposition from the privileged, which we could expect to be expressed mainly through the trade union movement, would almost certainly be vitriolic. In our judgment, however, that would be much less serious than the discontent which could be aroused among the beneficiaries. Nevertheless, plans must be framed to prevent the use of strikes in attempts to sabotage the scheme. But the better utilisation of the existing powers of the people, the greater scope for investment in human capital, the consequential rapid increase in the flow of wages and especially the rising standards of living of the lower-income groups would create an explosive situation among the beneficiaries unless all could expect ruthless protection against organised efforts to arouse and exploit resentments. The immediate enforcement of law and order at the first signs of intrigues to disturb the smooth operation of the transition would be needed.

The likelihood of the ideas we have put forward being seriously considered by the present parties (other than the Progressive Party) would seem very remote were it not for the obvious fact that the existing political and economic situation cannot indefinitely endure. And the hope that by piecemeal, pragmatic, groping changes, the basic reforms demanded can be indefinitely postponed is a dangerous illusion. But it persists largely because the politicians and the electorate are mostly convinced that the extension of political and economic equality must mean the destruction of what, if we consider the interests of the Whites alone, is a good and affluent society. If our argument is sound, what is of permanent value in the culture of the Republic *can* be conserved. Under a Constitution which is at least conceivable, with strongly entrenched and strict enforcement, the supposed 'miracle' of good relations under freedom in a racially complex society is not beyond attainment.

Notes

1. To distinguish them from those of "liberalism" in the sense widely acquired by this term during the present century, namely, "socialism" or "leftism."

2. A parallel development among the economists can be traced through Adam Smith, James Mill, J. Say, Ricardo, the other "classical" economists proper, and this century most clearly through the contributions of the Austrian School. The ideas of this school have crystallised in the praxeological studies which Mises has refined and synthesised in his monumental *Human Action.*

3. The enforcement of a contract freely entered into is not coercion; yet contracts to act in collusion *may* be a means of coercion. Boycotts or strikes do not differ essentially from the use of the baton or pistol for private ends.

4. Whether the objectives sought are privately or collectively determined is irrelevant; but for competition to exist appropriate rules, and institutions for the enforcement of those rules, may be essential.

5. For instance, the United States' Anti-Trust Laws are aimed at industry and commerce alone. Labour and agriculture are explicitly excluded.

6. The reader may ask, will not this leave the worker defenceless against exploitation? The present writer is engaged on a work which will show that the use of the strike-threat to influence wage-rates and conditions of work greatly reduces the flow of wages and the average wage-rate, causes avoidable inequity and inequality in the distribution of the wages flow (among races, classes, and individuals), destroys employment security, and is mainly responsible for the political expediency of monetary inflation.

7. All agree that *certain* coordinative rules must be centrally decided, such as whether we shall drive on the left-hand or the right-hand side of the road.

8. Because negotiation of the contracts needed for society's cooperative activity must necessarily involve large numbers of people.

9. In his great defence of the democratic system, *Representative Government* (The World's Classics, 1861), pp. 279-80.

10. A transferable privilege may become property, but property is not privilege.

11. Frequent resort to physical violence prior to that time *was*, of course, condemned.

12. The writer has always held that the peaceful achievement of a more just social order demands a *gradual* transition; for protected classes have often innocently inherited their privileges, which they have most frequently not recognised as such, and on the survival of which they have reasonably planned their lives. (See the writers' *Plan for Reconstruction* (London: Kegan Paul, 1943), and his *Economists and the Public* (London: Jonathan Cape, 1936), Chapter 21.

13. The injustices so perpetuated resemble those which are brought about in countries of more or less racially homogeneous population through the insistence

upon what trade unions term "established differentials" or "due relatives"—conventional ratios between the wage-rates for tasks of different supposed degrees of skill.

14. The chief attribute of the "Civilised Labour" policy was the denial (often explicit in argument) that any colour bar was intended or operative. The two "Colour Bar Acts" (Mines and Works Acts of 1911 and 1926) had been frank and honest defences of white privilege. Only in the recent recourse to "job reservation" has the admission of discriminatory intention again been so straightforward and candid.

15. "Employers' representatives" on the apprenticeship boards, anxious to maintain good relations with the labour unions, could usually be relied upon to refuse opportunities to the minority of non-Whites who might otherwise have qualified.

16. What misled many humanitarian supporters of the system was a failure to perceive that equality of remuneration for the production of output of equal quality is *the result of* a just economic system, not *a means of* securing justice.

17. The main exceptions have been (a) forcing Indians to abandon businesses in white areas, (b) forcing non-Whites generally to live at a distance from their work, and (c) control of Bantu labour. But we judge (c) to have been more than offset through increased opportunities in the Border Areas and within the Bantu homelands.

18. See the writer's *Economics of the Colour Bar* (London: Deuthsch, 1964), p. 173.

19. Ibid, pp. 159-60.

20. That Constitution was abandoned early in 1970. The responsibility for this change, which has been followed by a very hesitating move in the direction of *apartheid* by the Smith Government, must be laid on the shoulders of the British and American governments, and their press and television, which have disgracefully misrepresented one of the most enlightened experiments in multiracial relations that has ever been available for mankind. Had the amended Whitehead Constitution been effectively entrenched (and that was not out of the question), Rhodesian experience could have provided an object lesson for the whole world, both through its successes and its failures.

21. For instance, a minimum earned income or tax liability, an approved university degree or professional qualification, a minimum age (say forty) and so forth.

22. The speed at which this equality could be conceded would have to depend upon the predicted speed of attainment of equality of economic and educational opportunity.

23. Although some South African judges could not claim to qualify according to this criterion, in the present writer's opinion the traditions of judicial independence have almost invariably been honoured by judges, even by those whose appointments appeared to many to have been influenced by party political consideration.

24. The forbidding of discrimination on grounds of income and property implies the gradual abandonment of progressive taxation, except to the extent to which this is needed to countervail the regressive effects of indirect taxation. The recent recognition of *the inegalitarian nature of so-called progressive taxation* and the growing perception that that system has emerged as a form of vote-buying (to enrich majorities or those politically powerful for other reasons such as 'swing voters,' or large contributors to party funds) will have to be understood by those who set out to explain the reforms required. See F. A. Hayek, *Constitution of Liberty* (Chicago: University Press, 1960), Chapter 20.

25. Thus a university would retain the right to apply its own non-discriminatory academic admission standards.

26. Hutt, *Economists and the Public*, Chapter 17.

27. This tradition was weakening in a quite natural manner, a fact which explains all the legislative attempts of the last few decades to protect a threatened tradition.

28. Attempts would certainly be made to use integrated clubs as centres of subversion. The costs of preventing this would be one of the unavoidable costs which would have to be accepted.

29. If agriculture were covered by anti-trust, the many official agricultural control boards would have to be dissolved. But as, in the writer's judgement, this system has harmed consumers without benefiting farmers, its abandonment is certainly not impracticable under a scheme which would mean an unprecedented expansion of demand for the products of agriculture.

30. As distinct from certain business practices sometimes *called* "competition" but which have nothing to do with the process—such as fraudulent description, particularly in advertising; aggressive selling (i.e., discriminatory pricing); the slander of competitors, etc. It is essential to make this point mainly because the vested interests in discrimination have skillfully succeeded in associating the term *competition* with such practices.

31. We need not discuss here the special problems of patents, copyrights, and "externalities" (social costs and benefits). If there exists a case for protection of any activities by deliberately creating a monopoly, that protection should be provided, without discrimination, by the State, and not through private collusion to fix prices, outputs, etc.

32. We regard this as unlikely except for a mere handful of people; for as we have insisted, relaxation of the barriers, especially of the most vicious and powerful colour bar, "the rate for the job," will have released an unprecedentedly large flow of real income to make practicable the process of "levelling up."

33. In order, in particular, to reassure the Bantu of the justice of such an arrangement, it would be useful to include initially certain trusted friends of the Bantu, such as Helen Suzman, Alan Paton, and Margaret Ballinger. Thereafter, it

should consist of persons of eminence chosen by reason of a record of independence of politics.

34. W. Hutt, "The Economic Position of the Bantu in South Africa," in *Western Civilization and the Natives of South Africa,* ed. I Schapera (New York: Humanities Press, 1967), p. 202.

part II ● *THE CONSEQUENCES OF POLITICAL AND ECONOMIC POWER*

5 • *Economic Power and Labor Unions*

In the vocabulary of the social sciences, the term "power" has meaning onlyin the context of human freedom. But "freedom" is an elusive concept, and consideration of its relation to "power" raises issues of great conceptual complexity. Last century (1898) M. Pantaleoni[1] tried to clear up some of the difficulties in an article entitled "An Attempt to Analyze the Concepts of 'Strong' and 'Weak' in Their Economic Connection." Since World War II, three great scholars have returned to the topic. F. A. Hayek's[2] erudite *The Constitution of Liberty* has greatly helped us to clarify the issues; while Bertrand de Jouvenel[3] and Helmut Schoeck[4] have treated different aspects of the same problems in a remarkably different manner, but with comparable inspiration and logical rigor. They have reached very similar conclusions on the issues to be discussed in this paper.

We are here concerned with power-freedom relations in one of their most important manifestations. The issues are so complex that some reference to the broad question of "power" in relation to "freedom" (or "liberty") is called for. Certain of the complexities are semantic, arising through the use of words in a way which the reader understands perfectly well in the context, but which are inconsistent with the meaning of the same words in other contexts. "To be truly free," said Voltaire, "that is power." We all know, of course, what he meant. But, generally speaking, the word "power" implies a *potential* enemy of freedom, although it *may* be the means to freedom.

Original paper presented at the Association for Social Economy meeting, New York, 1973.

In the present article, "power" exerted will be conceived of as restricting the range of action of an individual, either in the interest of the freedom of all or for the special benefit of some. "Power" in the latter form will be regarded therefore as infringing on that condition of society that we call "free."

D. W. Brogan, in his Preface to Bertrand de Jouvenel's *On Power*, describes the book as "an argument for repeated stock-taking, for the scrutiny of every new proposal for extending the power of the state or of *any other power-monopolising body*."[5] Brogan's phrase seems to me to pinpoint the *practical* philosophic aspect of what may soon come to be accepted as *the* crucial economic problem of the present generation. Again in words from Brogan's preface, de Jouvenel insists on the need (from the angle of "freedom") of "making sure of making sure that effective power is not monopolised."[6]

Our concern here is with the two related forms of power "monopolisation" indicated in the passage just quoted: (a) what Herbert Spencer was envisaging in the title of his famous tract, "Man *versus* the State" and (b) what I think we should call "the man *versus* the private group." Our specific interest is in a particular manifestation of power wielded in form (b), namely, by labor unions. But this special problem of power "monopolisation" cannot be understood except in the light of a simultaneous awareness of the nature of governmental power. For the authority of the state may be used either to promote or restrain freedom. Thus, although the issue in this paper is possible abuse of power by monopolistic unions, it will be impossible to avoid recognition of and continuous concern with the authority exercised by and through those small groups of private people whom we call "governments."

The engrossing of power against which de Jouvenel has warned us has, then, to do with the accretion or seizure of the ability to restrain, control or "exploit"[7] others by (i) a person, or (ii) a group, or (iii) a government. Realism compels us to recognise that, in the contemporary world, both legislation and its administration are normally privately motivated, and that power has, indeed, been "monopolised."

Governmental power[8] to make and enforce the rules which all must obey is more often termed "sovereign"; and what is meant by that word is the power which actually gets obeyed, whether or not the "sovereignty" is defensible.

The complexities and dilemmas encountered in endeavors to reach conceptual clarity on the implications of "power" or "sovereignty" in relation to "human freedom" led the author of this paper, in a book published in 1936,[9] to insist that we cannot conceive of "liberty" as a condition in which every person is allowed to "do as he wishes" (in today's delightful vernacular, permitted to "do his own thing"). "When I can do what I want to do", said Voltaire, "there is my liberty for me."[10] But this notion is seriously incomplete; for one person might "want" to enslave others, or intimidate them, or steal from them.

It follows that, for individuals to be free, they must necessarily be subject to some restraints. This applies firstly to the group of people who have acquired the privileges and duties of the right to rule (i.e., governments). Secondly, it applies to individuals or groups operating in the market—selling, buying, or bartering services (inputs), products (outputs), or resources (assets). The purpose of the restraints is to ensure that one person or group shall not coerce another person or group, except in defense of the freedom of others. And the restraints applied through the market system are those imposed under the "democratic" form of what the writer calls "consumers' sovereignty."[11]

Sovereignty in this form can be envisaged as the exercise by persons in their consumers' role of their right to buy or refrain from buying outputs offered, at the prices asked. Consumers' choice then determines, *via* "market signals," the manner in which scarce resources can be profitably used by their owners. The discipline so administered, it is suggested, is a legitimate and "democratic" use of the individual's ability to contribute to the power which directs the employment of assets and of men.

In 1936, developing the ideas just expressed, the writer stressed two forms of *legitimate* power or sovereignty: (a) *democratic* governmental power and (b) free market power (i.e., "*democratic* consumers' sovereignty"). Both forms were, he maintained, compatible with that condition of the individual which, from the standpoint of the consensus of ethical opinion, would be accepted as "free."

Governmental power and market power can be seen to be essential for the orderly functioning of *any* form of society. But a slave economy and a slave market can operate in an orderly manner. Neither governmental institutions nor market institutions *need* be "democratic" for the virtue of *orderliness* in human relations to be won. We are to suggest, however, that for "freedom" from illegitimate power to be achieved, it is imperative that both governmental controls and market controls *shall* be "democratic" in a sense which we are to explain.

In respect of government, the term "democratic" does not mean simply that the rulers are chosen by counting votes. Still less does it mean universal suffrage ("one man, one vote").[12] Certainly it means that governments can be changed, without violence, through elections. But in a truly "democratic" *society*, the discretion of governments must be restrained through "rules for making rules." The restraints must have the purpose of preventing either (i) governmental institutions or (ii) market institutions from being used to subject some persons to the will of others. The most usual form in which such subjection occurs is through the transfer (or attempts to transfer) income or property from one group to another group.

Let us consider first in this context the required limitations on *governmental* discretion. Freedom, as we conceive of it here, will be achieved if constitutional enactments or strong conventions prevent the people who form governments from using their power for their own personal profit or for that of majorities or other favored groups. More positively, liberty is won if governments are allowed to act solely for the collective benefit, legislation being unconstitutional unless it is non-discriminatory. Thus legislation adopted or executive discretion exercised for the *special* advantage of, say, public servants, or the dairy industry, or the plumbers, or the teachers, or the unions, or the medical profession, or the Whites, or the Blacks, or importers, or exporters, or debtors, or creditors, or the rich, or the poor, or men, or women, or the rulers' friends, or contributors to "campaign expenses," or "swing voters," and so forth needs to be held unconstitutional if freedom in our sense is to be achieved and safeguarded.

To ensure that government operates for the collective interest, instead of, as today, largely (if not mainly) for private interests, its activity at all levels (e.g., in the U.S. at federal, state and municipal levels) needs to be restricted to its "classical" tasks: provision for the maintenance of peace (an army and armaments), the administration of police and justice, and the making and application of a framework of non-discriminatory rules under which disciplined entrepreneurs can plan and coordinate the economy. The required rules cover such diverse fields as contract enforcement (including any contract to maintain a money unit of defined value), weights and measures, traffic regulations, anti-trust, and the kind of activities supposed to be undertaken in the U.S.A. by agencies like the F.D.A., the S.E.C., the

F.T.C., the I.C.C., the Fed., and the like. For "freedom" to be assured, however, such agencies must be permitted only an interpretative discretion of the laws they administer; while their interpretations need to be checked by politically independent courts.

Under representative government, then, the voters have the right to choose and change rulers from time to time. That right *is* an important requirement for human freedom. But alone it does not cause political sovereignty to be effectively vested in "the people." We cannot place too much stress on the truth, enunciated by de Jouvenel, that ". . . Divine Right and Popular Sovereignty, which pass for opposites, stem in reality from the same trunk."[13] The safeguards of separation of powers—judicial, executive, and legislative independence—are insufficient alone to guarantee that government power will not be misused.

We have explained that whether or not governmental power over the individual can be said to be compatible with individual freedom is dependent upon the nature of the limitations imposed on the rulers. Very much the same limitations are needed for discipline in the free market. The constraints required on the individual in the satisfaction of his consumer preferences (i.e., the ends he pursues) are conducive to freedom when they are imposed either by the scarcity of means to ends, or by contract freely entered into in the absence of fraud. That is really what we imply when we use the term "free market."[14]

Both consumers and producers are disciplined by competition. Thus each consumer must ultimately compete against all other consumers for the *means* to the ends he seeks.[15] He competes either directly, or through entrepreneurial intermediaries. Under the institutional framework necessary, the producer-entrepreneur has an incentive to discover the least-cost method of responding to market-expressed ends. The consumer then enjoys "liberty" because the very restraints of market-determined values which limit *his* access to the things he may want discipline all other consumers in the same sort of way. Through rationing the distribution of the flow of outputs, the market operates in a non-violent, non-arbitrary way.

Similarly, in the individual's producer-entrepreneurial role, his discretion is limited only in the sense of being restrained by non-discriminatory market pressures. Through the commands of the free market, he has the strongest motive (the loss-avoidance, profit-seeking incentive) to use the community's resources for ends (products) which he forecasts the people will demand. He has a further, related motive to economize the resources he uses. And through the incentive to economize, he is also forced to "compete." (The term "compete" in this context means he must attempt to achieve each end which he seeks as entrepreneurial intermediary, so that the minimum sacrifice of other ends will be required.)

The process of competition can be defined as "the substitution of a lower cost method of producing and marketing any 'product,' irrespective of the institutional set-up which may be needed to create and/or protect incentives for the process." But when the framework of institutions releases and safeguards the loss-avoidance, profit-seeking incentives as far as is practicable, we can call the *consumers' sovereignty* exercised "democratic." The adjective "democratic" is apt when the sovereignty expressed reflects the forecast choices of all income receivers through a system of voting under which each person's vote about how the community's resources shall be utilized is weighted in proportion to the value of the productive services that he and his property (whether acquired through his thrift—or his parents') are contributing to the common pool of output.

In the absence of the overruling, *via* governmental or private monopolistic power of free market (i.e., "social") discipline, individuals whose "votes" are most heavily weighted are those whose assets, enterprise, energies and skills earn the most; and that, in turn, means those who are contributing most to the well-being of the rest. People as consumers, *choosing between ends*—"products," are viewed as *sovereign,* and people in their producer and entrepreneurial capacity are viewed as *choosing means to ends* and therefore as *subject.* That is, through the operation of this "consumers' sovereignty," persons in their producer capacity are governed by persons in their consumer capacity. In a money economy, consumers and producers must, to buy or sell, offer money's worth in one form in order to get money's worth in another form. When each consumer possesses a similar power to command other people in their "producer" role (his power being in proportion to the market-determined value of his contribution, as producer, to the common pool of wanted things), we have the "democratic form" of "consumers' sovereignty." Individuals are then constrained *via* a *social* sovereignty, as distinct from that *private* sovereignty exerted when some right to coerce others is vested in a monopolistic group, or when a government is commanded by pressure groups. Of course, because private power does today overrule social power, in practice consumers' sovereignty is far from perfectly "democratic."[16]

To ensure that consumers' sovereignty shall in fact be "democratic" and entrepreneurs truly "subject," the framework of law and law enforcement needs to have evolved, or to have been designed, so as to create or protect what I have called the loss-avoidance, profit-seeking incentives. Under the required framework, those entrepreneurs who are most successful in (i) observing consumers' current preferences, (ii) in forecasting their future preferences, and (iii) in achieving the least-cost response to them, are rewarded, while those entrepreneurs who (through defective judgment or bad luck) fail in this forecasting and economizing role are penalized.

Our use of the words "sovereignty" and "democratic" is, of course, metaphorical. Yet are not those attributes of *State sovereignty* which we have suggested contribute to the freedom of the individual just those which can be so clearly observed in the operation of *consumers' sovereignty* in "the free market"? If incentives could be released which subjected "the small groups of private people we call 'governments' " to a political discipline as effective as the social discipline I have called "democratic consumers' sovereignty," then the function of governing could indeed be viewed as "of the people, for the people, by the people" (although not in the common and naive connotation of this phrase).

In the background of the above discussion we can at last turn our attention to union power. There are various useful services the unions perform with which we are not concerned. Our interest here is solely with their organization of *privately motivated coercive power*. The power now under discussion is, in a broad sense, two-fold: firstly, personal intimidation and assault of managements and competitors (especially of non-strikers and strike-breakers) due to *de facto* exemption from society's normal sanctions against physical violence and sabotage;[17] and secondly, a form of coercion which is used for the same purposes but is less likely to be regarded as illegitimate, namely, through the right, by "peaceful threats," to disrupt the continuity of economic cooperation.

This power is the basis not only of the authority the unions have won to discipline their own members (willing or unwilling) and deny freedom to potential competitors, but it is of course used also against investors.[18] And it is often used detrimentally and ruthlessly against third parties, non-parties to the "dispute" (who have, in many countries, been denied the right to sue for damages). But, most important, union power is used against the community as a whole, as consumers and producers. For the disruption of one set of activities throws into disorder the work and life of others—sometimes huge numbers of others.[19] And because the strike is a form of warfare which, when resorted to, requires strategy and the maintenance of morale, it becomes essential during peace to keep alive the war spirit: mistrust and hostility towards the enemy—"the employer."

The threat to strike—"the gun under the table" as Mises called it, like all forms of warfare, can be used for good or noble purposes. Nevertheless, even when the objective is defensible, we are forced to regard all private use of coercive power (whether by boycott or strike) as an intolerable infringement of human freedom. As the present writer insisted in his recent book, *The Strike-Threat System*,[20] "we should have to condemn the Mafia even if it could be shown that the revenues of racketeering were being used to subsidize opera, cancer research or civil rights movements." The strike being a form of private warfare, as in all warfare, victory is to the strong, not to the righteous. Defenders of the right to strike are in fact accepting "Might is right!" as a principle.

Yet they typically contend that the workers are forced to strike to secure distributive justice. Hence we must face the question, how can the claims of the investors who provide the assets that multiply the yield of human effort be balanced against "labor's" claims on the value of the product?

In the textbooks of labor economics, the words "justice" and "injustice" constantly occur. The writer cannot recall ever having seen a reference to justice to investors who, as entrepreneurs, forecast the community's needs and take the risk of providing the assets required to satisfy those needs. And what about justice to consumers? In 1935, a book appeared entitled *Are Trade Unions Obstructive?*[21] The word "consumer" occurred once in the preface but was not used again anywhere in the book.

Moreover, because in so many cases duress-imposed labor costs reduce profitable outputs, what about justice to workers laid off? And can we disregard injustice to those who would otherwise have improved their productivity, earnings and prospects as additional recruits for the activities rendered less profitable? When costs are raised through union power, prospective yields to investment in labor's inputs are reduced; and then the loss-avoidance incentives force men and assets into inferior, "sub-optimal" employments.

Of course, the present attitude of the overwhelming majority of opinion-makers (or opinion-followers) in the press, broadcasting, television, the churches, the schools, politics, etc., is that the only relevant ethical consideration stems from their conviction that investors earn too much and the workers earn too little. But it can be shown that, when potential investors expect labor costs to be exposed to strike-threat coercion, they are unexploitable. There have certainly been periods during which some property transfers from investors to workers have been achieved *via* union aggression,[22] but that is simply because investors as a whole have failed to predict the extent to which they are exploitable.

When investors realistically forecast their vulnerability, they will make full allowance for the probability of union power being used to seize part of their capital. In assessing the value they can risk in assets to be used in any activity, they will rely on the unions' not wishing to kill the goose that lays the golden eggs, or unduly harm the goose's fertility. They will rely also upon the *probability* (a) that, although in a society which tolerates strike-threat coercion technological progress will be discouraged, it will not come to an end, so that labor-economizing and capital-saving achievements in non-competing fields will be raising the source of demands for most prospective outputs; and (b) that, in spite of the depressive effects of the use made of union power, aggregate income will continue to increase through continued thrift (provision for the future—the net accumulation of assets).

Investors today expect managements to be expert in (as far as possible) avoiding capitulations to strike-threat pressures, but they know they cannot rely on the managers' being wholly successful. They simply know that the avoidance of a future capitulation to union power will bring a windfall gain, while capitulation to a particularly heavy wage demand will bring a windfall loss; and, in every decision to retain, replace or accumulate assets in any productive activity, they must, if as entrepreneurs they are forecasting rationally, regard the property seizures referred to above as prospective costs which reduce profitable investment in that activity. From society's angle, the consequences of union power so used will be that the *composition* of the community's assets stock will be adversely affected. In general, the most productive and wage-multiplying types of assets are the least versatile, therefore the most exploitable, and hence most likely to be avoided until exploitation is forbidden. Investment in that form must certainly decline relatively to investment in non-union activities or in more versatile—less specialised—resources. The damage to the material well-being of labor as a whole is incalculable.

A related issue is the prices of those assets of which the accumulation has been continuously raising the yield to labor's efforts. The assets used in occupations producing goods of relatively short economic life (consumers goods) can be observed to be competing with the assets which are used in making goods of relatively long economic life (producers' goods). Duress-imposed "raises" or "hikes" in the former are in practice matched by similar "raises" or "hikes" in the latter. Now *ceteris paribus* the cheaper the assets needed in any activity, the greater will be the demand they express for the complementary factor—labor. That is, the higher will be the free market (natural scarcity) value of labor's services. For this reason alone, strike-threat pressures tend to defeat the objective at which the unions are aiming.

We referred earlier to the likelihood that there have been periods in which capital was widely confiscated through strike-threat power, and used as income by the union members. This was probably occurring, for instance, during the years which followed the Wagner Act in the United States. But the most careful empirical studies show that the proportion of income accruing to labor did not increase. As P. Sultan has commented, "It is surprising that at the very moment in history when unions enjoyed tremendous power and influence, the relative wage differential accruing to the union sector should appear to diminish."[23] The explanation seems to be that the swollen prospective costs of replacement of assets in capital-intensive activities, which on the whole are most important in the union sector, were reducing the relative profitability of that sector.

We must now give some attention to the suggestion that union power is "countervailing power." There are two conceptually distinct arguments here. Firstly, it is said that the unorganized worker has "inferior bargaining power" in the determination of wage-rates unless he can resort to the strike threat. The fallacy was put very lucidly by a famous judge—Lord Francis Jeffrey— in 1825, very shortly after the repeal of the British Combination Laws.[24] He said:

> A single master was at liberty at any time to turn off the whole of his workmen at once—100 or 1000 in number—if they would not accept the wages he chose to offer. But it was made an offense for the whole of the workmen to leave the master at once if he refused to give the wages they chose to require.[25]

This sounds, of course, like an intolerable injustice, and so it appeared to that famous judge. But that word "master," like the word "employer" today, really refers to *the residual claimant* (in the twentieth century most frequently a corporation) on the value of what is being produced.

Through the managers, who are responsible to their stockholders, decisions about how much to invest in the labor inputs required to produce any commodity or service will be determined in the light of the point at which marginal prospective yields will equal the rate of interest. But just as Molière's *bourgeois gentilhomme* was astonished when told that he had always spoken prose, so will most managements be surprised when told that they are continuously thinking of the marginal increment when deciding on how much to retain, replace or add to the value of different inputs in different combinations. Yet that *is* what they are doing when they are planning to use the resources at their command to the greatest advantage. And the value the managers will put at risk (i.e., the magnitude of outputs planned) will depend *inter alia* upon what they judge they will have to offer in order (1) to attract additional workers (a) from their existing employments (and this will mean a higher offer than the workers' present wage-rates), or (b) from the ranks of the unemployed (and this will mean at wage-rates not lower than those which the unemployed expect they will be able to command, sooner or later, if they do not accept the offer); and (2) to retain such of their existing employees as they judge can provide profitably priced inputs at wage-rates at least as high as the workers believe they can command elsewhere (allowance made for the costs and inconveniences of movement).

In the absence of monopsonistic (or oligopsonistic) abuse, and provided there is no government restraint on the loss-avoidance, profit-seeking incentives, it will be to the investors' advantage that managers shall attract or retain all workers the value of whose inputs permits a yield above, or not less than, their predicted output values. And, under the *assumption* that there is no monopsonistic or oligopsonistic abuse, *a corporation will have no power to influence the wage-rates which it will be to its advantage to offer*, although the managements' purely interpretative discretion in judging what that wage-rate is may well be wrong, *in either direction*.

We are now brought to the possibility of the abuse of monopsonistic power which we have so far assumed away. To see the problem in its full setting, we must recognise that it is very easy (where the law allows) to raise the value of inputs and/or outputs by excluding competing resources—men or assets—from an occupation, industry or area. In other words, it is very easy to exploit competitors in this way. But it is very difficult indeed to exploit *complementary or non-competing* factors, such as labor by capital or capital by labor. We have already seen how the flow of capital into non-versatile or otherwise exploitable assets is reduced when investors are served by vigilant managements.

For similar reasons, labor is unexploitable, unless managements can somehow suppress competing demands for the labor they acquire. The circumstances required for monopsonistic action to reduce wage-rates are those which cause labor to be shut into a firm, occupation, industry or area. This *has* occurred and may again occur. The most obvious case concerns what is known as the "lock-in contract," under which an employee who leaves a corporation is subject to some penalty, such as loss of pension rights. But if abuses of this kind are indeed important, they are easily remedied. Lock-in contracts can be declared void and illegal except when they are a protection for investment in human capital (resembling patents to protect investment in research), or unless the contract is a means of repayment of beneficial loans to the employees, such as removal expenses, and so forth.

Nevertheless, in theory, monopsonistic exploitation of labor is *conceivable.* This is not a matter of controversy. The *most likely form* in which such exploitation of labor might happen (otherwise than through lock-in contracts) is where, by subtle fraud, workers are inveigled into specialised training for an occupation so that they find themselves trapped in it, so to speak. We know of no concrete illustration of such a situation. But if it should occur, it would still not justify the private use of force as "countervailing power."

Fortunately, there is one simple test for determining whether strike-threat power has countervailed an exploitation which has forced or maintained the price of labor below its free market value.[26] The test is whether any workers not presently employed in firms paying the increased wage-rates would be prepared to accept work of the same quality and quantity for lower wage-rates. But after nearly half a century of interest in this subject, the present writer has discovered no case studies in which proof of previous monopsonistic exploitation has been demonstrated in this way. Only if, at the increased wage-rate, or at any lower wage-rate offered, no firm could recruit additional labor if it wanted to, is there evidence of any previous monopsonistic exploitation.

Nevertheless, this problem has been discussed at great length by pure theorists, as well as labor economists, during the last three decades. We have therefore tried elsewhere[27] to consider such objections as we have found to the thesis that it is virtually impossible to exploit *complementary* (as distinct from competing) parties.

Oligopsonistic exploitation is rather different in some ways. But for most purposes it can be regarded simply as a much weaker form of monopsony. In practice, effective exploitation of any kind seems to require iron-clad agreements, secret when vigilant anti-trust is present, so that explicit restraints on individual demands for or supplies of outputs can be applied. Effective monopolies or monopsonies must, it seems, rely on penalties.

It is very easy to mistake ordinary entrepreneurial caution in bidding up the value of inputs as oligopsonistic. In reality, we suggest, the caution so misinterpreted is nothing more than a realistic representation of Walras' "groping" process, which he described as "the mechanism of competition" (or "market competition," or "free competition").

Concrete allegations, illustrated examples of either oligopsony or monopsony always seem rather unconvincing to the writer. Thus, there have been secret "no poaching" or "hands off" agreements relating to the recruitment of highly specialised and skilled craftsmen, or of executives. But they all imply conduct of patent illegality under the anti-trust laws. Yet we do not call to mind any prosecutions for such reasons in the United States. Can the problem then be of any importance?

Among the many misconceptions on this issue, we can here mention just two. Certain areas are isolated from others by distance and physical barriers. For this reason the costs of labor mobility over space are high. But this does *not* facilitate exploitation of labor within the area unless the barriers are man-made. The general principle here, as the writer has explained elsewhere,[28] is that, unless labor is somehow "shut in" by managements, "within any area sheltered by economic distance, by human inertias and by union-imposed restraints on mobility, the flow of wages will be highest and the distribution of the flow most equal and equitable, when every wage-rate is fixed at the lowest level necessary to retain and attract labor for every activity judged to be profitable." And on this issue, the reader should consider whether it is not true that all man-made obstacles to labor mobility between occupations, industries and areas are the consequence of strike-threat power or labor union lobby power.

In spite of the strong probability that monopsonistic exploitation of labor is of minimal importance, there are bound to be many who will feel that, in particular circumstances, it could occur, so that the need for some countervailing power remains. Even so, strike-threat power would not be an acceptable countervailing force. What *can* be done is to bring monopsonistic exploitation explicitly within the scope of anti-trust. Unions could then assume responsibility for the initiation of proceedings against observable collusive monopsony where they believe it is damaging to their members. And the unions could also take the initiative against non-contractual lock-in practices which they can show are harmful to their members.

We can now consider the regressive effects of strike-threat power. When wage-rates are raised by privately motivated coercion, the burdensome effects must almost universally be borne by individuals in proportion to their poverty.

Consider first the consequences upon the community as consumers. The following illustration has proved useful in explaining what happens. If the price of leather rises, the prices of footwear products will rise. If the price of labor producing footwear rises, the prices of footwear will rise for the same reason. The circumstances in which these consequences do not follow are unimportant. The effects are obviously regressive.

The sheer arbitrariness of consumer exploitation ought to be enough to cause universal condemnation of the use of strike-threat power. Thus, workers making products confronted with inelastic demands have a differential advantage because consumer exploitation is facilitated. Nearly all labor economists recognise that inelastic demand for the product constitutes an advantage for labor in collective bargaining; but we cannot remember any condemnation in such contexts of the injustice and arbitrariness of the exploitation envisaged.

And what are the consequences upon the wage-earning classes of duress-imposed labor costs? A regressive effect is brought about as profitable outputs are reduced, (a) through lay-offs which drive the displaced workers into less well-paid, "sub-optimal" employments, or into unemployment when it is collectively purchased through income transfers (e.g., unemployment compensation not based upon actuarially sound insurance); and (b) through the exclusion of those who could have improved their earnings, and prospects of earnings, by entering the protected employment, as they could have done if competition had been allowed to influence labor costs.

The most important freedom that is denied through union power is that of the right of every individual to accept any employment which he believes will improve his earnings and prospects. The "closed shop" or the "union shop'' which have been inflicted on managements in so many parts of the world must appear to any detached student not only as flagrantly regressive but as an intolerable negation of individual freedom. But even under what are called "right to work laws," union power can force managements to deny the right of those persons who wish to raise their contributions to the common pool of income from doing so. Juveniles and the less fortunate adults, and especially those who are initially less well qualified, or those who belong to what Demsetz has called "non-preferred groups" (e.g., non-whites, Jews, ugly women, elderly women, etc.) can be prevented by various subterfuges (like color bars, demarcation obstacles, apprenticeship barriers, occupational licensing and—most effective of all—enforcement of "the rate for the job")[29] from improving their earnings and prospects of earning. Hence if by "union power" we mean the ability to coerce managements through the threat of organized disruption, the use of that power may enable potential strikers to engross for themselves the effective ability to achieve skills in, or to become "attached" to occupations which would otherwise be open to interlopers. The privileges so gained must be balanced against the detriments suffered by those who are debarred from employment at wage-rates which they believe could raise their earnings and prospects.

Again, because of the incentive for a union's power to be used so as not unduly to endanger the employment of its existing members, the strike-threat has been most ruthlessly aimed at industries, or branches of industries, which would otherwise have expanded most rapidly. Unions appear in practice to be little concerned about their demands hampering the growth of their industry, and they seem to inhibit concern with their suppression of countless better-paid openings for less privileged workers which would have been available through growing outputs in a free labor market. Moreover, the composition of the stock of skills and the workers' familiarization and adaptation to the best available employment outlets must be influenced in a similar manner. The composition of the assets stock largely determines the composition of the labor stock. Durress-imposed costs are compatible with "full employment," but only in "sub-optimal" activities.

Many contributions critical of the use of strike-threat power place great stress on the enormous social cost of actual strikes—the community's losses in the form of outputs of men and assets during the stoppages. But the detriment suffered in this form, although obvious to all, and deplorable, is of small importance in relation to the harm inflicted on the capital structure caused through fear of future strike-threat pressures.

It is often felt that the individual's freedom is infringed because in any firm in which he works he has no voice in the making of the rules to which he is subject or in the administration of those rules. Elliott J. Berg attributes to such well-known "labor economists" as J. Dunlop, Clark Kerr, F. Harbison, and C. Myers the view that workers "live in a state of perennial protest arising from the frustrations implicit in being governed by a web of rules they usually have little to do with making."[30] But as the present writer has explained, there is nothing to protest about![31] There is no legal or other barrier to the workers' accepting most of the risks, by accepting the residual share, if they so wish. They will then automatically have the right to make and administer all the rules under which they work, appoint all the managers, hire all the assets, and borrow all the circulating capital required. In that case, their earnings will be wages *plus* profits or *minus* losses, just as the investors' earnings are interest *plus* profits or *minus* losses. But the workers will then sacrifice the security of earnings and employment continuity which the wage system provides. It would, of course, entail an inappropriate division of function; for investors can spread their risks over many ventures, while workers who put their future earnings at risk cannot spread risks in that form. A *sharing* of risk and management is, however, by no means out of the question, as has been shown elsewhere.[32] But what is really important is that the rules and their administration by the managers would be unlikely to differ one iota from what they are with investors taking the residue.

Unfortunately, that word "employer" suggests subordination to the "owners." But the suppliers of the assets and circulating capital are just as subordinate as the workers to the power of consumers' sovereignty. Consumers are the true "employers." A firm's assets are employed just as the workers are. The services of both are embodied in output. The investors willingly submit to the ruthlessness of market discipline. Seen from this angle, the investors' acceptance of the residual share from the sale of output is the most important form of social security for the workers that society provides. Our stressing of this truth does not of course imply that there is no problem of justice in the application of social discipline through managerial authority.

Union power is expressed partly through the promise of votes to or the subsidization of legislators at all levels (federal, state and municipal) and reliance on lobby power generally. In this form, it has conferred on the unions far-reaching immunities before the law. Secondly, it has, over the years, acquired protection for union members from the competition of the under-privileged. *Via* minimum wage enactments *plus* "welfare" hand-outs, occupational licensing, prolonged useless schooling, etc., private objectives sought through government have displaced social objectives sought through the market.

But even if the unions could no longer dictate to legislators, they could, as the law now stands in most countries, continue to restrain market freedom; and, as we have seen, that means to withhold the civil and human rights of some individuals both as consumers and potential producers. Through strike-threat power, millions are denied the right of access to the bargaining table, and those who suffer most are the initially less able and the "non-preferred." *Via* subterfuges such as apprenticeship requirements, "the rate for the job," and so forth, strike-threat power has, through such freedom-suppressing devices, been impoverishing millions. The unions have, in-deed, erected what seems to be an almost unscalable wall against the right of all to obtain the valuable general education and technical training which it would be profitable for managements to supply under unrestrained recruitment. Through society's tolerance of a usurpation—the private use of coercive power—freedom of access to the public as consumers (mainly *via* corporate intermediaries) has been withheld.

Union power, whether exercised through government or through the strike-threat, far from redistributing income from the rich to the poor has had exactly the opposite effect. Yet opinion-makers and the public have been brain-washed into believing that greater distributive justice has been its aim and achievement. Although at times, through private coercion, some part of investors' property has been seized and squandered, backlash reactions upon the subsequent composition of the assets stock have countervailed the gains. Any benefits which some unions have won for their members have been at the expense of their competitors—laid-off or excluded workers—and at the expense of all as consumers. The system has had a formidable depressive effect upon aggregate purchasing power (as distinct from aggregate money-spending power), i.e., upon the magnitude of the wages-flow and real income. It has therefore caused creeping, crawling, chronic inflation to be politically expedient. And finally, when governments resort to incomes policies as a crude attempt to mitigate the harm, union power simply comes to be exercised in a different way, *via* government power instead of through the market.

Appendix

In the ideal, an *unenfranchised* minority would be guaranteed the freedom of the enfranchised. The right to vote alone has never conferred freedom. The writer has been a resident alien (and hence unenfranchised) for eight years in the United States. Yet he has throughout felt that he has been sharing in all the freedoms enjoyed by American citizens. Such freedoms would be greatly enhanced (for the unenfranchised as well as for the rest) (a) by protection of those citizens most liable to be used for the private benefit of politicians exploiting their ignorance, and (b) by denying the right of government employees to vote for candidates who offer them most at the taxpayers' expense. This could probably be achievable by some special form of electoral franchise. Otherwise, for the eradication of exploitation *via* government power, the unenfranchised should include the following: (i) public servants; (ii) beneficiaries from government-arranged income-transfers (such as subsidies, or any kind of relief payments); (iii) those who, by reason of defects of intelligence, or will, or health, or through bad luck, have failed to achieve an appropriate level of literacy, ability to calculate and general knowledge; and (iv) those who, failing to qualify under (iii), are unable to produce evidence of an incentive for responsibility (indicated by a certain level of income or property—accumulated or inherited).

Notes

1. M. Pantaleoni, "An Attempt to Analyze the Concepts of 'Strong' and 'Weak' in their Economic Connection," *Economic Journal* 8 (June 1898), pp. 183-205.

2. F. Hayek, *Constitution of Liberty* (Chicago: University Press, 1960).

3. Bertrand de Jouvenel, *On Power* (Boston: Beacon Press, 1962). Also *Sovereignty: An Inquiry into the Political Good* (Chicago: University of Chicago Press, 3rd impression, 1963).

4. Helmut Schoeck, *Envy* (New York: Harcourt, Brace & World, 1969). This

book shows that the urge to power abuse is the very human attribute of envy.

5. De Jouvenel, *On Power*, p. 15.

6. Ibid., p. 18.

7. A rigorous definition of "exploitation" is essential. As used here it means: any action taken, whether or not through discernible private coercion (collusion) or governmental coercion, or whether through monopolistic or monopsonistic power, which, under a given availability of resources (including the stock of knowledge and skills), reduces the value of the property or income of another person or group of persons, or prevents that value from rising as rapidly as it otherwise would, *unless this effect is brought about through* (a) the dissolution of some monopolistic or monopsonistic privilege, or (b) the substitution of some cheaper method (labor-saving or capital-saving) of achieving any objective (including the production and marketing of any output); or (c) the expression of a change in consumers' preference; or (d) through taxation authorized by explicit legislation accepted as legitimate in any context.

8. For simplicity, we shall not treat separately a wealthy individual's power. It corresponds exactly to that of a group.

9. W. Hutt, *Economists and the Public* (London: Jonathan Cape, 1936), Chapter 15.

10. De Jouvenel, *Sovereignty,* p. 248n.

11. The writer believes he was the first to use this term. See Hutt, *Economists and the Public*, Chapter 16, and Hutt, "The Concept of Consumers' Sovereignty," *Economic Journal* 50 (March 1940), pp. 66-77.

12. See Appendix.

13. De Jouvenel, *On Power*, p. 27.

14. The case for government restraint of traffic in drugs, or in pornographic material and the like is, according to the philosophy here explained, the protection of the individual from a form of assault.

15. All ends of which the means are scarce are "products."

16. That is, the expression of consumers' sovereignty is molded by private interests which work either through government or through government toleration of privately contrived coercion. Even so, consumers' preferences can never be wholly ignored.

17. There is a large literature dealing with coercion of this type. Sylvester Petro's contributions are most important. E. Schmidt's recently published *Union Power* (Los Angeles: Nash Publishers, 1973), especially Chapter 9, is an outstanding analysis and exposure of the situation as it is today.

18. Yet investors have taken the risk of providing labor's tools—the assets which multiply the yield to human effort. Moreover, investors continuously finance replacement of materials and work in progress.

19. The New York transit strike of 1966 is an apt example. The British coal strike of 1926 was almost as disastrous as the general strike of that year.

20. W. Hutt, *The Strike-Threat System: The Economic Consequences of Collective Bargaining* (Arlington, Va.: Arlington Publishing House, 1973), p. 44.

21. J. Hilton, et al., *Are Trade Unions Obstructive?* (Gollancz, 1935).

22. The words "property transfers" here may need explanation. If, through a strike-threat, the aggregate value of a corporation's shares declines by $x, *ceteris paribus* the successful strikers will have gained an additon to their income which, when capitalized, will equal $x. In practice, the capital transferred is (with unimportant exceptions) treated as income by the unionists who receive it, and consumed.

23. P. Sultan, *Labor Economics* (New York: Henry Holt, 1957), p. 73.

24. Between 1799 and 1825, these laws had tried to strengthen the ancient common law and about forty statutes applying to particular trades or industries which were enacted against monopolistic pricing or wage-rate fixing.

25. Quoted in S. and B. Webb, *History of Trade Unionism* (London: Longmans, 1920), p. 72.

26. I.e., below the wage-rates which would be determined in the light of wage-rates in alternative employments open to the workers concerned.

27. W. Hutt, *The Strike-Threat System*, Chapters 8-9.

28. Ibid., p. 103.

29. Sometimes called "equal pay for equal work" or "the standard rate."

30. E. Bakke, et al., *Unions, Management, and the Public* (New York: Harcourt, Brace, and World, 1967), p. 19.

31. Hutt, *The Strike-Threat System*, Chapter 6.

32. Ibid., pp. 80-82.

6 • *Misgivings and Casuistry on Strikes*

In mediaeval England, it was felt to be imperative to protect the common people from practices known as "forestalling, regrating and engrossing"— activities believed to have the effect of withholding nature's bounty against the common good. The contrivances (which various ordinances and statutes forbade) were believed to make food and other necessities scarce and expensive. In the same spirit, the common law and a number of statutes[1] prohibited "conspiracy," namely, agreements not to sell any kind of product at less than a certain price, including the output of labor. While associations of people for peaceful purposes were never discouraged, associations which aimed at making any kind of products dearer for the benefit of those associating were regarded as criminal.

The law was far from consistent. Gilds (merchant or craft) were constituted by charter, and their restrictive powers persisted in spite of occasional vitriolic attacks on them for conspiracy and the use of their privileges to oppress others. "They conspire," charged Wycliff, "that no man practicing their craft shall take less payment daily than they have agreed among themselves," and they "oppress other men who are in the right" (i.e., anxious to work for less). Moreover, although the common law and general statutes against conspiracy applied when there was no gild privilege, they were very difficult and costly to enforce. This led masters in certain trades during the 17th and 18th centuries to petition Parliament for special Acts to outlaw "combinations" (a synonym for "conspiracy" until well into the

Reprinted with permission from *Modern Age* 12 (1968).

19th century) in their specific trades. About 40 special Acts of this kind were passed until, in 1799, a Bill to forbid combinations among millwrights came before Parliament, and Wilberforce (of anti-slavery fame) moved unexpectedly that its provisions should be generalized. His amendment was accepted; but the resulting Act (which merely reiterated the illegality of what was already criminal) was very leniently and half-heartedly enforced, a fact which the slanted teaching of history has hidden.[2] Moreover, it was shortlived. It was repealed in 1824 because Parliament naively accepted assurances that the legalization of trade unions would discourage strikes; and during the 19th and the present centuries, in gradual stages, political pressures led to the unions achieving immunities from criminal and civil prosecution and other general privileges before the law.

In the United States, similar immunities and privileges have been won and are currently creating problems of major economic and political import. The turning point in this country was a disastrous policy blunder which resulted in wage-rates being maintained (due to what we now call "Keynesian" notions) under conditions of incipient recession during 1929 and 1930. This economic solecism forced an unavoidable contraction of credit,[3] of an unprecedented contraction in the flow of wages and incomes generally; it forced millions into avoidable unemployment and hunger; it precipitated the worst depression of history; and it induced the inauguration, from 1933, of the chronic, creeping, crawling inflation which still persists.

In the background of the depression as it was in 1932, the Norris-LaGuardia Act was passed. Since then, a fantastic network of federal legislation, judge-made law, and administrative jurisdiction, complicated by state legislation and diametrically opposed in aim and content to anti-trust law, has been gradually woven into the fabric of the American economy. Based on five major Acts,[4] it has been a copy-book example of a response to what Walter Lippmann once called "the polity of pressure groups." Introduced largely in return for "campaign expenses" and the formidable support of labor unions in elections, these laws were passed with the assistance of explicit assurances from their sponsors that they did not mean what they have proved to mean.[5]

The proclaimed intention of the legislative hotch-potch to which I have referred was to ensure the workers' "bargaining freedom," but each Act was introduced in order to achieve some specific *sectional* advantage, without any regard for self-consistency, as far as I can see. The word "hotch-potch" is no careless exaggeration. Largely owing to the defects of the law itself, administration and enforcement have become increasingly arbitrary and the consequences increasingly ominous. It is hardly surprising that misgivings about the strike-threat as an influence in wage-rate determination have been growing. The misgivings have been expressed in various quarters, but it is their significant expression recently by several "labor economists" and industrial relations consultants with which I propose to deal.

Evidence of grave misgivings can be found in a symposium published early in 1967 by The American Assembly, entitled *Challenges to Collective Bargaining*. Edited by Lloyd Ulman, this volume contains nine articles by active "labor consultants" or "labor correspondents." They are mostly also professors of labor economics or industrial relations. Their deep perturbation is obvious throughout.

Early in 1931, Sidney Webb (Lord Passfield), then a member of the British Labor Cabinet, came home and growled to Beatrice Webb (his co-author in the two most influential books aimed at justification of the labor union movement), "the (trade union) General Council are pigs." And Beatrice Webb commented bitterly on "the sabotage of British industry by trade union pig-headedness."[6] Yet in Sidney Webb's *public* pronouncements at that time there was no hint of his true judgement which, had it been frankly disclosed, could have brought down his government, possibly have saved the pound sterling, and thereby have staved off the era of competitive devaluation which began in September 1931 and soon involved the dollar!

Now it seems to me that most of today's academic advisers of the labor movement and teachers of "labor economics" would have applauded Sidney Webb's silence. If I judge them fairly, they want to speak sternly to the unions but not to appear to do so. The contributors to Ulman's symposium seem to be warning the union rulers, in language of studied caution and occasionally calculated ambiguity, that the community is coming to perceive the ultimate responsiblity of strike-threat activities for the economic difficulties which were developing last year (and have since led to the present plight of the dollar). They are tactfully hinting that legislative or administrative constraint may soon become unavoidable through a sudden revulsion of influential opinion. They recognize that serious displacement of labor is today avoidable only through chronic inflation and ever-worsening balance of payments difficulties. They know that strike-threat pressures are continuously creating the menace of deepening unemployment, with the deliberate depreciation of the dollar appearing to offer the only way of crudely rectifying the situation. They perceive also the hopeless failure (in the United States) of the "guidelines." Hence they seem to fear that, sooner or later, more effective legislative steps will have to be taken. The normal tendency of union policy to reduce the flow of uninflated wages and income, and thereby to precipitate recession in the absence of validating inflation, is likely to become more widely understood; and this will, they feel, give rise to demand for some really drastic curb on contemporary policy. It might even result in a dissolution of the present labor union privileges and immunities.

For instance, J. T. Dunlop writes: "The community must learn to give up desired, but second ranked objectives. Free collective bargaining, democratic unions, industrial peace, full employment, . . . the present price of gold . . . price stability . . . are simply not fully compatible. . . . The abandonment of our present international monetary policy would provide collective bargaining with more elbow room.'"[7] But after thus suggesting that it might be to the advantage of the union rulers to use their financial resources and lobby strength to work for the devaluation of the dollar, he warns that, in his estimation "the dominant view of the American community, as expressed in the political process, is that a degree of freedom in collective bargaining and in the setting of both wage rates and prices at the margin is more expendable than a closer approach to full employment, more jobs and higher income for Negroes, a degree of price stability, the Viet Nam expenditures and the price of gold." And as a sort of further warning, he says: "My own preferences would be to give up some of the exaggerated views of union democracy expressed in the spirit of the Landrum Griffin statute"; but he tempers this unpopular admission with a recommendation that the United States should give up her commitment to exchange dollars and gold at a fixed price, which would give a further lease of life to the policies he is obliquely condemning.[8]

Other contributors to the symposium are a little more explicit on the crucial issue. Ulman warns that the prohibition of strikes in the "public sector" might come to be applied generally. His warning is naturally carefully worded, e.g., to the effect that such prohibitions "might turn out to be a prototype rather than a curiosum.'"[9] The Greek derivative and the Latin noun here are obviously not pedantry, but intended to soothe the anger which his admonition is likely to evoke among union rulers.

A. H. Raskin, after assuring the labor union establishment that he is "a great believer in collective bargaining,'' goes on nevertheless to describe it as "a dangerous weapon" which, through "incompetence at the bargaining table," or "lack of social responsibility," can inflict serious damage on the economy."[10] And, again showing his impartiality by blaming both sides equally for "the willfulness or ineptitude of economic power blocks," he suggests that "it is an affirmation—not a denial—of democracy to provide effective government machinery for breaking deadlocks."[11] Yet did not the ancient statutes and common law against restraint of trade and "conspiracy" do precisely this? Indeed, did they not do even more—tend to prevent the deadlock from arising at all? Aren't we beginning to look for new methods when old, perfectly satisfactory methods are available? Raskin at least sees the absurdity of the situation in which we "exalt the right to make war as the hall-mark of industrial civilization" in the collective bargaining field "when we seek to exorcise it everywhere else."[12] And he says that he cannot accept "the hands-off view of economic power struggles that damage the public more than they do the parties."[13] But he fights shy of getting to grips with the real issue. He remarks weakly that "there is no standard to measure what is fair and what is extortionate, even when the community itself is the employer,"[14] and he is careful to make it clear that he does not challenge "labor's view that government is still not doing enough to . . . compensate for the inadequacies and imbalances that condemn millions to lives of squalor."[15] Once again the reason is, I guess, that to obtain a hearing he feels bound to make a gesture of impartiality by repeating the shibboleths of union apologists.

For what are the "inadequacies and imbalances that condemn millions to lives of squalor?" The only such forces which I myself, after a lifetime of study in this field, can discern are in the study of restraints which prevent under-privileged workers from bettering their condition and prospects by offering their labor in competition with the privileged. I see first, and by all odds most important, the restraint of entry to occupations through the enforcement of "the rate for the job"; and the imposition of minimum wage-rates (aggravated by demoralizing handouts), some apprenticeship rules, and certain other restrictive labor practices can be recognized as *subsidiary* causes of the perpetuation of squalor.

But is it true that "there is no standard to measure what is fair and what is extortionate?" If universally accepted ethics are allied to economic insights, there *is* a perfectly clear criterion of justice in this sphere, namely, *all man-made scarcities are wrong, and all prices determined by such scarcities reflect extortion.* Similarly, values determined under natural scarcity are good. Hence any wage-rate is unfair if its enforcement excludes from the bargaining process those workers who are of less than average inborn or developed ability.

Raskin says that the difficulty here arises "even when the community itself is the employer."[16] But if the community in its consumer role were identified as the true "employer" in every case, we should see the problem in due perspective. Under governmental enterprises, with which Raskin is mainly concerned, the intermediary between consumers and labor is less effectively subjected to social or market discipline than when the intermediary operates under what we misleadingly call "private enterprise." That is the main difference.

In apparently condemning strikes that "damage the public more than they do the parties,"[17] Raskin seems to suggest that there are two different kinds of power struggles: first, those that damage non-participants less than participants (which, presumably, are acceptable), and second, those that damage non-participants more than participants (which, presumably, are unacceptable). But why should any *reluctant* participant be expected to acquiesce in damage unless he submits to coercion? Moreover, there is a lack of any coherent principle for drawing a line between stoppages which create an "emergency" or "jeopardise" the public interest and stoppages which, like the recent New York transport and garbage collection strikes, merely "inconvenience" the community. Is one not forced to recognize that *all* harm to the public and not *some* harm needs to be prevented? After all, we do our best to prevent small thefts as well as large thefts; and there are indeed grounds for believing that petty pilfering is a greater burden on the community than bank robberies. There is a good case for the view that small strikes, each of which does not in itself cause grievous harm to the community, are responsible in the aggregate for a greater social detriment than the sensational stoppages which make the newspaper headlines.[18] The detriment to the flow of wages and other incomes from inconspicuous strikes and strike-threat pressures is probably far greater than that due to prominent stoppages.

The power *to delay* strikes which has been taken in some countries, where national safety or national health are threatened (one assumes with the aim of giving governments or administrations a chance to take some sort of defensive action), is power to postpone or mitigate an evil which could, in the same manner, be eradicated. For physical safety and health are merely special aspects of the community's well-being, and all aspects of that well-being are, in a degree, harmed through strike-caused disruption.

Raskin refers to "the long list of settlements in which Presidents, Governors, Mayors, Secretaries of Labor *et al.*, have pushed up the price of peace"; and he regards such intervention as "a virtually inescapable ingredient." "Government does have a rare talent for making a hash of things in labor management relations," he admits; but, he adds, "that is true of almost any other field, and we have never concluded that the answer is to repeal government."[19]

Is that not a facetious dodging of the whole issue? Defining the role of the legislature and the administration is not *repealing* it. If the function of government is to play a part in the achievement of wages equity and wage-maximization (with the concomitant achievement of the greatest possible measure of income security and employment security), the legitimate sphere of centralized initiative can be fairly easily envisaged. The task of government is to ensure that the valuation of labor shall be free of restraints imposed by managements (in collusion or otherwise) or restraints imposed by unions, *so that all justification for the private use of coercive power shall fall away;* that the terms of wage-contracts shall be honored; that those harmed by the breach of wage-contracts shall not be denied the common law right of all citizens to sue for damages; that labor union tyranny or managerial tyranny or injustices shall be capable of rectification and redress; and that no one shall be required, as a condition for admission to any employment, to contribute to a fund used for purposes of which he disapproves. But simply to ask, as Raskin does, that governments should have "adequate powers in the interests of the public," or that they should exercise the function of "impartial appraisal" is to ask for arbitrary authority. For what are the criteria of "public interest?" And what are the criteria of "impartial appraisal?"

Although deeply worried, Raskin is unable to offer any rigorously thought-out solution. The reader hopes in vain that he will ultimately point to some *rule of law*—some principle which will enable a clear-cut judicial remedy for the sectionalist chaos in which the western world is expected today to acquiesce. In the end, all he can offer is some vaguely conceived extension of the present nauseating system in which mayors, governors, and even the President of the United States himself, humble themselves before the AFL-CIO rulers and ask them, possibly with the assistance of veiled threats, to bring particularly disastrous strikes to an end. He has no guidance to offer those whom he expects to implore, reproach, or threaten.

"It would be a mistake," Raskin says, "to decree any single remedy as immutably right . . . in every contingency. I would put everything anyone can think of in the bag, from doing nothing to compulsory arbitration." He hesitates about giving the government a whole "arsenal of weapons," although he mentions injunctions and/or seizure covering a whole industry or parts of it "deemed essential to meet national requirements."[20] But why does he not suggest giving these "weapons" to the courts?

Dunlop looks forward, rather similarly, to "some form of *ad hoc* legislative intervention, after established procedures have been exhausted . . . becoming a characteristic feature of our system . . . (but) generalized legislation is not likely to be very useful or resolve all cases . . . the legislative body is representative of the people."[21]

Even if the legislature and administration *were* in some acceptable sense representative of the people (as distinct from representative of those who contribute to "campaign expenses"), have we any grounds at all for expecting that it could settle disputes "on their merits?" Why should we not rely on principle—"the rule of law?" Will not interventions normally be such as are judged likely to influence the electoral ballot box in a manner which favors the intervener? These special pleaders for the unions all seem to me to be confessing to intellectual bankruptcy on the issue. They are shrinking from any courageous consideration of fundamentals.

These attitudes of Raskin and Dunlop are not, I think, untypical of most of the labor unions' friends in the universities. Yet I interpret them as saying, in guarded phrases: "You have gone too far. The community is worried and you must watch your step. We academics have given you all the arguments needed to make your policies appear reasonable. But these arguments will be rejected if you show quite so clearly your lack of concern for the well-being of the community as a whole. You don't want your empires to fall. You must make some effort to improve your image. You must find formulae to satisfy a disquieted public." And Dunlop *seems* to be saying also: "You should realize that the devaluation of the dollar could postpone your day of reckoning for years; and the public *would* fall for that. If you don't get a devaluation, you may be forced to go slow in your demands—unless you want a backlash."

Some contributors who feel compelled to admit the obvious indefensibility of contemporary arrangements suggest that reform merely demands the refashioning of more effective organizations for bargaining—a suggestion which turns out only to mean the designing of organizations under which threats can be exchanged with less friction! Others place stress on the importance of communications—fact-finding and the passing of the facts to the parties. "Fact-finding committees" are, we know, time-honored devices for delaying action, including strikes. But if the negotiations are concerned simply with how much of the contractual remuneration shall be deducted and removed from voluntary spending (e.g., devoted to "fringe benefits," such as pension contributions to finance "paid holidays," etc.), that is obviously a matter which *need* not concern managements at all.[22] The managers are solely concerned with, and all the difficulties and controversies arise out of, the contractual *gross* labor cost. And as far as I can see, the only relevant data in a dispute about what this cost *should* be concern the gross earnings of labor in *competing* fields.

A different approach which has been heard is that while collective bargaining must be recognized as a "fundamental democratic right," which public employees can claim as much as the employees of private enterprise, it does not imply the right to use the strike or the strike-threat. But what can be the role of collective bargaining if the strike is forbidden? Does the notion of "no-strike bargaining" make sense? I can conceive of two possible meanings only.

First, the union representatives may, in the course of "negotiations," threaten discontent and unrest instead of the strike unless their demands are met (and that is, of course, simply a special form of strike disruption). *Second,* they may threaten to advise some of those employed to take higher-paid jobs available elsewhere. And here we have, indeed, what I suggest is the only legitimate role of "no-strike" collective bargaining, a point to which I shall return.

It may be argued that the strike-threat may be used defensively against a similar coercive power exercised by managements (on behalf of consumers or investors). Even so, that method of trying to rectify a defect in market organization is still indefensible, in the sense that the set-up is intolerable. To rely on private force to fight private force is to resign ourselves to the expectation that government cannot be expected to perform its usually accepted functions.

Others groping for some better alternative than the present system have argued that the wise approach is to regard strike-threat phenomena as *symptoms* of a disease of society. We are told that strikes must not be regarded as evils in themselves, but as expressions of conflicts which are inevitable in an injust social order.[23] But here also it is preposterous to recommend acquiescence in privately wielded coercive power in the hope that injustices will somehow be righted. For instance, if it is believed that market-determined distribution of income, as affected by the inheritance of capital, is unjust in some defined sense, surely any defensible redistribution would tax the wealthy in proportion to their wealth and distribute to the poor in proportion to their poverty. Is there any case at all for taking from those consumers, excluded workers, or investors who just happen to be vulnerable to exploitation through strikes and giving to those who just happen to possess an exceptional power to disrupt the economy by the concerted withdrawal of labor?

We occasionally hear the claim that the purpose of the strike-threat system is to replace by *an ethically more acceptable process* the "sordid" procedure under which, in making wage offers, managements are motivated solely by their legal duty to find the cheapest labor suitable for their purpose. But if the economizing of human effort (by offering the minimum needed to achieve any output) can be shown to tend towards the achievement of the ideal response to democratically expressed demands in the market, and to tend thereby to maximize the flow of wages and the employment available at different levels of wage-rates for various kinds of skill, why should the process be termed "sordid?" And the lesson of disinterested economic teaching is, I believe, that entrepreneurial incentives to economize have just that effect. The flow of wages (and of other incomes) is rendered greatest when every product, including the product purchased through wage contracts, is valued no higher than the resources which make it are believed to be able to command elsewhere in the economy. Moreover, under that condition, the distribution of wages seems likely to come nearest to satisfying the egalitarian ideal.

Naturally, propagandist writers describe reliance upon the strike-threat as a means of "restraining the excesses" or the "ruthlessness" of the free market. But we must not allow them to get away with such phrases unless they are explicit about the "excesses." For the free market can be said to be "ruthless" only in its intolerance of privilege and the outmoded. And the alternative is sheer economic warfare while there are no principles to tell us what the results of a war or a threatened war *ought* to be (as distinct from what the results are *likely* to be).

As things are, virtually all who write on this topic dismiss as unworthy of discussion the notion that the market mechanism should be allowed to determine all prices, those of labor included. Later generations will, I predict, regard this as astonishing; for the supposed "opposition of interests"—the real cause of the continuous economic warfare of today—would disappear if wage-rates, like other prices, were determined under free market pressures and not under the influence of private coercion. It is because society acquiesces in the strike-threat method of evaluating labor that we nearly all resign ourselves to the assumption that *tensions* must exist between the residual and the contractual claimants to the value of output. The so-called "tensions" are in evidence only when the threat of economic violence (strike, boycott, or lockout) is an influence determining prices or wage-rates. Is it not significant that we do not assume that anything resembling similar "tensions" must arise over the prices at which commodities are offered to the public in shops? Some parallel is experienced only on the rare occasions on which housewives have been incited into organizing a boycott of stores.

It is the duty of government, I suggest, to provide a framework of legislation and administration under which consumers, investors (organized through the firms which, subject to market discipline, offer wage contracts), and the workers (organized through unions) are all equally impotent to influence the values (prices and wage-rates) which imerge in a free market.[24] The social discipline exercised by unencumbered consumers' choice and substitution, and by unencumbered entrepreneurial judgement, is the sole guarantee of justice in the division of the value of the product. All other determinations involve the principle of "might is right"—either political might or the might of the power to disrupt.

While it is true that there must always be some imperfections in the best designed institutions, including the coordinative machinery of a free society, there is not the slightest reason to believe that the strike-threat system can bring about more sensitive adjustments to changes in preferences and changes in the availability of resources or mitigate (let alone eliminate) privilege. The apparatus of economic warfare was never designed for such purposes.[25]

I have referred above to "the legitimate role of non-strike collective bargaining." The power which a "workers' association" can legitimately wield is that of reducing the amount of labor available to any undertaking which is paying or offering wage-rates (*plus* "fringe benefits") which are less favorable than those available elsewhere. This function can be carried out without *compelling* any worker to leave his job, simply by finding a better-paid opening for him. An enterprise which is offering less than is available elsewhere will then find numbers of its employees withdrawing as their contracts expire. Through such a service for its members, a union will be in a position to apply ever-mounting pressure on a firm which is "under-paying" any of its personnel. The difference from the strike-threat system is that the withdrawal of labor will be gradual, not disruptive—unless the discrepancy is exceptional.[26] The withdrawal will be voluntary in every case. Union pressures will have been purged of their coercive intention.[27]

The Webbs referred (in 1920) to what they described as "the uncontrolled power wielded by the owners of the means of production, able to withhold from the manual worker all chances of subsistence unless he accepted their terms."[28] In writing this passage, the Webbs excluded from their minds all consideration of the "manual workers' " alternatives. And if the purpose of the unions had merely been to seek out the alternatives, who would have objected? In the absence of strike-threat pressures, managements (representing intermediaries between consumers and workers) have never been able to offer wage contracts effectively, except at labor costs which have been determined under the social forces of the market. If managements happen to have possessed "monopsonistic" power (that is, the ability to restrain competition for labor from their rivals, or to arrange collusive restraints so as to fence in those whom they are employing), then what I have suggested as "legitimate" functions for union-type organizations could effectively overcome the "monopsony."

To suggest the outlawing of the strike-threat as an element in wage determination is not to question the right of workers to organize for the purpose of improving their status and earning powers *via* activity directed at the non-violent removal of privileges on the part of other organizations— possibly other unions. The objection is solely to the private use of coercive power to increase the incomes of particular groups at the expense of consumers of the products and at the expense of displaced comrades or those confined to lower-paid occupations.

I have referred to "disinterested economists." Unfortunately, the labor economists who have written nearly all the textbooks of "labor economics" in current use, and who dominate the teaching of the subject in the major universities, cannot be described as "disinterested." They are labor consultants, arbitrators, conciliators, and mediators. As such they have a vested interest in the survival of the strike-threat system. Industrial warfare is, directly or indirectly, the source of a large part of their income. Their ability to play a useful role in moderating union demands will vanish if, in their writings and teachings, they are known to have questioned the right to use the strike-threat. In spite of the word "challenge" in the title of the symposium which has prompted this article, the contributors have been careful *themselves* not to challenge the right to disrupt. They are suavely warning the union rulers that *others* are likely to make such a challenge. The greatest tragedy is that, on this vital issue, subtly biased teaching is indoctrinating most university students into acquiescence in an intolerable system.

Notes

1. The most explicit seems to have been the Act of Conspiracies of Victuallers and Craftsmen, 1549, but the first statutes date from the fourteenth century.

2. The facts are summarized by M. D. George in the *Economic Journal, Economic History Supplement,* 1927.

3. For when outputs are being generally priced higher than uninflated incomes can afford, or higher than is consistent with price expectations, credit contraction can alone prevent inflation.

4. The Norris-LaGuardia Act, 1932; the National Industrial Recovery Act, 1933; the Wagner Act (National Labor Relations Act), 1935; the Taft-Hartley Act (Labor Management Relations Act), 1947; the Landrum-Griffin Act, 1959.

5. E.g., Senator Wagner assured the Committee on Labor of the House of Representatives in 1935 that "nothing could be more false than the charge that a gigantic closed shop would be forced upon industry . . . the terms of the bill do not compel or even encourage a man to join any union."

6. M. Cole, *Beatrice Webb's Diaries* (London: Longman, 1956), pp. 283-84.

7. Dunlop in Ulman (ed.), *Challenges to Collective Bargaining* (Englewood Cliffs, N. J.: Prentice-Hall, 1967).

8. Ibid., p. 179. Dunlop was writing, of course, more than a year before the semi-devaluation of March 1968.

9. Ulman, *Challenges to Collective Bargaining*, p. 10.

10. Raskin, in Ulman, *Challenges to Collective Bargaining*, p. 155.

11. Ibid., p. 156.

12. Ibid., p. 156.

13. Ibid., p. 157.

14. Ibid., p. 156.

15. Ibid., p. 157.

16. Ibid., p. 156.

17. Ibid., p. 157.

18. We have here an example of what has been called "the law of the importance of being unimportant." It can be illustrated by the case of the cost of the metal tin in an automobile, which might amount to, say, only 50¢. Suppose the price of tin is doubled by a cartel. This would hardly affect the price of the final product and nobody would be likely to protest. Yet, *for that very reason*, the community ought to be especially vigilant in preventing any forced price increase under such conditions.

19. Ibid., pp. 158-59.

20. Ibid., p. 167.

21. Ibid., pp. 177-78.

22. Although virtually all managements would *prefer* the workers' earnings to be used in this manner, the union members would be more likely to object, as several economists (not contributors to the symposium under discussion) have stressed.

23. There is much that is unjust in the existing social order, but labor-union apologists appear never to perceive its origins. It is rooted in the strike-threat system itself and can be discerned to be nothing more than plain human greed. For greed is fostered whenever the laws which define property (and hence theft) fail to restrain the natural cupidity of man.

24. I am assuming here defensible anti-trust activity, not the degeneration of antitrust which has resulted through the misuse of the regulatory agencies of government for political ends. If these functions are wisely and disinterestedly carried out, even the largest corporations will seldom have any discretion in respect of the prices which, in the light of input costs, it will pay them to charge for output. Countless imponderables will determine such prices; but large undertakings know that (given anti-trust) if they overcharge, instead of their finding it profitable to add to their capacity, they will merely stimulate development against them, and the growth of their own undertaking will be slowed down, stopped, or reversed. Through what I interpret as anti-trust blunders, probably due to lobby-inspired motivation, there are some large corporations which have inhibited the price-reductions needed to render growth profitable, in order to avoid anti-trust charges.

25. Theoretically, it *could* be used for this purpose. For instance, we can imagine a strike by school teachers and public servants demanding legislation to forbid strikes on the part of other sections (from which the groups concerned are among those who are most obviously harmed).

26. With such withdrawals, the first to leave would presumably be the most seriously underpaid. Those remaining would then be likely to be workers of lower efficiency and not *necessarily* underpaid at all.

27. S. and B. Webb, *Industrial Democracy* (London: Longman, 1920), II, p. 84.

7 • *Critics of the "Classical Tradition"*

This article discusses certain fundamental points raised by Dr. D. J. J. Botha in his interesting review of *The Critics of Keynesian Economics*, edited by Henry Hazlitt and published in 1960.[1] That review[2] does me the honour of devoting chief attention to my contribution to the symposium, an essay which had been published previously in this Journal in 1954.

In a recent book[3] I have discussed in detail the fallacies (as they appear to me) of Keynes and his disciples, and there would be no point in repeating any part of that discussion in answer to Dr. Botha's defence of Keynesian economics. In the present article I propose instead to deal solely with certain common Keynesian misconceptions, well illustrated in Dr. Botha's article, about teachings in the 'classical' or 'orthodox' tradition.

It was about 25 to 30 years ago that most of the younger sceptics who expressed misgivings about the 'new economics' began to be eliminated from academic life. There was no inquisition, no discernible or intentional suspension of academic freedom; but young non-conformists could seldom expect promotion. They appeared rather like young physicists who were arrogant enough to challenge the basic validity of revolutionary developments which they did not properly understand. To suggest that Keynes was all wrong was like questioning the soundness of Einstein or Bohr. The older economists could declare their doubts without serious loss of prestige, but any dissatisfaction on the part of the younger men seemed to be evidence of intellectual limitations. Dr. Botha's ideas are typical of a vast

Reprinted with permission from *South African Journal of Economics* 31 (1963).

111

number of economists whose training has been wholly in what I believe to have been a fallacious tradition; and in replying to him I shall be answering Keynesians in general. The school of thought I shall criticise is one from which, if my judgement is correct, there is a belated retreat in progress.[4] It is my hope that the present essay will help to accelerate the retreat.

In conformity with the presently dominant doctrines which I am challenging, Dr. Botha says that Keynes aimed at "discrediting the 'invisible hand' approach of the *laissez-faire* theorists."[5] Justly expressed this should be: Keynes aimed at discrediting an explanation (which he called 'classical economics') of the process by means of which—*through the performance by the State of its appropriate rôle*—price adjustments permit the responsible planning and co-ordination of the economic system.

Economic planning can be said to be 'responsible' when it is controlled through the social discipline of the loss-avoidance, profit-seeking incentives to which the crucial decision-makers may be subjected by the people in their consumers' rôle. When this discipline is exerted, the complex activity of free society seems to be co-ordinated so effectively that Adam Smith was moved to use the metaphor of the 'invisible hand.'[6]

Keynes' method of refutation was not that of carefully and dispassionately examining the critical, rigorous analysis which constituted the 'classical' or 'orthodox' explanation, but the devising of a wholly new approach, employing *concepts* and models which obscured issues that several generations of thinkers had regarded as vital.[7] Through the so-called macro-economic apparatus, he and his disciples extended to the economy as a whole types of reasoning which have meaning only in relation to particular sectors. Indeed, Dr. Botha's criticisms of the non-Keynesians seem to me to stem largely from his attempts to think macro-economically where macro-economic concepts conceal the problem.

I propose, however, to discuss first Dr. Botha's suggestion that economists who regard the Keynesian system as defective are influenced by a dogmatic attitude towards the rôle of the State in the co-ordination of the economy. He asserts: "Planning is, of course, anathema to all anti-Keynesians."[8] But *as economists*, those whom I would classify as 'orthodox' are neutral in respect of controversies about the merits of 'capitalism,' 'socialism' or other *isms*. They realise that all valid praxeological generalisations are equally applicable whatever the institutional framework of the societies studied. The relevance of their basic teachings is not upset because, under 'economic democracy,' the determination of economic ends (consumers' sovereignty) is mainly vested in the people, whereas in 'totalitarian' societies a small group of persons (whom we call 'the State') ultimately determines most ends, the detailed expression of which, as well as responsibility for entrepreneurship, being delegated to 'planning commissions' and officials. The rational use of scarce means for the satisfaction of ends (whoever may ultimately determine the ends) is subject to the same economic rules in both types of economic system.[9]

Where the misunderstandings arise is that, in advising supposedly democratic communities about how to achieve their professed ideals, economists have necessarily spoken as *political* economists, or as political philosophers recognising the relevance of the economic relationship. In this rôle they have perceived that Keynesian policies encourage the trend to totalitarianism—an outcome which Keynes himself appeared at times to deplore. It is as political philosophers that, in the volume which Dr. Botha has reviewed, Mises and Hazlitt in particular have emphasised this judgement.[10] Accepting the standards of the West, economists as advisers must often appear to be reproaching the State for its passivity in face of the private exploitation of coercive power and economic sectionalism generally. The tragedy of the Keynesian exposition of economics (which dominates teaching today) is that it is expressed in concepts and models which veil—even if they were not purposely designed to veil—the nature of government responsibility for the discoordination which is expressed either as inflation or in the form of unemployment.

It is true that orthodox economists deny that governments can 'foster' private enterprise or 'create confidence' (as governments not unnaturally like to claim they can, and as Dr. Botha assumes that they can) in any other manner than (a) providing a framework of institutions and administration to promote faith in contract (private or State) and price flexibility[11] (in order to facilitate responsible entrepreneurial determination of resource use), or (b) resorting to inflation; and method (b) is simply a very crude, unjust and essentially dishonest[12] method of bringing about less discoordinative price-cost ratios and hence more favourable prospects of yield to replacement or net accumulation.[13] Inflationary action—although politically easier than the alternative in communities which persistently underestimate the rate at which governments engineer inflation—is much less effective than the free market in establishing such confidence. The only justification for resort to co-ordination through the depreciation of the money unit is the emergence of the electoral vote-buying process. Under the present system, in which governments over-rule the public interest for the benefit of politically powerful insitutions or classes, it may seem to be essential, in order to prevent disastrous depression and unemployment, to *confiscate* some of the conspicuous sectionalist gains expressed in the enhanced money incomes of favoured groups.[14] The method of confiscation is to reduce the real claims conferred on the money unit, i.e., in Keynes' euphemism, "allowing the standard of value to be subject to deliberate decision."

If the Keynesian case had been frankly founded on grounds of this kind, there would have been no controversy within the sphere of economic theory. But Keynes' concepts and models are not necessary to explain the co-ordinative effect of such currency depreciation as occurs more rapidly than the public expect. Indeed, they hinder a full understanding of the process.

There was never any doubt in the minds of Keynes' orthodox critics that an inflationary policy could be successful, *provided either (a) the public could be continuously misled about the speed at which the money unit was losing 'real value,' or (b) totalitarian controls could prevent the politically least powerful sections of the population from reacting to expectations of inflation.* Nor were non-Keynesians ever in doubt about the possibility that, when a great deal of productive capacity had been priced out of reach of uninflated demands, the Keynesian remedy could assist in restoring the *status quo* with little immediately discernible inflation (even in the absence of controls to repress the evidence of inflationary pressures).

Admittedly, in the Britain of the 1930's the public had become accustomed to and acquiescent in a state of chronic unemployment, just as they have today become accustomed to and acquiescent in a state of chronic inflation. As Dr. Botha has put it, "at that time ten per cent unemployment was regarded as a tolerable percentage."[15] But to the orthodox economists it was a scandalous, not a tolerable percentage—a reflection of governmental appeasement of man's cupidity. They understood that just a little reasonableness on the part of a minority of the community could have turned the depression into boom.[16] At the same time, they knew how hopeless it would have been to rail publicly against the trade unions, just as the modern anti-Keynesians know how unrewarding it would be to campaign against inflation.

I do not think that Keynes' motive was so much the "bolstering of the basic economic structure of Western democratic society" (Dr. Botha's words) as that of bolstering those governments which were embarrassed by the politically difficult rôle of the State in the co-ordination of the economy. In the old liberal tradition, when orthodox teachings had some influence, the province of the State in the co-ordination of the economy involved, *inter alia*, the designing and administering of institutions under which sectional interests could be over-ruled for the common good. *Keynes' message was that this burdensome task could be avoided through the "maintenance of effective demand,"* which could dissolve all the difficulties—he might have said, "as though guided by an invisible hand!" If labour unions or other collusive monopolies were tending to price output out of reach of uninflated income (as they were doing in Britain in the 1930's), you must increase money expenditure; but you must not *call* any rise of prices caused in the process 'inflation' as long as it brings any resources in price-induced idleness into activity.

To the orthodox economists, a country's attempt *to spend* its way out of depression must inevitably be inflationary, whilst the Keynesians clothed their central thesis in formulations which diguised this reality and enabled them to claim a revolution in economic insight. What may be called the 'orthodox' solution of the depression problem is the restoration of the flow of uninflated income, and any criticism of the 'orthodox' case which fails to recognise this is based on a complete misconception. The method of restoring the flow which is implied *under economic democracy* is that of rendering market pressures more effective, so as to secure the downward adjustment of those prices which are higher than the people are *able* to pay (or, in the light of their price expectations, *willing to* pay) for valuable productive services.

The Keynesian solution is to render people able to and willing to purchase the full potential flow of output, not by direct co-ordinative price adjustment, but by means of fiscal and monetary policy through which entrepreneurial margins are widened, the prices of final products being raised relatively to those of the basic services which are embodied into them. I can illustrate the point by reference to the usually admitted Keynesian device of reducing *real* wage-rates generally without differentiating against those particular *money* wage-rates which have most seriously discoordinated the economy. The vital difference between the remedy *implied* by orthodox teaching and that adopted on the authority of Keynesian teachings is that in the former the reduction of wage-rates which have been too high (e.g., as in the sheltered industries generally in Britain during 1930-31) will be accompanied by a raising of wage-rates or an increase of aggregate earnings in *other* industries (e.g., in the British coal-mining industry and other un-sheltered industries during the same period).

Dr. Botha thinks that my exposition shows that I myself have some doubts about the efficacy of price adjustment.[17] He charges me with having relegated to a footnote the grounds for my misgivings, partly through my admission that selective wage-rate reductions *on a small scale* could involve "severe distributive injustices." "We are not," he says, "given an indication as to the nature of the selective reductions that would *not* cause distributive injustices."[18] I am afraid I did not realise that, to those who have been nurtured in Keynesian economics, the point I made briefly in the footnote referred to would not be self-evident. It can be explained as follows.

Whenever a particular wage-rate has been pricing some part of the flow of productive services beyond the reach of income or inconsistently with expectations, its reduction will, I have argued, always bring about an increase in aggregate real income. But the benefits may be enjoyed mainly by those whose efforts or assets are employed in non-competing industries. Injustice arises when wage-rates and prices in non-competing industries have been holding even more resources out of utilisation than those which have been withheld by any industry which takes the first step towards pricing for fuller employment. Equity demands therefore that all cases of resources which have been priced into idleness shall be tackled more or less simultaneously.

For instance, the general employment situation in Britain during early 1931 could have been immediately *improved* if the money wage-rates of the miners had been reduced to a level nearer to those then ruling in the mines of competing European countries. But although such a step might be held to have been to the material advantage of the British miners *as a whole* (through lessening the inequity of the differences in income enjoyed by an unemployed miner 'on the dole' and one in employment), it could still be held to have been unjust; for the high wage-rates which the unions had enforced in the sheltered industries were not only reducing the demand for coal but maintaining *relatively* high prices for the products which miners (like the rest of the community) had to buy. Had money wage-rates in the sheltered industries been reduced by, say, 10 percent on the average (which would still have left their employees better off in real terms than they had been a few years previously), normal employment among the miners could probably have been restored without wage-cuts. The employed miners had been maintaining their wage-rates unjustly high from the standpoint of their unemployed comrades; but their aggregate real earnings—of employed and unemployed miners together—having been reduced because of the contrived scarcities enforced by unions in the sheltered industries, they would have been victims of injustice if they alone had been persuaded or forced to make a contribution to the restoration of activity. The elimination of one contrived scarcity may, indeed, not only validate what had previously been a contrived scarcity wage-rate in another field but effect a rise in its natural scarcity value.

Selective reductions are those of prices which are diverting resources into less productive forms of use (or, under price rigidity, into idleness). As I showed in this Journal thirty years ago,[19] every *contrived scarcity* involves an *incidental plenitude*; for resources which are excluded from any field of operation become cheaper (i.e., relatively plentiful) for non-competing fields of operation (and unemployed if their prices are maintained). Blanket reductions of *money* wage-rates or (as implied in the Keynesian remedy) of *real* wage-rates, penalise those who work in, or who have invested in the industries or occupations in which the magnitude of their outputs has depended upon an unjust cheapness (caused by the protection of labour or other resources employed elsewhere). Selective reductions are aimed at 'contrived scarcity prices,' not at the 'incidental plenitude prices.' And it is not the State or a planning commission which can appropriately decide which are the contrived scarcity prices. The free market alone can be relied upon to do that.

Admittedly, during a purposeful deflation (such as that pursued by Britain during her return to gold in 1925 and her subsequent endeavour to remain on gold), one cannot dogmatically rule out the desirability of State action directly to overrule such trade union pressures as seem obviously to be reducing the flow of wages and causing an inequitable distribution of wages. But how much more effective would be a governmental promise to protect every management which is able to reduce wage-rates and product prices simultaneously. If British managements had felt in the thirties that they were safe from the private exercise of coercive power (on the part of those unions which, by resisting, disclosed their blame for a self-perpetuating contraction of the flow of wages, inequitable distribution and the deepening of chronic depression), they could have engineered an explosive recovery,[20] and in doing so they would almost certainly have raised the real standards of workers in the unsheltered industries like coal-mining.

The Keynesian failure to understand the orthodox approach on this question is reflected, I think, in Dr. Botha's discussion of the Say Law. He refers to the arguments of James Mill, J. S. Mill and Say himself on the Law, but still rejects it. It seems to me that the Keynesians' blind spot on the Law of Markets (a law which, to orthodox economists, is as fundamental as the law of gravity to astronomers) can be traced mainly to their attempt to persevere with the inherently defective concept of 'aggregate demand.' For Say was dealing with *demands in general*, i.e., a complex of separate phenomena of preference which are *quite incapable of any meaningful aggregation.* The demand for a particular service is merely the value (which may be measured and expressed in money but is otherwise completely unconnected with money[21]) of whatever services or assets happen to be exchanged for it.

The process of production is that of providing a *flow* of services, the greater part of which is embodied into a *stock* (of inventories and other assets), a stock which is in current process of decumulation (consumption), full or partial replacement, or net accumulation. Keynesian theories of general over-production maintain that *this whole flow can be too big in some sense.*[22] The Say Law suggests that any such notion is meaningless because demands consist simply of the offer of one part of this flow for other parts. Each demand expressed and effected is a supply offered and accepted.

Demands may be classified as follows: (a) demands from the offer of some part of the flow of productive services for other parts of the flow of services; (b) demands from the offer of certain assets for other assets; (c) demands for certain services by the offer of certain assets and *vice-versa.* Changes in the demands which fall under category (a) influence the relative values of different portions of the flow of services; those expressed under category (b) influence the relative values of different portions of the stock of assets; and those expressed under category (c) influence only the rate of interest unless they happen to be a medium through which particular services are offered for other services or particular assets for other assets. But none of these demands can have the slightest effect upon the value of the money unit (even when all these demands are *measured* in money) except when they are demands for monetary services (for immediate consumption or for embodiment into assets).

Say himself did not assume that the value of the money unit had to be constant, or that the hoarding of money (due to abnormal demand for its services) could not occur. Hence his thesis is not in the least upset (as Dr. Botha suggests) because society happens to express values in terms of any particular commodity or instrument such as the pound, dollar or rand.

Demand for monetary *services* may rise or fall in relation to demands for non-money services, and demand for money *assets* may rise or fall in relation to demands for non-money assets: and if we make the absurd assumption (for the modern world in which the credit system operates) that the number of money units is constant, changes in preference as between satisfactions from money and from non-money, or changes in judgement about the relative productiveness of money and non-money, must lead to a change in the non-money value of the money unit. Yet there is nothing in the Say Law to suggest that the *relative* values of different kinds of services or assets may not change; changes in the aggregate real value of money are simply one such instance; and the mere possibility of such a change does not make sense of the notion of a general deficiency or excess of demands, evisaged as an excess or deficiency respectively in the flow of services or the stock of assets.

Of course, every change in demands (effective preference) must lead to the wasteful idleness of resources under defective co-ordination; and disco-ordination so caused in one sector of the economy may (under price rigidity) have a cumulative effect, the decline in the flow of services in that sector inducing a decline in another sector. That is, however, an illustration of the *operation* of the Say Law, not of its failure to operate. It is the cumulative withdrawal of supplies (by the pricing of services out of range of income and expectations) which may lead the economy into depression; for that is the withdrawal of demands.

This is the answer to Dr. Botha's argument that the value adjustments which, in an abstractly conceived barter system would (if permitted) result in the full utilisation of resources are not likely to achieve this result in a monetary economy.[23] In reality, far from the monetary system constituting a hindrance to adjustment, it is a mechanism for facilitating and rendering more sensitive the process of co-ordinating value ratios which, my critic perceives, *can* operate successfully under barter.

The failure to demand the full flow of valuable services (and services *are* always valuable or they are not to be classified as services, whilst being valuable means being demanded) must be due to the pricing of part of the flow too high in relation to the rest of the flow (either by the direct withholding of supply or by fixing a price at which some part of the flow remains unpurchased); and 'too high' has reference to the income and the expectations of the rest of the community.

It follows that depression is the consequence not of over-production but of the cumulative results of refusals to sell at prices consistent with uninflated income and expectations. Indeed, we may define depression as a situation in which each act of pricing for unemployment induces, under general price rigidity, other withholdings of capacity elsewhere in the economy.[24]

Marx's truism, "no one can sell unless someone else purchases," which Dr. Botha appears to believe illustrates the defect of the Say Law,[25] needs completion by the addition of the converse: "no one can purchase unless someone else sells"; and every act of selling requires that the *seller* prices his product to permit the sale (or that he *accepts* the buyer's offer[26]). The root co-ordinative act which keeps the economy in activity is obviously this price determination.

When Mill admitted that a seller need "not buy at the same moment when he sells"[27] (to someone who simultaneously purchases!) he was dealing with the case in which the community happens temporarily to *prefer* relatively more monetary services or money, and hence *prefer* relatively less of non-money services or assets. Whether or not such a bidding up of the aggregate real value of money means also a bidding up of the real value of the money *unit* (as under monetary rigidity), it is difficult to see in what sense "*both* commodities and money may then be in excess supply."[28] If the rise in the aggregate value of money is due to expectations that monetary policy intends to raise the real value of the money unit and the expectations are correct, the 'hoarding' is assisting the monetary aim. Similarly, when the value of inventories of non-money assets increases because people expect their money value to rise, that does not mean that there is an 'excess' of such goods. The only case in which the word 'excess' has meaning in this context is when it refers to inventories which are generally accumulating because (owing to entrepreneurial misjudgement) they are not being disposed of at prices sufficiently low to maximise the yield (or minimise a realised loss) from their sale. That is the orthodox notion of 'excess.' And the *prices* of such goods, rather than their *volume* (as rates of output or stocks) are then 'excessive.'[29]

If over-pricing is ruled out, then although *misdirected* production can occur (in the sense of particular over-productions and under-productions which may cause some assets—including inventories of final products—to be valued at less than they had cost, or even valueless), this is a defect in the *composition* of output, not of its *quantity*. And even so, each particular over-production implies the under-production of some other output, to which the flow of valuable services would otherwise have been devoted. Moreover, the effect of such misdirection of production will be *inflationary*, on the assumption of monetary rigidity, a decline in T being accompanied by an unchanged MV.

The exposition of the early classical economists was often far from rigorous, indeed, occasionally quite woolly on this issue.[30] In his controversy with Malthus, and in his *Cours Complet*, Say was certainly muddled on an issue which, although irrelevant to the Law of Markets, has provided critics of that law with ammunition with which to attack it.[31] In an attempt to show the folly of regarding mere additions to physical output as 'production,' Say defined a product as a thing of which the value exceeds its cost of production, and then got into a serious intellectual entanglement in an attempt to explain the implications for his theory.[32] But a thing which is worth less than it has cost may still have a positive value and be demanded; and the fact that such things may exist (indeed, every student of business administration knows that they normally do exist) does not weaken the vital law for which Say has been given credit. It does not detract from the reality that the sole source of demand for any part of valuable output is the flow of non-competing output.

I expect to be charged, however, with having admitted the possibility of the free, uncontrolled market permitting serious deflation and depression. My answer is that the market can do nothing more than co-ordinate the factors which, *monetary policy being given* (or private contracts to convert on the part of banks of issue being given) determine the value of the money unit. But no free economic system would choose as its monetary standard any commodity or token, the value of which, *under wise monetary management*, would be subject to disconcerting fluctuations in real value. Thus, the gold standard was adopted officially in the nineteenth century because it had for long served mankind satisfactorily as a privately concluded contract; and its virtues depended upon the fact that the standard was merely the measure of value in a credit system, under which a public or private contract (to convert into gold) enforced changes in the volume of deposits and currency in circulation (and in a manner which, in normal times, maintained an approximate constancy in the scale of prices).

If Keynes had merely extolled the virtues of a more stable money unit than it was believed the gold standard could offer, controversy of a quite different nature would have followed.[33] But a principal feature of Keynesian teaching was the conviction that any money unit of defined or contractual value, however stable that value might be, must constitute a barrier to the central action required for the maintenance of effective demand. Keynes wanted the value of the money unit to be a matter of governmental discretion (see above, page 113). His controversy with F. D. Graham and Hayek made that doubly clear.

The root controversy between Keynesians and non-Keynesians centres, then, around the denial of the former that the downward adjustment of certain prices (towards the point at which people, as savers or consumers, are *able to* purchase and, in the light of their expectations, *willing to* purchase the full flow of valuable services) can restore full employment when unemployment has occurred. The concept of 'willingness to purchase' covers the full consequences of expectations. That is, the price adjustments which non-Keynesians hold are implied in a co-ordinated system are such as bring about consistency between spot and future prices as well as consistency between prices in different parts of the economy and at different stages of production.

It is, I think, symptomatic of the extent to which the Keynesians have failed to understand orthodox theory that Dr. Botha can remark of my exposition of that theory: "expectations apparently play no rôle."[34] This charge of neglected expectations is repeated several times, on one occasion surprisingly immediately after my critic has referred to my insistence that price flexibility requires the continuous adjustment of prices so as to establish harmony between current and expected prices.[35]

The neglect of expectations would, indeed, have been responsible for serious fallacy; for it is true that the process of price adjustment has time dimensions. But it is not true that "pre-Keynesian theorists (and anti-Keynesian) theorists failed to recognise 'the transitional process.' "[36] One has to be just to them. Dr. Botha and other Keynesians have seized on minor inconsistencies in the thinking or exposition of a few in order to refute a thesis which shows the most profound insight.[37]

I myself have laid stress on "the transitional process" through the concept of "unstable price rigidity,"[38] but I claim no *originality* for the ideas so treated. Far from "expectations being ruled out altogether," their consideration is essential for any understanding of the orthodox viewpoint.

The question can be best discussed by consideration of the cases in which

(i) *in a particular industry* from which demand has been transferred to other industries, drastic price (and wage-rate) reductions can minimise the burden on employees when their skills are non-versatile; and (ii) *in the economy as a whole*, obligations of honour demand drastic deflation following an inflation which a monetary authority has admitted the obligation to rectify,[39] whilst substantial reductions of certain prices with simultaneous reductions of certain money wage-rates (to restore previously existing real wage-rates) can remove the price barriers between valuable services and the demands which create their value (hence permitting deflation without depression).[40] In both such circumstances, the pains of re-coordination are likely to be least if the adjustments are so boldly undertaken that the new prices established (of labour and products) are those which people expect ultimately to be realised.

In case (i) each price or wage-rate reduction will have lessened the prospective yield from investment in the costs of postponed transactions— i.e., the inconvenience of temporarily acquiring less of the commodity in question. It follows (on the assumption that the expected price does not then fall further) that the pressure to additional reductions, although still present, will be reduced. The fact that *ceteris paribus* the pressure to adjust prices is greater the further any price diverges from its generally forecast level means that expectations are a powerful co-ordinative factor.[41]

In case (ii) this is equally true; for co-ordination under deflation (deflation being regarded as a collectively sought product, acquired at a cost) requires, in a régime which seeks competing ends with consistency, that all prices subject to re-contract shall be adjusted to the projected new value of the money unit.[42] Difficulties arise when the *expected* scale of prices (a forecast ultimate *real* value of the money unit), not itself being an explicit declared objective, is changing. The mere fact of the actual scale of prices falling may create new expectations. Now if the aim is to reduce the scale of prices by more than the public would be prepared to accept at the outset, such a gradual change in expectations may assist policy. But the first requisite of any rational monetary policy under the credit system (unless it relies upon the continuous deception of the public) is that of creating complete confidence in an existing, permanent and defined value of the money unit or, in the case of a purposeful deflation, in a similarly defined future value of that unit. In such circumstances, the obligations of convertibility, although not creating absolute certainty about the ultimate scale of prices, will create limits to the extent to which prices in general can fall. Each decline will reduce the probability of a further decline. But any fall in the demand for non-money services as a whole in favour of monetary services, caused by the belief that monetary policy is aiming at establishing a higher real value of the money unit, must assist the correct discernment of that policy.[43]

I turn now to what seems to me to be a separate point. Dr. Botha objects that when, through downward price adjustment, less has to be spent in the aggregate to obtain what the community demands of a particular product, "more may be spent on other goods *or savings may increase.*"[44] I shall assume first that the word 'savings' here is not intended to mean an increased demand for money. The italicising of the last four words in the sentence then appears to imply that, if the services to which demands are shifted are such that the rate of net accumulation of income-producing assets increases (an increase of 'savings'), the orthodox price adjustment thesis is somehow upset. But an increased rate of economic growth (a rise in 'savings') is merely a response to induced or autonomous changes in time preference. It is on a par with responses to all other changes of preference.

My critic goes on to say, however, that savings may increase "when consumers desire to increase their cash reserves . . ."[45] Well, as one may obviously accumulate money without saving, the need for money (as distinct from assets in general) can hardly be a *special* motive for saving. Nevertheless a saver must choose some assets to acquire, and on occasion so many savers *may* regard money as the most productive form of assets that the aggregate real value of money will be bid up. There is, however, no good reason why a change in time preference *should* cause any change at all in the valuation of monetary services and money assets. But if an increased desire to save, or a rise in realised savings *does* have this effect, it is still quite wrong to say that "classical theory will not hold."[46] Classical theory no more assumes that the demand for money is constant than it assumes that the demand for any other kind of asset is constant; and it relies on no *dogma* about the factors which determine that demand.

But my assumption in the paragraph before last about the meaning of 'savings' may not be legitimate. Dr. Botha has, I think, been trapped at this stage in a confusion between time preference (saving preference) and liquidity preference. The confusion, which the use of Keynesian concepts has rendered conventional, is not purely Keynesian. It has probably arisen because, in a money economy, a normal step in a person's acquisition of *additional* assets (out of income) or *different* assets (out of existing capital) is the temporary accumulation (in a bank, till or purse) of the money to pay for them. Such temporary money accumulations are acquired through an exchange of the services which constitute income for money held by others or through the exchange of assets for money held by others. But this process is in continuous operation; and a change in *the type of assets*[47] into which the flow of services is embodied (for replacement or net accumulation), such as is the result of a response to a change in time preference, has no necessary tendency to cause the demand for money to rise. Time preference and liquidity preference are as independent and unconnected as are the preferences for bubble gum and monocles. *Saving more* is not spending less: it is increased bidding for assets by the offer of services, and in a money economy it involves *spending on different things* (ultimately, on different services).

Another point on which Dr. Botha finds my exposition 'perplexing' arises out of my explanation that, although any monetary policy which aims at changing the value of the money unit necessarily throws the price system out of co-ordination, that is no final argument against such a policy. He says that "having sown the seeds of doubt," I "leave the reader to fend for himself."[48] But every change in economic objectives, whether privately or collectively sought, throws the system out of co-ordination in the sense that activities and hence prices have to be adjusted in conformity. Thus, if a country has persuaded other countries to enter into contracts with her by promising, say, to restore the suspended convertibility of her currency into gold (and thenceforth to maintain that convertibility), and she wishes to honour her obligations, she may legitimately expect that her activities will be so moulded that this objective will be attained at least cost. The folly of the British return to gold in 1925 and the attempt to persevere with the gold standard until 1931 was that policy permitted trade unions and price rings *to frustrate the required co-ordinative pressures*, thereby reducing the flow of wages and other incomes and preventing a more equitable distribution.

Dr. Botha quotes my assertion that a policy of restoring employment by bringing the full flow of service into price consistency with incomes and expectations, is one which has never been experimentally tested (in spite of its having been implied by the disinterested teachings of a century of scientifically minded scholars). He says that I ask the reader to accept "in good faith" the suggestion that it is *possible* to price all valuable services so that the demands which create their value can reach them, and that "the evidence against it is overwhelming."[49] I am unaware of that evidence. Classical teachings have been derived from and have survived through careful, critical interpretation of concrete price experience; the whole record of the great depression of the 1930's seems to confirm these teachings; and since 1936 the results of Keynesian policy appear to have amply justified the warnings of those economists who had the intellectual courage or confidence to refrain from conforming to the Keynesian fashion.

Notes

1. H. Hazlitt, *The Critics of Keynesian Economics* (Princeton: van Nostrand, 1960).

2. D. Botha, "The Critics of Keynesian Economics," *South African Journal of Economics* 31 (June 1963), pp. 81-102.

3. W. Hutt, *Keynesianism—Retrospect and Prospect* (Chicago: Henry Regnery Company, 1963).

4. Ibid., Chapter 19, entitled, "The Retreat."

5. Botha, "The Critics of Keynesian Economics," p. 81.

6. The same perception caused the pious, didactic Bastiat to claim (about 1850) that the price system was "a celestial mechanism which reveals the wisdom of God and tells of his glory." This phrase is quoted by P. Lambert (*L'Oeuvre de J. M. Keynes*, p. 123), to suggest that the classical case somehow rested upon the assumption of heavenly control. But references of this kind no more detract from the rational insight of the early classical economists than similar irrelevant references to the Almighty detract from the soundness of Bach's writings on harmony or Newton's treatment of gravity. See my *Economists and the Public* (London: Jonathan Cape, 1936), pp. 135-7. In fact, Bastiat explicitly recognized the similarity of his position to that of Newton. See *Harmonics Economiques* (Paris: Guillaumin, 1893), p. 49.

7. I ignore here the support which Keynes—and *some* of his successors—won for his methods by misrepresentation and ridicule of the disinterested economists whose authority they were successful in destroying. But Dr. Botha's own phrase, "discrediting the 'invisible hand' approach," illustrates the effectiveness with which the typical student of economics today has been indoctrinated with the belief that the classical or orthodox school somehow relied upon divinely enacted guidance— "mythical automatic stabilizers" as one Keynesian has put it, to produce order out of laissez-faire chaos.

8. Botha, "The Critics of Keynesian Economics," p. 98.

9. Although the market test of achievement is largely absent under the totalitarian system, whereas under economic democracy decision-makers are subject to the discipline of loss-avoidance, profit-seeking incentives.

10. See my *Keynesianism*, Chapter 3, Section 7.

11. I do not mention here (i) the provision of a money unit of defined value or (ii)

the guaranteeing of such a value; for (i) is not an essential State function (thus, the gold standard emerged through purely private enterprise) and (ii) is merely the uncontroversial State function of the enforcement of contract (control of weights and measures being the most appropriate parallel).

12. It is dishonest because the technique of creeping inflation (such as has followed the adoption of Keynesian policies) involves the perpetual deception of the public. An announced inflation of say, 5 percent per annum would be self-defeating because costs would tend to rise ahead of final prices, and contracts would offset the gradual, deliberate extermination of the value of the money unit. (See my *Keynesianism*, Chapter 18.)

13. In this connection it is important to insist that contrary to what Dr. Botha assumes, J. S. Mill was perfectly correct in maintaining that a government cannot *encourage* production by taking some of the people's income *via* taxation and then buying their goods with it (ibid., p. 84). The Keynesians are tricked by their method into supposing that such a transference of income can generate a stimulus. Only if the collective exercise of entrepreneurial judgement succeeds in the achievement of a more productive (greater income-earning) replacement or net accumulation of assets than the responsible decision-making of private entrepreneurs, can a non-inflationary impetus to productive activity result from state expenditure.

14. Won, for example, by threats to strike, by other forms of privately used coercive power, or through sheer political favouritism.

15. Botha, "The Critics of Keynesian Economics," p. 100.

16. I refer again below to the situation in Britain in the 1930s. This was at the time when even Sidney Webb could remark to Beatrice Webb (his co-historian of the trade union movement, and his co-author of the most influential attempt at justification of the private use of coercive power by the unions): "The (trade union) General Council are pigs." Mrs. Webb went on bitterly to comment on "the sabotage of British industry by trade union pigheadedness," and added that "the wage-earner is so irresponsible that idleness, with a regular pittance is comparatively attractive to large bodies of men." M. Cole, *Beatrice Webb's Diaries* (London: Longman, 1956), II, pp. 253-4.

17. Botha, "The Critics of Keynesian Economics," p. 95. I have no doubts whatsoever! What I do doubt is the practicability of getting governments to perform their crucial role in the coordinative process until economists begin to speak with unanimity on the subject.

18. Ibid., p. 95.

19. W. Hutt, "Natural and Contrived Scarcities," *South African Journal of Economics* 3 (September 1935), pp. 345-53.

20. Equity would have demanded simultaneous anti-monopoly action against the many manufacturers' and dealers' price rings which existed in Britain at that time. But I assume, as indeed did Keynes, that the unions were principally responsible.

21. I have defended this thesis against several misconceptions in my *Keynesianism,* especially in Chapters 5 and 8.

22. Or (the "capital saturation" or "stagnation" thesis) that *the stock* can be too big; and sometimes the suggestion is that the rate of flow of services into income-producing assets can exceed some undefined optimum—the notion of "excessive savings."

23. Botha, "The Critics of Keynesian Economics," p. 94.

24. The vague notion of "over-full employment" which the Keynesian approach has introduced into economics seems to have nothing to do with the equally defective idea of "over-production." It refers in practice to the boom condition in which the repressed form of latent inflation is tending to break out into open inflation.

25. Ibid., p. 85.

26. I am assuming here that "contrived plenitude" (as opposed to "contrived scarcity") is unimportant. This assumption is based on an empirical judgment. If buyers everywhere had been "organized" as so many sellers are "organized," the problems of finding markets in which to buy would have received as much discussion in the literature as the problems of finding markets in which to sell.

27. Ibid., p. 85.

28. Dr. Botha's phrase and his italics, ibid., p. 86.

29. *Particular* inventories may have been "over-produced" in the sense that other kinds of output would have been productive and profitable. But this notion cannot be generalized to apply to *all* assets.

30. The most enthusiastic admirer of the founders of our science must admit their unsatisfactory treatment of some issues. Thus Edwin Cannan, whose great sudy of early classical economics is thought by some to have been hypercritical, came to be regarded as a leading exponent of that teaching.

31. I have dealt fully with this weakness in Say's exposition in my *Keynesianism,* pp. 395-401.

32. For some reason Dr. Botha refers to this definition as "mere prevarication."

33. In his *Monetary Reform* which appeared at a time (1923) when Britain had, so to speak, contracted with the world to deflate her currency in the measure necessary to restore and maintain the traditional gold standard, Keynes *had* argued for this stability.

34. Botha, "The Critics of Keynesian Economics," p. 93.

35. Ibid., p. 96.

36. Ibid., p. 97.

37. Thus, there are passages where J. S. Mill seems to have been confounding the situation in which the value of non-money tends to fall in terms of money (so that—through monetary rigidity—the real value of the money unit tends to rise) with the situation in which there is a greater increase in the flow of non-money services

than can be absorbed by the demands expressed (i.e., even when the real value of the money unit is not rising). But these conceptually distinct situations were equally confused by the Keynesians of Mill's generation, such as Sismondi and Malthus.

38. See my *Keynesianism*, especially pages 170-171 and 174-176. But I have found it essential to use this concept in many contexts.

39. E.g., in Britain between 1918 and 1931, a rise in the real value of the money unit was rendered necessary by the determination to keep faith with the world— originally in order to permit the return to gold and later to permit the continued honouring of the convertibility contract. A complicating factor was that, after 1925, politically determined unemployment was increasing the deflationary burden by weakening faith in convertibility.

40. Professor A. F. Burns reminded the world a few years ago of the possibility of "prosperity without inflation" in a book by that title. But "deflation without depression" is equally possible unless governments are committed to the Keynesian variety of laissez-faire.

41. This disposes of Dr. Botha's difficulty that, when the price of a commodity falls, expenditure on it may diminish, even if the demand for it happens to be elastic, "if a further drop in price is *expected.*" Of course. But when the demand for a particular commodity falls because its price is expected to fall relatively to prices in general (i.e., by more than the average), the transfer of preference to other things (including, perhaps, money) *assists* price adjustment by exerting the required pressure.

42. This does not necessarily mean that *all* prices must fall.

43. Dr. Botha says that I have "surprisingly" failed to criticize Patinkin's analysis of the role of time in adjustment (ibid., p. 97). But I had no occasion to do this; for my contention is that Patinkin's attempt to rehabilitate Keynesian teaching, in spite of his having just rejected the unemployment equilibrium thesis, is still based on the assumption of "unstable price rigidities" *somewhere* in the economy. That being so, the analysis which leads him to his unemployment *dis*equilibrium notion does not contradict my own argument.

44. Ibid., p. 94 (Dr. Botha's italics).

45. Ibid., p. 94.

46. Ibid., p. 94

47. This reference to the "type of assets" may need further explanation. Response to a rise in time preference will cause a greater flow of services into assets of which a larger stock can be profitably carried through time, and a smaller flow into assets of which a larger stock cannot be profitably carried through time. (See my *Keynesianism*, pp. 229, 232f, 299-300.)

48. Botha, "The Critics of Keynesian Economics," p. 95.

49. Ibid., p. 96.

8 • *The Significance of Price Flexibility*

The period 1932-1953 has witnessed a revolution and counter-revolution in thought on the function and consequences of price flexibility.

In considering this remarkable phase in the history of theory, it is useful to begin by referring to a related field of hardly disturbed agreement. There has been no controversy during the period of our survey among serious economists about the desirability of a system which tends to ensure that different kinds of prices shall stand in a certain optimum relation to one another, or about the desirability, in a changing world, of continuous *relative* price adjustment in order to bring about some conformance to the ideal relation. From the so-called "socialist economists" of the Lange-Lerner type to the so-called "individualist economists" of the Mises-Röpke type, there has been agreement that the price system has important equilibrating and co-ordinative functions. Moreover, until the appearance of Keynes's *General Theory* in 1936, the measure of agreement about the *aims* of institutional reform for the better working of the price system seemed to be slowly but definitely growing.

There was not the same marked tendency towards agreement about *methods*. Some thought that improved pricing could be achieved through a greater centralisation or sectionalisation of economic power, with the final voice to decide both preferences (choice of ends) and productive policy (choice of means) entrusted to elected representatives or syndicates. Others thought that the required reforms involved exactly the reverse—the breaking

Reprinted with permission from *South African Journal of Economics* 22 (1954).

up and diffusion of economic authority so that the final voice about ends rested with the people as consumers, whilst the final voice about the choice of means rested with those who stood to gain or lose according to the success with which they allocated scarce resources in accordance with consumer-determined ends. But in spite of this apparently basic clash, as soon as explicit plans for the devising of a workable economic system were attempted, even the divergence of opinion about methods appeared to be narrowing. The so-called "socialist economists" were clearly attempting to restore *the market* and the *power of substitution.* So much was this so, that I believed the result of their labours would ultimately be the re-building of *laissez-faire* institutions, in elaborate disguises of name and superficial form, the result being regarded as the perfect socialist pricing system.[1]

This interesting trend towards unanimity of opinion in several fields was overlapped by and rudely disturbed by Keynes's *General Theory.* Since 1936, the economists have become sharply divided about the nature of the price changes which ought, in the interests of "full employment," to take place in any given situation.[2] Consider trade union or State-enforced wage-rates. At one extreme, we have the Keynesians who argue that, in maintaining wage-rates, we are maintaining consumer demand, creating a justification for new investment, and so preventing the emergence of depression. At the other extreme, we have those who argue that each successive increase of wage-rates so brought about renders essential a further element of inflation in order to maintain "full employment"—a development which tends permanently to dilute the money unit.

The Keynesian theory on this point proved enormously attractive. The idea as such was not novel; but before *The General Theory* it had enjoyed a negligible following in respectable economic circles. After 1936, it gave many economists what they seemed to have been waiting for, a non-casuistic argument for the tolerance of the collective enforcement or State fixation of minimum wage-rates.

Curiously enough, Keynes's challenge was based on a sort of admission of the evils of current collective bargaining and a further admission (by no means explicit, but an inevitable inference[3]) that labour in general was unable to benefit in real terms at the expense of other parties to production by forcing a rise in the price of labour. Gains achieved by individual groups of organised workers were paid out of the pockets of other workers. At the same time, Keynes's new teachings seemed to support strongly those who cried, "Hands off the unions!" Although his thesis was accompanied by the charge—not wholly without foundation—that orthodox economists had closed their eyes to the consequences of the wage rigidity caused by trade union action, he always seemed to range himself on the side of the unions in their resistance to wage-rate adjustments. The reasons for his views on this question were two-fold.

Firstly, he argued that the price of labour had to be regarded as *inevitably* rigid. This empirical judgment about economic reality is, of course, not confined to the Keynesians. Where Keynes was original was in the subsidiary and supporting assumption that what other economists have called "the money illusion" was a basic cause of the rigidity.

Secondly, he argued that, in any case, wage-rate flexibility downwards, even if other prices were flexible, would aggravate and not alleviate depression. For even under perfect wage-rate flexibility and perfect flexibility generally, an equilibrium with unemployment could exist.[4] As I have previously argued,[5] Keynes would have preferred to rely wholly upon the second argument. But he kept the first, as Schumpeter has put it, "on reserve." In this survey I shall be dealing only with this second argument.

The contention is that wage-rate cuts must in any case be ineffective, as a means of restoring employment in labour, because it is possible to cut money rates only and not real wage-rates. Reduced money rates, Keynes explained, would mean reduced wages in the aggregate and reduced demand. Hence the wage-rate rigidity, which former economists had been inclined to criticise ought, in his opinion, to be regarded as a virtue in times of depression.

At two points, Keynes appeared to have some misgivings about this thesis. He admitted firstly that if the price of labour *could* be flexible, things would be different, i.e., "if it were always open to labour to reduce its real wage by accepting a reduction in its money wage. . . ." This condition assumed, he said, ". . . free competition among employers and no restrictive combinations among workers."[6] And he explicitly admitted later that, if there were competition between unemployed workers, "there might be no position of stable equilibrium except in conditions consistent with full employment. . . ."[7] But he did not attempt to reconcile these passages with apparently contradictory passages.

We are left, then, with the principal contention, namely, that changes in wage-rates are "double-edged," affecting both individual outputs and general demand. As this infectious doctrine has been developed by Keynes's disciples, costs as a whole are no longer regarded as merely *limiting* output, but as *calling forth* output through demand.

The objection to regarding costs as a source of demand can be simply stated. The only cost adjustments which defenders of price flexibility advocate are those which must always increase real income, and hence always increase money income under any system in which the value of the money unit remains constant. If we concentrate attention upon wages, it can be said that, on the reasonable assumption that the growth of real income will not mean a re-distribution against the *absolute* advantage of the wage-earners, the effect of the wage-rate reductions which are advocated must always mean an increase and not a decrease in aggregate wages received, and hence an increased demand for wage-goods. (The possibility of hoarding being induced is discussed later.)

In part, the Keynesian attempt to handle the problem in terms of the crude concept of "the price of labour" has confused the issue. We are concerned with the prices of different kinds of labour, whilst the index number concept of "the wage level" screens off from scrutiny all the issues which seem to me to be important.[8] Throughout Chapter 19 of *The General Theory* Keynes talked simply of "reduction of money wages." And he discussed the orthodox view of the desirability of price adjustments as though it was based on a "demand schedule for labour in industry as a whole relating the quantity of employment to different levels of wages."[9]

Through thus thinking rather uncritically about aggregates, the Keynesians appear to have *assumed* that wage-rate reductions imply reduction of aggregate earnings,[10] irrespective of whether the labour price which is cut is that of workers in an exclusive, well-paid trade, or that of workers doing poorly paid work because they are excluded from well-paid opportunities. When the Keynesians do think of adjustments in individual wage-rates, they think of blanket changes. At one point Keynes objected to price flexibility as a remedy for idleness in labour on the grounds that "there is, as a rule, no means of securing a simultaneous and equal reduction of money wages in all industries."[11] But it is not *uniform* reductions which are wanted, it is selective reductions, the appropriate selection of which can be entrusted to markets when non-market *minima* have been adjusted.[12]

But even if equi-proportional wage-cuts were enacted, in a régime in which there was much unemployment, aggregate and average earnings might still tend to increase,[13] owing to the redistribution of workers over the different wage-rate groups. It would become profitable to employ more in the higher-paid types of work, whilst in the lower-paid types there would have to be rationing.[14] Keynes's static, short-term methods exclude consideration of these reactions.[15] Clarity will not be gained whilst we try to think in terms of "wage levels." We have to think in terms of changing frequency distributions. This is important enough for the consideration of employment in individual industries, but still more important in relation to employment as a whole.

The Keynesian argument is that it is no use cutting the wage-rates of say, carpenters, if there is unemployment among them because, even if *their* employment fully recovers, their incomes and expenditure will fall and so cause the demand for the labour of other workers to fall.[16] But the case for price flexibility by no means assumes that a moderate fall in carpenters' wage-rates, together with a corresponding fall in the price of the product will, in itself, greatly increase the employment of *carpenters*. Such a reaction, although *possible*, is most unlikely.[17]

The correct proposition can be put this way. *Increased employment among carpenters can be most easily induced as the result of wage-rate and price reductions on the part of those persons who ultimately buy the carpenters' services.* The assumption is that the reductions result in the release of withheld capacity in the industries which do not compete with carpenters, whilst the increasing flow of products becomes demand through being priced to permit its full sale. This is the argument which the Keynesians should answer.

In his *Prosperity and Depression*, Haberler expressed doubts about this type of argument. He stated the case for it briefly, in a footnote,[18] but added that it assumed MV to be constant. I shall try to show that whatever MV may be, the value adjustments needed to secure the consumption or use of all goods and services may still be brought about. Haberler argues also that we cannot infer the truth of the proposition from facts which appear to support it. During the depression, outputs and employment were maintained in the agricultural field, in which the fall of prices *could not be* effectively resisted, but shrank in industry, in which prices *could be* effectively maintained. It would seem, then, that full employment and outputs could have been maintained in industry also, had price competition been effective. That, says Haberler, "has not yet been rigorously proven."[19] But is it not self-evident that, given any monetary policy, *selective* reduction of the prices of industrial goods would, in general, have made smaller reductions of agricultural prices necessary (in order to secure full employment in that field), whilst the maintenance of outputs as a whole would have eased the task of financing full production without diluting the money unit?[20] And is it not equally obvious that, had the price of agricultural products been maintained, so that these products absorbed a greater proportion of the total power to purchase, industrial unemployment would have been still more serious?

The relations between wage-rates and the aggregate pay-roll cannot, I suggest, be effectively considered, except in relation to the price system as a whole. But the Keynesians appear to take the co-ordinative effects of the value mechanism for granted and concentrate upon what they regard as the motive power behind it, namely, money income. They do not continuously envisage and consider the *synchronising function* of prices, the fact that the prices attaching to individual commodities or services determine the *rate of flow* at which these commodities or services move into consumption or into the next stage of production. The co-ordination of the rates of flow of materials, services, etc., is brought about through the raising or lowering of prices. *Ceteris paribus* a rise in price causes a falling off in the rate of flow, and a fall in price causes a rise in the rate of flow of any thing through the stage of production at which it is priced. If certain prices cannot change, other prices (i.e., other rates of flow) must adjust themselves accordingly if the economy is to be synchronised in any sense.[21]

"Full employment" is secured when all services and products are so priced that they are (i) brought within the reach of people's pockets (i.e., so that they are purchasable by existing money incomes) or (ii) brought into such a relation to predicted prices, that no postponement of expenditure on them is induced. For instance, the products and services used in the manufacture of investment goods must be so priced that anticipated future money incomes will be able to buy the services and depreciation of new equipment or replacements.

Admittedly, the view that co-ordinative reductions or increases of wage-rates must always tend to increase real income (and probably real wages in the aggregate also) does not imply that money income (and money wages) will *also* increase, except on certain assumptions about the nature of the monetary system which exists. Perhaps the pre-Keynesian economists could be criticised for having made tacit instead of explicit assumptions on this point. But orthodox economics (as I understand it) did not overlook what is now called "the income effect." The tacit assumption[22] was that the monetary system was of such a nature that the increased real income due to the release of productive power in individual trades (through the acceptance of lower wage rates) would not result in a reduction of money income. No one suggested that the monetary system *had* necessarily to be like that; but from the actual working of the credit system, it seemed to be unnecessary to consider the case in which an expansion of production would not be accompanied by an increase in money income induced by this expansion. The assumption on which Keynes built, namely, that the number of money units is fixed, would have seemed absurd to most pre-Keynesian economists, unless they were considering the economics of a community so primitive that a fixed number of tokens (shells, for instance) served as the sole medium of exchange, whilst no lending or credit of any kind existed.

In a credit economy, there could never be any difficulty, due to the mere fact that outputs had increased, about purchasing the full flow of production at ruling prices. That is, expanding real income could not have, in itself, any price depressing tendencies. Only monetary policy was believed to be able to explain that. But given any monetary policy, they believed that unemployment of any type of labour was due to wage-rates being wrongly related to the "amount of money" existing at any time.[23] It followed that downward adjustments of minimum wage-rates and prices could never *aggravate*—on the contrary would always *mitigate*—the consequences of any deflationary tendency caused by monetary policy.

Ought we not now to recognize that it is unnecessary to modify this pre-Keynesian view? Under *any* monetary system, the price situation which permits ideal co-ordination, in the sense which I have explained, must maximise the source of real demand—real income. Whilst this may be clear enough in the case in which monetary policy precipitates *primary* deflation, it may be less obvious when *secondary* deflation is induced. But postponements of demand, with their self-perpetuating consequences, arise when current costs or prices are higher than anticipated costs or prices.[24]

In more general terms, expected changes in costs or prices, unaccompanied by immediate cost and price co-ordination to meet expectations, lead to "secondary" reactions. A *cut in costs* does not induce demand postponement; nor, indeed, do *falling costs* have this effect. Postponements arise because it is judged that a cut in costs (or other prices) is less than will eventually have to take place, or because the rate of fall of costs (or other prices) is insufficiently rapid. It follows that "secondary" deflations are attributable to the unstable rigidities which prevent continuous co-ordination of prices. Confusion arises because secondary deflation can be brought to an end, not by true co-ordination, but at the expense of a prospective permanent sacrifice of real income, i.e., through the imposition of cost and price rigidities (in the form of minima) which are expected to continue indefinitely.[25]

Now if, for any reason, a change in the value of the money unit becomes the declared object of policy, or the expected consequence of policy, *the whole price system is immediately thrown out of co-ordination*. Thus, if the value of the money unit is expected to rise, then until the necessary adjustments have all taken place, "willingness to buy" must necessarily fall off—most seriously where values of services and materials in the investment goods industries do not at once respond.[26]

We turn finally to explicit criticisms of the reasoning on which Keynes based his suggestion of unemployment equilibrium under wage-rate flexibility or, as his disciples were later forced to argue, under price flexibility.

Through the attempts of disciples[27] like Lange, Smithies, Tobin, Samuelson, Modigliani and Patinkin to defend or strengthen the new creed, successive refinements have gradually paved the way for the ultimate abandonment, by would-be Keynesians, of the view that wage-rate and price adjustments are powerless to secure full employment. The contributions of these very friendly critics, said Schumpeter, "might have been turned into very serious criticisms" if they had been "less in sympathy with the spirit of Keynesian economics."[28] He added that this is particularly true of Modigliani's contribution. He could have made the same remark about that of Patinkin, which appeared two years later. But the criticisms of these writers *were* very serious in any case. Their apparent reluctance to abandon standpoints which their own logic was urging them to reject clouded their exposition; but it did not weaken the implications of their reasoning.

Modigliani (whose 1944 article[29] quietly caused more harm to the Keynesian thesis than any other single contribution) seems, almost unintentionally, to reduce to the absurd the notion of the co-existence of idle resources and price flexibility. He does this by showing that its validity is limited to the position which exists when there is an *infinitely elastic* demand for money units ("the Keynesian case"). Modigliani does not regard this extreme case as absurd and, indeed, declares that interest in such a possibility is "not purely theoretical."[30] Yet Keynes himself, in dealing explicitly with this case, described it as a "possibility" of which he knew of no example, but which "might become practically important in future,"[31] although there are many passages in *The General Theory* which (as Haberler has pointed out[32]) rely upon the assumption of an infinitely elastic demand. "The New Keynesians" appear to be trying to substitute this "special theory" (Hicks's description) for the "general theory" which they admit must be abandoned.

It is my present view that any attempt to envisage the "special theory" operating in the concrete realities of the world we know—even under depression conditions—must bring out its inherent absurdity.[33] But let us keep the discussion to the theoretical plane. If one can seriously imagine a situation in which heavy net saving persists in spite of it being judged unprofitable to acquire non-money assets, with the aggregate real value of money assets being inflated, and prices being driven down catastrophically, then one may equally legitimately (and equally extravagantly) imagine continuous price co-ordination accompanying the emergence of such a position. We can conceive, that is, of prices falling rapidly, keeping pace with expectations of price changes, but never reaching zero, with full utilisation of resources persisting all the way.[34] We do not really need the answer which first Haberler, and then Pigou, gave on this point, namely, that the increase in the real value of cash balances if inversely related to the extent to which the individual (or for that matter the business firm) prefers to save, whilst the rate of saving is a diminishing function of the accumulation of assets which the individual holds.[35]

I have argued above that the weakness of Keynes's case rests on his static assumptions; and that once we bring dynamic repercussions into the reckoning (*via* the co-ordination or discoordination of the economic system), his arguments for unemployment equilibrium under price flexibility fall away. Strangely enough the new Keynesians have themselves transferred the fight to the dynamic field. The position they now seem to assume is that, whilst Keynes's own analysis (essentially static) cannot be defended, his propositions survive if they are explained through dynamic analysis. But in their attempt to retain Keynes's conclusions, they have abandoned the very roots of his own reasoning.

Thus, Patinkin[36] is equally specific in rejecting the original Keynesian arguments concerning unemployment equilibrium. He says, "it should now be definitely recognised that this is an indefensible position."[37] Even so, Keynes's errors on this point, and the similar errors of his manifold enthusiastic supporters over the period 1936-1946, are represented by Patinkin as quite unimportant. The truth which the early critics of *The*

General Theory fought so hard to establish (against stubborn opposition at almost every point[38]), namely, that price flexibility is inconsistent with unemployment, he describes as "uninteresting, unimportant and uninformative about the real problems of economic policy."[39] In spite of the mistakes which led Keynes to his conclusions, he did stumble upon the truth.

Let us consider, then, the conclusions concerning price flexibility of what Patinkin continues to describe as "Keynesian economics" (meaning by that an economics which rejects the logic but retains the conclusions of *The General Theory*). This version of "the New Keynesianism" contends—again in Patinkin's words—"that the economic system may be in a position of under-employment *dis*equilibrium (in the sense that wages, prices, and the amount of unemployment are continuously changing over time) for long or even indefinite, periods of time"[40] (Patinkin's italics). "In a dynamic world of uncertainty and adverse anticipations, even if we were to allow an infinite adjustment period, there is no certainty that full employment will be generated. I.e., we may remain indefinitely in a position of under-employment dis-equilibrium."[41]

This sounds like pure orthodoxy. Indeed, the use of the word "*dis*-equilibrium" implies that some Keynesians have now completely retreated. And the reference to "uncertainty and adverse anticipations" seems to refer to hypothetical situations which, using my own terminology, can be described as follows:

> Given price rigidities regarded as unstable, deflation will cause the emergence of withheld capacity. Three cases arise: (a) general expectations (i.e., typical or average expectations) envisage a fall of prices towards a definite ultimate scale which is regarded as most probable; or (b) general expectations are constantly changing so that the generally expected ultimate scale of prices becomes continuously lower; or (c) general expectations envisage a certain rate of decline of the scale of prices in perpetuity.
>
> In case (a), a withholding of capacity will last over a period which will be longer the more slowly the predicted price adjustments come about. In cases (b) and (c), the withholding of capacity will last over an indefinite period, *unless downward price adjustments take place as rapidly as or more rapidly than (i) the changes in expectations, or (ii) the generally expected rate of decline,* in which case full employment will persist throughout. In short, when the scale of prices is moving or is expected to

move in any direction, the notion of perfect price flexibility must envisage current prices being adjusted sufficiently rapidly in the same direction, if the full utilisation of all productive capacity is sought.

In admitting that Keynes cannot be said "to have demonstrated the co-existence of unemployment equilibrium and flexible prices," Patinkin explains that this is because "flexibility means that the money wage falls with excess supply, and rises with excess demand; and equilibrium means that the system can continue through time without change. Hence, *by definition*, a system with price flexibility cannot be in equilibrium if there is unemployment."[42] Now if by "excess supply" is meant more than can be sold at current prices, and by "excess demand" more than can be bought at current prices, *it remains true, equally "by definition," that price flexibility so conceived is inconsistent with wasteful idleness, even when we take into account the full dynamic reactions which are theoretically conceivable under a condition of falling or rising prices.* For price flexibility then requires that all prices shall be continuously adjusted so as to bring the spot and future values of the money unit into consistency; in other words, to establish harmony between current and expected prices. Under such adjustments, even enemployment *dis*equilibrium is ruled out.

Do not the words "adjustment period" in the passage quoted above show that Patinkin, in using the term "*dis*equilibrium," is in fact still envisaging some price rigidity? What other adjustments, apart from changes in prices and effective exchange values, can he be envisaging? How else can the terms "uncertainty" and "adverse expectations" be explained, unless in relation to unstable price rigidities? And the same tacit assumption of rigidity is present in his statement of what he terms, "the Keynesian position, closest to the 'classics' ." In this position, he says, although price flexibility would eventually "generate" full employment, "the length of time that might be necessary for the adjustment makes the policy impractical."[43] He tells us that this statement (like that in the previous quotation) is *not* "dependent upon the assumption of wage rigidities."[44] But what "adjustments" other than tardy cuts in rigid wage-rates has he in mind? He must be thinking of unstable price rigidities *somewhere* in the system.

A critic writes that this argument seems to overlook *inevitable* rigidities. In practice, contracts cannot be varied constantly, so that costs tend to follow prices with some interval. Thus, copper miners' wages can hardly change every time the price of copper changes. But for Patinkin's argument to hold, it would be essential for the wage-rates of the miners to be maintained when actual or expected copper prices had fallen to such an extent that formerly marginal seams became unworkable at current costs. The most complete measure of price flexibility practically attainable involves discontinuities at both the cost and the final product ends.[45] But periodic adjustments through recontract (as idleness threatens) can meet that situation.[46]

In short, the kind of price flexibility for which we can reasonably hope is one in which the price inconsistencies which must exist at any point of time *are never in process of material or cumulative worsening.* That need not mean unemployment. Contract covers the short run. And inconsistencies need not accumulate: they can be in process of rectification at about the same rate as that at which they arise.

Hence, "the dynamic approach" does not, as Patinkin maintains, obviate the necessity for the assumption of rigidities and revalidate the Keynesian fallacies. On the contrary, it was largely Keynes's neglect of the dynamic co-ordinative consequences of price adjustment which led him into the error that wage-rate and price adjustments are no remedy for unemployment.[47]

What are the implications? In my judgement, the abandonment of the theory of unemployment equilibrium under price flexibility means that the Say Law stands once again inviolate as the basic economic reality in the light of which all economic thinking is illuminated. But I do not think that all the critics of Keynes on the point at issue will immediately accept this inference. Indeed, Haberler adheres to a rejection of the Law at the very stage at which his own reasoning seems to be prompting him to recognise it.[48]

Yet even so extreme a Keynesian as Sweezy has been rash enough (and right enough) to admit, in his obituary article on Keynes, that the arguments of *The General Theory* "all fall to the ground if the validity of the Say Law is assumed."[49] If my own view is right, then the apparent revolution wrought by Keynes after 1936 has been reversed by a bloodless counter-revolution conducted unwittingly by higher critics who tried very hard to be faithful. Whether some permanent benefit to our science will have made up for the destruction which the revolution left in its train is a question which economic historians of the future will have to answer.

We are now forced back to the stark truth that the elimination of wasteful idleness in productive capacity is attainable only through the continuous adjustment of prices or the continuous dilution of the money unit. But the latter is a tragically evil method of attempting to rectify discoordination due to inertias or sectionalism. For the harmful repercussions of inflation become the more serious (and force an accelerated inflation) the more successfully entrepreneurs and consumers, in the free sectors of the economy, correctly forecast monetary policy. But the new Keynesians, like the old, appear to believe that monetary or fiscal policy, through the control of spending, can act as a universal solvent of all price disharmonies and, like an invisible hand, make unnecessary, or less necessary, the difficult task of overhauling the institutions which make up the price system.

We must remember that the attack on wage-rate adjustment as a policy of securing full employment in labour is an attack on a policy which has never been experimentally tested. For whilst there is a great deal of evidence of wage-rate adjustments forced by depression being followed by recovery, no deliberate attempt to increase income (including the flow of wages) by reducing all prices which appear to be above the natural scarcity level (including wage-rates) so that all prices and wage-rates below the natural scarcity level may rise, has ever been purposely pursued. Actual policies have, for decades, been based precisely upon the politically attractive rule, justified by Keynesian teaching, that disharmony in the wage-rate structure must not be tackled but offset; whilst the current tendency is to assume dogmatically, with no examination of the institutional and sociological factors involved, that to advocate wage and price adjustments is to recommend the conquest of the moon.

Notes

1. In a discussion with A. P. Lerner about 1933, I pointed out to him that however opposed our approaches might seem superficially to be, the institutions which we were seeking would, in the end, turn out to be exactly the same things. He refers to this conversation in the Preface to his *Economics of Control.*

2. J. Viner, "The Role of Costs in a System of Economic Liberalism," in *Wage Determination and the Economics of Liberalism* (Washington: U. S. Chamber of Commerce), p. 31; today, different groups of economists "give diametrically opposite advice as to policy when unemployment prevails or is anticipated."

3. Compare A. Smithies's statement of the implications of *The General Theory,* in his article, "Effective Demand and Employment," in Harris, *The New Economics* (New York: A. A. Knopf, 1947), p. 561: ". . . concerted action by the whole labour movement to increase money wages will leave real wages unchanged. Real wage gains by a single union are won at the expense of real wages elsewhere."

4. These two propositions were very much confused in Keynes's exposition and it is usually difficult to know, at any point, on which proposition he was relying. The exceptions are in passages which are rather puzzling, when related to the rest of his argument, as on pages 191 and 267 of *The General Theory.*

5. In "The Nature of Money," *The South African Journal of Economics* 20 (March 1952), p. 53.

6. J. Keynes, *The General Theory* (London: Macmillan and Co., 1936).

7. Ibid., p. 253.

8. Compare criticisms of "the wage level" concept by R. A. Gordon in the *American Economic Review* 38 (May 1948), who refers to ". . . the concentration of attention upon aggregates and upon distressingly broad and vaguely defined index number concepts—with insufficient attention being paid to those interrelationships among components which may throw light upon the behaviour of those aggregates" (p. 353).

9. Keynes, *The General Theory*, p. 259.

10. It is an interesting commentary on the uncritical nature of current assumptions that Professor Viner has felt it necessary to remind economists that it does not necessarily follow, "and I think that many economists have taken that step without further argument," that an increase of wage-rates at a time of unemployment will increase the pay-roll. "An increase of Wage rates may quite conceivably reduce the pay-roll." Viner, "The Role of Costs in a System of Economic Liberalism," p. 32.

11. Keynes, *The General Theory*, p. 264. It was partly this which led him to argue that wage-rate adjustment would be possible only in a Communist or Fascist State. (Ibid., p. 269).

12. Actually, Professor Pigou has shown that equiproportional wage-cuts, even under Keynes's other assumptions, must mean increased employment of labour if the reaction is a reduction of the rate of interest. Professor Pigou suggests that this reaction is "fairly likely." "Money Wages and Unemployment," *Economic Journal* 48 (March 1938), p. 137.

13. As measured by money units of unchanging value.

14. For simplicity, I am assuming that *maxima* are enacted.

15. The possibilities of transfers of workers from low-paid to high-paid work are magnified in the long run, because it will be possible to train for the well-paid employment opportunities which are brought within reach of income.

16. Professor K. Boulding has used this actual example and argument in his *Economics of Peace* (New York: Prentice-Hall, Inc., 1947).

17. Moreover, while wage-rate and price adjustments are required to dissolve withheld capacity among carpenters, to adopt that remedy *in individual trades* and on a small scale would bring severe distributive injustices in its train. Indeed, the

aggregate wage receipts of the larger number employed in any trade might be smaller than before the increased employment.

18. G. Haberler, *Prosperity and Depression* (Cambridge: Harvard University Press, 1958).

19. Ibid., p. 243.

20. I feel that Haberler would now admit this argument, in view of his unequivocal rejection, in 1951, of Keynesian teaching about unemployment equilibrium under price flexibility. "Welfare and Freer Trade," *Economic Journal* 61 (December 1951), pp. 779-80.

21. What is commonly expressed as changes in cost-price ratios, e.g., in the price of output in relation to the price of labour, I think of in terms of divergencies from, or conformance with, synchronising prices at various stages of production. (The last stage is, of course, sale for consumption.)

22. Some economists in the pre-Keynesian era, in attempting to deal with the relations of employment and wage-rates, made *explicit*, highly simplified assumptions consistent with the assumption as I have worded it, for purposes of abstract analysis. But I do not know of any economist who has stated the fundamental assumption as I have done. Quite possibly the point was made.

23. Compare F. Modigliani, "Liquidity Preferences and the Theory of Interest and Money," *Econometrica* 12 (January 1944), pp. 45-88.

24. My article in the December 1953 issue of this Journal is an attempt to deal rigorously with this situation.

25. Imposed cost and price rigidities in the form of maxima (i.e., ceilings) may similarly prevent secondary inflation, but in this case the effect is the opposite. Insofar as the maxima force down monopoly prices nearer to marginal cost, there is a mitigating coordinative and deflationary action which creates an incentive to increased outputs (i.e., increased real income).

26. It should be stressed, however, that this is no conclusive argument against policies seeking to increase the value of the money unit, as tardy rectifications of the distributive injustices of inflations. Nor is it a good argument against rectifying price disharmonies which have been allowed to develop and strain the ability to honour a convertibility obligation.

27. I do not include Haberler, whose criticisms have been damaging, as a Keynesian. It is difficult to pick out the other non-Keynesian economists who have been most influential on the point at issue; but Margot, Knight, Viner, and Simons must take much of the credit.

28. Schumpeter, in *The New Economics*, p. 92.

29. Modigliani, "Liquidity Preference and the Theory of Interest and Money."

30. Pigou regards the contemplation of this possibility as "an academic exercise." He describes the situation envisaged (although he is not criticising Modigliani) as extremely improbable, and he adds, "Thus the puzzles we have been considering

. . . are academic exercises, of some slight use perhaps for clarifying thought, but with very little chance of ever being posed on the chequer board of actual life." See "Economic Progress in a Stable Environment," *Economica* 14, (1947), pp. 187-8.

31. Keynes, *The General Theory*, p. 207.

32. Ibid., p. 221.

33. No condition which even distantly resembles infinite elasticity of demand for money assets has even been recognised, I believe, because general expectations have always envisaged either (a) the attainment in the not too distant future of some definite scale of prices, or (b) so gradual a decline of prices that no cumulative postponement of expenditure has seemed profitable. General expectations appear to have rejected the possibility of a scale of prices which sags without limit, because of such things as convertibility obligations, or the necessity to maintain exchanges, or the political inexpediency of permitting prices to continue to fall.

34. Compare the argument here to Pigou, "Economic Progress in a Stable Environment," pp. 183-184, and Haberler, *Prosperity and Depression*, pp. 499-500.

35. In any case, this argument is no answer to the case in which the nature of saving is speculative hoarding. For this reason Haberler claims only that there is "a strong probability" and no "absolute certainty" of there being a lower limit to MV so caused. See Haberler, *Prosperity and Depression*, p. 390.

36. J. Patinkin, "Price Felxibility and Full Employment," in *Readings in Monetary Theory* (Homewood, Ill.: Irwin, 1951).

37. Ibid., p. 279.

38. For an example of the stubborness, see Keynes's reply to criticisms in his "Relative Movements of Real Wages and Output," *Economic Journal* 49 (March 1939), pp. 34-51.

39. Patinkin, "Price Flexibility and Full Employment," p. 279.

40. Ibid., p. 280.

41. Ibid., p. 281.

42. Ibid., p. 279.

43. Ibid., p. 282.

44. Ibid., p. 282.

45. That is not, in itself, likely to mean discontinuity in movements of the scale of prices (i.e., in a price index).

46. Sliding scales can render the need for recontract less frequent.

47. The confusion in this field ultimately stems, I feel, from a failure to achieve conceptual clarity, and particularly owing to the absence of price flexibility. definition of price flexibility.

48. Haberler, *The New Economics,* pp. 173-76. The acceptance of the Say Law does not imply, as Haberler suggests, the absurd assumption that the phenomena of hoarding or dishoarding cannot exist. It merely accords to money assets and the

services which they provide the same economic status and significance as all other assets and the services which they provide. Nor does the existence of depression or idle resources (under unstable price rigidity) prove that this law does not hold, any more than balloons and aeroplanes invalidate the law of gravity.

49. S. Bernstein (ed.), "Marxism," *Science and Society* (New York: Science and Society, 1946), p. 400.

9 • *The Significance of State Interference with Interest Rates*

Recent developments in this and other countries in the direction of legislative interference with rates of interest have led to some misconceptions as to the nature of this intervention. To understand the question, we must consider it in relation to the general problem of authoritarian price-fixing; for a rate of interest is simply an agreed price for the loan of capital for a certain purpose. The view of orthodox economic theory is that the fixation by the State of any price, be it the price of a commodity, a wage rate, a rent or a rate of interest, must usually be detrimental to the general good. This view rests upon certain philosophic assumptions as to the rightness of that manifestation of the social will, which, being the expression of individual wills unrestricted by State or other deliberately imposed and collectively enforced impedimenta, is the determinant of "market price." On the basis of these assumptions it is reasoned that what we may call "contrived" (i.e., monopolistic or State-controlled) prices, as opposed to "competitive" prices, are a reflection of "contrived scarcities." By "contrived scarcities" is meant relative deficiencies of wanted things which would not have been experienced had the distribution and utilization of productive resources been subject to the social force that we know as "competition." Thus the main objection to State-fixed prices lies in the belief that behind them the flow of those goods and services *most desired* [1] by the community is checked, and that capacity to add to wealth is kept in idleness.

Reprinted with permission from *South African Journal of Economics* 1 (1933).

The second main objection to official price-fixing is that the system of "contrived scarcities" is inevitably unstable and bound, ultimately, to break down. The drawback of that is that, in the meantime, it must mislead entrepreneurs, and so eventually bring about serious private losses. High commodity prices induce too much investment in fields to which capital funds would never be attracted under the guidance of competitive prices. The tendency of this reaction is, it is recognized, to break down "contrived scarcities," but when a great deal of the misdirected funds have been immobilized (as in specialized fixed plant or farm improvements), severe depreciation of capital values may have to be borne by unfortunate investors.

The third objection to Government-fixed prices is their rigidity. A price represents a rate at which a certain commodity or service can be exchanged for other goods. It has social significance in two ways: first, it represents a ratio of exchange; and second, it implies a certain rate of transactions per unit of time at that ratio. Apologists for State-fixed prices commonly overlook the second implication; or they assume, sometimes quite wrongly, that it is an inelastic factor. Now price rigidity is thought by orthodox economic theorists to be socially harmful for three types of reasons: (*a*) even if producers were reasonable, the relation of different sets of prices to one another ought (in the interests of effective co-ordination of production and consumption) to be allowed free adjustment; (*b*) producers are not reasonable, and when one price moves against them and another remains unaltered, they are apt to slacken the rate of production, and so to create further maladjustment; (*c*) in times of monetary disturbances, price rigidity leads to avoidable injustice in the division of the value of the product.

There is a fourth argument against authoritarian prices, also based largely on the assumption that the community desires distributive justice. The investor whose capital is immobilized may be "exploited" by any unexpected adverse price-fixation subsequent to his investment. This is felt to be most unjust, for the exploited development was voluntarily undertaken in response to a social demand, and the decrement thus imposed upon the enterprise appears to be an arbitrary one from the standpoint of any distributive principle. It is here that ethical and economic precepts can be seen to merge, since under a State which practises such price-fixation, a great deal of development in easily exploitable forms is deterred. We can regard this class of case as intermediate between that in which capital resources are mobile and that (yet to be considered) in which it is the terms of existing *contracts* that are modified by the State.

But authoritarian prices are not the only "contrived" prices in modern society. The frustration of the general good in the struggle for increased income rights may, indeed, be more effective through private monopolistic or ganization than through the scramble for private advantage *via* the medium of socialistic enactments. In these circumstances, the *simple* case against State interference goes. Let us assume for a moment that there exists a wise and disinterested Government. The present writers's opinion is that whilst in those circumstances State passivity cannot be defended, *price-fixation* with the motive of restoring a competitive situation is still indefensible, because it will only make matters worse. The remedy is to be sought along a different adminstrative path. But the grounds for this view cannot be pleaded here. Authorities differ on the point.

Finally, we must consider authoritarian price-fixations which, whilst they do not directly determine the conditions of future contracts, alter the terms of contracts already concluded.[2] The question of interference with interest rates has its principal relevance here. The clearest and most typical illustration of it is, however, that of deliberate currency devaluation (say, of a gold standard), which, *ipso facto*, modifies a consideration relevant to all contracts other than barter obligations, but affects each agreement only to the extent to which it is related to markets where gold continues to be the measure of value. Another example is that of the reduction by legislative enactment of interest rates on bonds.

Again, assuming the existence of a disinterested Government seeking "the general good," the object of any such general or particular revision of contractual terms must be either the procuring of distributive justice or the achievement of more desirable price relations between different kinds of things. The search for distributive justice in this manner involves the dangerous principle that established expectations ought not to be disappointed. The assumption is that subsequent to the conclusion of some or all contracts made during a certain period, a number of changed circumstances, both unpredictable and uncontemplated by the parties, have intervened to alter the original significance of the agreements. The State then endeavours to restore the former position. The difficulty is, however, to say how far the changes that it is desired to countervail were really uncontemplated by both parties. The risk is that far from obtaining justice by these means, there will be a penalization of those who have exercised foresight, for the benefit of those whose policy has been blindly based on the assumption of a static world.

The *economic* case for the compulsory revision of the terms of a pledged bargain rests either on a fallacy or else on the assumption that the parties are irrational. Contractual obligations between rational co-operant producers and others with claims on the value of the product can have no effect upon productive policy unless they restrict purchasing or selling to certain monopolized channels, or unless the parties are stimulated to act aggressively. Thus the "burden" of bond interest on a farm will have no effect on its activity if we have an intelligent bond-holder and a reasonable farmer both seeking their own good. The farmer's interest commitments determine how much of his receipts he must pay away. But it is still to his and the bond-holder's advantage that those receipts shall be at a maximum. As we cannot assume universal reasonableness, however, it may be that the amendment of contracts which have become onerous will have a psychologically beneficial effect upon productivity. This is a matter upon which the economist as such is not specially qualified to pass judgment. Neither is the economic specialist necessarily the best one to judge whether the indirect repercussions of large losses to important classes who have been unwise in the past can sufficiently extenuate an otherwise undesirable policy.

Thus our final verdict as to how far the compulsory revision of contractual terms (either by interference with interest rates or in other ways) is justifiable will depend in the first place upon our estimate of the extent to which the provisions of the original agreement have been upset by happenings genuinely uncontemplated at the outset by all parties affected (as perhaps might be so in the case of war, famine and unparalleled depressions or booms). In the second place, we must have recourse to an estimate of the repercussions of such intervention upon the motive of those responsible for private policy to take judicious risks and to expend effort and energy in attempts to predict and anticipate future changes.

But we cannot assume a disinterested Government. In practice, such interferences are made in the interests of the income rights of organized groups controlling publicity and hence possessing political power; and in countries of heterogeneous and clearly defined racial and economic classes like our own, certain classes have political strength out of proportion to their numbers, and are held, for this or other reasons, to be worthy of special consideration.

Notes

1. For the relative scarcities of different things are determined by human taste and choice on the one hand and natural abundance on the other. Any forced restriction of the plenitude of Nature must lead (on the basis of accepted assumption) to a less desired composition of the flow of welfare which constitutes the response to social choice.

2. This class of case must be sharply distinguished from agreements subject to re-contract.

part III   •   *THE CONSEQUENCES OF FREE COMPETITION*

10. *The Sanctions for Privacy under Private Enterprise*[1]

My object is to examine the sanctions for business privacy under what is called "private enterprise." I shall endeavour to show that, whilst privacy has traditionally performed an important but hardly noticed function, it has led to certain weaknesses in capitalistic organisation which are seldom discussed by critics of modern society.

That the works of the theorist economists have not forced the practising economists to face this issue appears to have been due to the inadequate attention which has been given to the *factor of knowledge* as an element in general equilibrium analysis. For firstly, traditional theoretical treatment has built on the convenient, but for the most part inappropriate, assumption "that the data . . . will be equally given to all individuals and that their acting on the same premises will somehow lead to their plans becoming adapted to each other";[2] and secondly, whilst some of the "welfare economists" (most notably Edwin Cannan) have given adequate importance to the accumulated stock of knowledge as an element in man's *welfare*, insufficient attention has been given to the fact that the stock of knowledge as such (i.e., as opposed to "skill" in the sense of "knowledge assimilated for action") is gratuitous, and therefore not an economic good (although the accumulation of the stock may involve costs).

As theorist economists we have recognised that the process of decision-making is complicated by the fact that one person's decisions may be another person's data; and as practising economists we have tried realistically to face

Reprinted with permission from *Economica* 19 (1942).

the consequences and avoid circular reasoning. But, as Professor Hayek has pointed out, we have not seen sufficiently clearly that the true concepts of data, "on the one hand in the sense of the objective real facts, as the observing economist is supposed to know them, and on the other in the subjective sense, as things known to the persons whose behaviour we try to explain, are really fundamentally different and ought to be kept carefully apart''; and that one of the main problems which we have to answer is "why the data in the subjective sense of the term should ever come to correspond to the objective data."[3] Professor Hayek concludes that the problem of the *Division of Knowledge*, the fact that all individuals cannot know the relevant data of all fields, "is quite analogous to, and at least as important as, the problem of the division of labour''; and the problem of division of knowledge ought really to be "the central problem of economics as a social science."[4]

Now I am concerned with certain of the institutional issues which these theoretical questions lead the student to consider, and mainly with what I may call the negative aspect, i.e., the problem of privacy within the larger problem of access to, the accumulation of, and the productive use of knowledge in general. The appropriate collective functions of the State or other agencies in gathering and disseminating data is not my principal concern, although it is a very important part of the larger problem. Nor am I concerned with the full implications of the principle of *Division of Knowledge* as bearing on the relative efficiency of centralised and decentralised entrepreneurship, although the question should really be reckoned as fundamental in some of the major controversies of to-day.[5] What is the significance of *privacy* in relation to the data of decision-making?

Let us first consider the *notion* of "private enterprise." This has always been a common sense rather than a conceptually clear notion. "Private" enterprise has been contrasted with "State" enterprise. Sometimes it has been regarded as a system of economic organisation of which the *laissez-faire*, or individualistic, or capitalist doctrines approve. But no particular attention seems to have been centred on the problem of the nature of and the justification for *the attribute of privacy*. It is arguable that the term "private enterprise" has no necessary connection with the notion of privacy, but that it has really meant "individual enterprise," which may be quite a different thing. But most people, if questioned about it, would certainly state that the sanctions for private enterprise involve the recognition of the desirability of privacy. On the face of it, however, the term hardly suggests a defensible social order. It implies that private rights or individual interests can be superior to the rights or interests of society; whilst liberal apologists for private enterprise must, in fact, plead that under that system the individual is most effectively subjected to the social will.

Privacy in general is demanded for several reasons. In some of its manifestations, the psychologists can help to explain it. Other aspects are of interest to the political historian. The historical philosopher would probably regard the demand for privacy as due mainly to the intolerance of man. And the grounds for this view are obviously strong. The right of acting according to one's own conscience, or of communicating one's private judgments, not only on religion, but on countless other subjects, can be secured only by secrecy in an intolerant society. And this right is widely treasured. It is a right which preserves independent judgment, opinion and conduct in a community in which the State, or individuals themselves (or the majorities which they form) are intolerant. History appears to record one long, chequered, yet gradually succeeding struggle against intolerance; and during those struggles secrecy has been, and still is, the bulwark of unshackled thought. Hence the growth of ideas concerning the sanctity of privacy is easily understandable. The community and the State have been feared as *inquisitors.*

Now the term "private enterprise" probably arose owing to the State having been feared not so much as inquisitor as *despoiler.* The objection to the State in this role gives rise to claims for a different sort of immunity. It is the individual's *property* which is claimed as *private.* He asserts the right to a certain autonomy in respect of the disposal and exchange of resources and services; and law and custom have accorded him this right.

What are the sanctions for and the defensible scope of *privacy* in respect of the diffused entrepreneurial power which makes up "private enterprise?" To discuss this point, we must have some accepted ideal. Strange as it may seem, in many contributions relevant to this topic, the ultimate ideal is discernible only in the haziest form. The criterion of the social good which I propose to apply is that of "consumers' sovereignty," which I have enunciated and explained elsewhere.[6] Applying this standard, we must regard property-owners as the custodians of the community's scarce resources. The powers they possess in dealing with these resources must be regarded as delegated to them by society in its consumer aspect. So conceived, the system which is variously known as "private enterprise" or the "private property system" is simply one in which the task of deciding upon action in response to consumers' will is diffused by a more or less automatic devolution throughout the community. For the property system is regarded (to use the words of Professor F. H. Knight) as but "one method of selecting, motivating and remunerating the functionaries who actually direct a social-economic organisation."

This being so, is there any case for the existing right to almost unlimited privacy in business matters? That right is, of course, practically universally assumed to be an axiom of an individualistic society; yet I feel that it is a right which must be sceptically examined. For, *prima facie*, there is no case for permitting the concealment of any knowledge which any individual may possess about the facts or results of the pricing system. I say *prima facie*, for the final conclusion of studies in this field may well be different. It is *possible,* for instance, that a sympathetic and discerning study of the psychology of individuals co-operating through exchange might disclose good and sufficient grounds for the careful guarding of the secrets which are usually hidden away in a firm's accounts. But I have certainly failed to trace any attempt to give adequate consideration to this problem. Moreover, I have also been unable to conceive of any arguments for the tolerance of business privacy that are not equally valid in defence of monopoly. Hence I am driven to the conclusion that there is a definite gap in recorded speculations in the philosophy of commerical institutions.

That existing practices in respect of business secrecy are indefensible has certainly been pointed out from time to time. In the United States, the right of secrecy in respect of corporation accounts has often been challenged by the more far-seeing critics of society. I do not know, however, of any contributions which have attempted to formulate general principles respecting such rights. All will admit that the activities and degree of success of *entrepreneurs* are a matter of social concern. Why, then, should knowledge of their activities and their successes or failures be withheld by those who possess it?

Perhaps the most important bearings of this question have reference to the relative economies achievable through the co-ordination of production under independent and under centralised ownership, that is, the relative efficiencies of different entrepreneurial concentrations. Yet the problem has received hardly any consideration in discussions about the relative advantages of small and large firms. In my own judgment, it is lack of knowledge arising from privacy which constitutes the most obvious element of inferiority in the small enterprise. The management of an amalgamation (or sometimes even of a cartel) has an efficiency advantage over a number of separate competing or co-operant firms in the access it has to the accounts and plans of the associated firms. The degree of advantage which the large amalgamation obtains in this way is, of course, not easy to estimate. But it is clear that the most efficient *conceivable* working of society, from the purely administrative point of view, is one in which the privacy or secrecy which surrounds the affairs of "firms" has been overcome. Conventional business secrecy certainly appears to be inimical to the most effective functioning of contemporary institutions.

Among those who have recognised this point is Mr. H. D. Dickinson, who has argued that "the chief cause of the instability found under competitive conditions (*sic*) is the mutual ignorance in which competing firms work; each plans for the market or introduces new methods without regard to the similar activities of the others."[7] But resistance to the idea of making public the internally acquired data of business is simply a form of *resistance* to competitive conditions. Mr. Dickinson stresses the wrong point. Indeed, however unconscious, *the masking of profitableness* appears to be the very motive for business privacy in most cases. Certainly the opposition to reforms attempting to mitigate conventional secrecy would be motivated mainly by fear of the competition which would be precipitated. If the argument for greater and more independent publicity is based on the necessity for protecting investors, one may expect considerable support. But if the same reform is advocated on the grounds that it would enable the better utilisation and co-ordination of productive activities, it is less likely to be sympathetically considered. "Ruinous competition" will seem to be threatened as soon as the general aim of any such reform is contemplated.

For the next stage of this discussion, let us ignore the conventional arguments in defence of "secret reserves" and assume that the full exposure of profitableness has actually been achieved. This involves the assumption that the technical difficulties of determining, from the point of view of an accountant, what constitutes "secret reserves" have been sufficiently overcome. To give objective clarity to the assumption let us imagine that auditors declaring profits have become independent State servants, and that, in the endeavour to abolish secrecy, the law has gone much further than insisting upon the revealment of profits, namely, that it has granted to the public, competitors, co-operant concerns, and consumers' organisations the right actually to have access (through expert agents if required) to the accounts of any private undertaking.

If such reforms were administratively and politically achievable, the social gain which would arise from them is obvious. They would enable entrepreneurs, whether standing in a competitive or in a co-operant relationship to one another, to make their plans and enter into commitments with access to incomparably more complete data. I do not propose to dwell on a host of misconceived objections which I anticipate will be urged against the suggestion of enforced and full publicity, namely, objections based on the usual misconceptions respecting competition. I shall also ignore certain valid objections to attempts to abolish privacy *suddenly*. (It is clear that even if indefensible in principle, business privacy is so bound up with institutions as they are that clumsy attempts to get rid of it would have effects worse than its presence. It cannot be too frequently emphasised that to strive blindly for the fullest effectiveness for competitive forces would be to court social disaster.) And I shall pass over other practical obstacles which must be overcome in reforms along these lines. My object in the remainder of this article is to deal with a fundamental difficulty which would arise if the dissemination of what is at present private knowledge were perfect.

The chief question to which any discussion of the abolition of privacy must give rise is that of knowledge as property. For knowledge, unless it can be kept secret, is available for all. Hence, in a society in which secrecy was eliminated and in which monopolies were dissolved, could the function of adding to knowledge, at a cost, still be remunerated? It is obvious that the *published* idea which can be easily copied is not *naturally* property. In the absence of patents or copyrights, it will have no more scarcity than that due to the costs of printing, or running libraries, or other means of disseminating knowledge. And although knowledge of this kind possessed by the community is of immense importance to general well-being, it is often as gratuitous as the air that we breathe.

This brings me to an important form of knowledge which apparently falls into this category, but which is not usually thought of in this connection. When any plan under consideration is essentially *experimental*, the willingness to undertake risks (which is an essential factor in all business decision-making) will be present only through the recognition that there exists some inertia in the attainment of equilibrium or some indefinite privately contrived scarcity element in the value of the product.[8] For if the plan is experimental and the result known, interlopers will be attracted in when it is successful, but avoid it when it is unsuccessful. Hence, if the community demands that the supply of knowledge shall be added to through experiment, it may be necessary, under a system in which secrecy and monopoly have been abolished, to create institutions which confer property on knowledge by preventing it from being used (or rather acted upon) without payment. And it appears that in such a society, payment for adding to knowledge can only be arranged collectively, through the State. Even in *existing* society, patents and copyrights are almost universally regarded as essential; and the problem seems likely to become more urgent as secrecy is overcome and competition stimulated.[9]

A good example is that of the introduction of an entirely new type of commodity into a market. It is impossible to know in advance whether it will appeal to consumers or not. A considerable capital expenditure may be required to produce it and much advertising expense may be necessary to inform consumers of its existence and to persuade them to be enterprising in trying it. But once their demand for it has been established, interlopers may be able to add to the supply, not without all the other initial expenses, but without the *risk* which the pioneers undertook. There is little doubt that, even outside the field covered by patent and copyright legislation, the framework of *existing* institutions does provide adequate protection to the creator of innovations in a large number of cases, perhaps in most cases. Things like fashion stealing are said to be common in respect of dress designing, and interlopers frequently do intervene to produce products the existence of the demand for which has been established by means of enterprise and risk-bearing to which they have not contributed. But it may be that in practice such interlopers are only attracted in when the original entrepreneurs have tried to make undue profits out of their innovations or connected activities. It may even be argued that existing institutions give *too much* protection to those who are only incidentally originators, and that apparently parasitic interloping is nothing more than the normal operation of competition in the consumer's interests. Nevertheless, the necessity for some protection must be recognised.

The problem which arises is, therefore, that of distinguishing between those elements of income derived from scarcities which frustrate consumers' sovereignty, and those which are in the nature of payment for the experimental policies which must inevitably accompany all innovating, prospecting, inventing, and cognate activities. What may well be regarded as the most live force in a dynamic industrial and trading regime—the exercise of originality and an important type of enterprise—appears to have been traditionally remunerated as a result of arbitrary conditions arising from the advantages of site and size (natural monopoly) of sets of productive operations, inertia in the attainment of equilibrium, collusion in price and output policy, and finally the exercise of business secrecy. The remuneration of experimental investment has been inextricably bound up with the creation and maintenance of scarcities in a given state of knowledge. That these scarcities have brought a private return much greater than the rate of payment necessary is a conclusion to which I believe all disinterested students of the existing world must be forced. The imagination, research, enterprise and venturesomeness in planning, and the pioneer and prospecting services which have been at the world's disposal have certainly been too dearly bought.

If *enterprise* could be held to be less essential to-day than it was in earlier times, the task of reform would be relatively easy. But in these days of more static conditions of supply, it seems that the service of originating and prospecting is more than ever able to serve the interests of mankind. And in so far as economic inertia, in which business secrecy plays a part, acts as the medium through which the incentive that brings forth the supply of intelligent initiative is exercised, policies which aim rashly at the promotion of equilibrium under natural scarcities might do much harm. The invention of competitive institutions to serve consumers' sovereignty must build on a recognition of the curious fact that inertias and secrecies enable some return to be reaped by pioneers, prospectors and innovators. That the existing system works depends, apparently, largely upon the fact of its slowness. *Risk-bearers through experiment* do obtain rewards which arise through their being pioneers. For a while, partly owing to inertia, and partly because they *can* conceal initial profitableness, they obtain remuneration sufficient to compensate for failures, as well as to pay for successes.

This conclusion constitutes one of the biggest difficulties which I have tried to surmount in my own efforts at visualising the institutions of a more complete economic freedom. In thinking out methods of eliminating the avoidable uncertainties and consequent instabilities due to business privacy, and in attempting to improvise other devices for the removal of official and monopolistic arbitrariness and hindrances to the full utilisation of productive power, I have felt it essential (*a*) to leave all enterprises submitted to anti-monopoly ''control'' a measure of autonomy deemed sufficient to permit remuneration for *risk-bearing through experiment,* and (*b*) to invent procedures which will permit the protection of "registered innovations." The latter is intended to cover novelties which cannot be practically brought within the scope of patent and copyright legislation.[10]

The problem of remunerating this type of innovation is, however, one which has hardly been encountered yet in society as it is. At any rate, if recognised, the problem has always seemed to be one of small urgency. Only when the framework of the property system has been refashioned, with a view to enabling diffused and decentralised entrepreneurship under conditions of much fuller knowledge, is the necessity for some solution likely to become apparent. And experience alone can determine the practical importance of conferring the functions of property upon the results of this kind of risk-bearing.

Notes

1. This article represents a development and revision of ideas which I first explained in an article entitled "Privacy and Private Enterprise," published in the *South African Journal of Economics* 7 (November 1939), pp. 375-88.

2. F. Hayek, "Economics and Knowledge," *Economica* 4 (February 1937), p. 38.

3. Ibid., p. 39.

4. Ibid., p. 49.

5. I have touched on one aspect of that larger problem in my article "War Demand, Entrepreneurship and the Distributive Problem," *South African Journal of Economics* 9 (November 1941), p. 353: "The managements of firms are more likely to be in a position to understand the local supply situation in respect of labour, materials, housing, transport, etc., than any central administration; that is, of course, provided that the State does its job of gathering and making known the main facts concerning national supplies. If the supply situation as a whole can be envisaged, the managements of firms will understand the cost significance of the relevant facts much better than would be possible for any centralised administration. All the war production must be solved in the light of detailed and local technicalities, the knowledge of which cannot be effectively centralised."

6. *Economists and the Public* (London: Jonathan Cape, 1936), Chapter 16, "The Concept of Consumers' Sovereignty," *Economic Journal* 50 (March 1940), pp. 66-77.

7. H. D. Dickinson, *Institutional Revenue* (New York: A. M. Kelley, 1966).

8. The recognition is not very specific in practice. But if the inertia or privately

contrived scarcity elements were not present in some way, such risks would not be undertaken.

9. "The sacred right of every man to possess exclusive ownership in his own secret or discovery is a sort of inalienable right which has come down to us from ancient times, and which has more recently been hedged about with legal barriers," C. J. Foreman, *Efficiency and Scarcity Profits,* p. 280.

10. Needless to say, a reform along such lines must attempt to eliminate the gross and obvious abuses of patents and copyrights in their present legal form.

11 • *Discriminating Monopoly and the Consumer*

1. The purpose of this article is to refute the view (which seems to be obtaining currency without opposition) that when all productive resources are free to be applied according to the dictates of forces expressed through free markets, the most effective response to consumers' preferences is frustrated. It is more usual to express the contention that we are disputing by saying that "*laissez-faire* fails to maximise total utility," which is the phrase used by Mrs. Robinson.[1] Free exchange is alleged to fail because, under it, the advantages of discriminating monopoly are unrealisable.

2. Because discrimination is prevented where there is free exchange, and because it happens to maximise a monopolist's return, does not prove that it is opposed to consumers' advantage. On the contrary, it may be beneficial. The uniformity which is the product of the purchaser's right to re-sell may, on occasions, conceal some important elements of arbitrariness. This is possible because successive increments of a particular kind of commodity may be regarded as having a different "urgency" to a particular buyer—as occupying a different place on his scale of preferences; and as between different buyers, we may regard the increments that are purchased at a uniform price at any moment as being wanted with different degrees of urgency—as occupying different *relative* positions on the individuals' scales of preference.[2] Now it has been suggested that the ideal production and exchange system, if planned by a divine hand—by one completely conscious of every individual's scales of preference (that is, of his aspirations

Reprinted with permission from *Economic Journal* 46 (1936).

and strivings, and his powers and resources), would lead to a set of prices for each commodity which in certain circumstances also varied for each individual. In so far as this could be so, it follows that a social loss might be incurred as a result of the uniformity imposed by competitive conditions.[3] A set of prices other than the uniform prices enforced by the consumers' right to re-sell *could* serve their "real desires" more effectively.

3. For detailed consideration and a pioneer development of this thesis, economists are indebted to the work of Edgeworth (who received his inspiration on the subject largely from the writings of Dupuit). The question lent itself to a form of treatment which gave great scope to his mathematical talents. His case was that discrimination would enable the maximisation of "total utility," and it was this, and not "final utility," which was the real measure of consumers' welfare. Mrs. Robinson's fundamental case against *laissez-faire* is derived from the same idea. She says: "The choice of what commodities to produce should be made, not by applying the criterion of marginal utility (price), which only serves to regulate the ideal amounts of output, but by applying the criterion of total utility." Orthodox economics, according to Edgeworth, had tended largely to overlook this important aspect of the question. In bringing total utility into discussion he stated his position as follows: "The corner-stone of this building is formed by a conception which Dupuit introduced under the designation of 'rente des acheteurs': the money-measure of the benefit accruing to purchasers from obtaining articles which they purchase at a certain price, while they would have been willing to give more for those articles rather than go without them altogether. The sum of money designated by the term in question may, I think, be an object of science as well as the sum designated by the more familiar term *price*. The monetary equivalent of total utility may be as objective as the monetary equivalent of final utility."[4]

4. The conception of "total utility" or "consumers' surplus" (as opposed to "final" or "marginal" utility) is defective. Mrs. Robinson admits at the commencement of her note that "there are serious objections to the notion of aggregating utilities and the notion of utility itself, but a very serious, though very simple, objection to the presumption in favour of *laissez-faire* arises after the notion of utility has been accepted." The case against total utility is that the surplus which diagrammatic treatment shows in the case of an individual's demand for a particular commodity is one which depends upon a schedule representing the utility of the commodity as a function of price. Now every change in price affecting a particular surplus

must alter the individual's utility schedules for all other things. Hence any surplus represented is a purely fictitious conception. When price in respect of any one schedule is altered, every other schedule must be regarded as changed. Thus any truth and definiteness in the meaning of one schedule implies that the utilities of no other commodities which the individual may want can be represented as functions of price. To each point on one schedule there exists a different set of other schedules. It follows that it is really impossible to conceive of the maximisation of an individual's total utility as a sort of summation of surpluses representing for each commodity the difference between aggregate utility and aggregate cost. Still less is it valid to attempt an aggregation of individual aggregates of surpluses. The logical inadequacy of the notion of "utility" may not, however, invalidate Edgeworth's argument, and Mrs. Robinson's objections to *laissez-faire* cannot be simply refuted by the denial of assumptions of which she expresses her own doubts. We know that the scales of individual preferences do in fact differ from person to person; and although these differences are conceptions inappropriate for mathematical treatment as utility functions, we can accept the implication that occasions may exist in which the imposition of the uniformity of values brought about by competition *may* lead to some loss *in the effectiveness of the response of social effort* to the complexities of individual preference. In spite of the deficiencies of the idea of "total utility," it is convenient in this discussion to accept it as roughly corresponding to that measure of effectiveness for the consumer's satisfactions which the ideal pricing system would tend to maximise.[5]

5. The implication of the suggestion is, then, that unrestricted transactions would diminish the power of consumers to command those things which they want. The fact that A and B find it profitable to exchange products bartered or purchased from others does not prove, according to the theory we are examining, that the degree of satisfaction realised by the whole may not suffer in certain circumstances if they do, although the two parties concerned can always gain from the immediate transaction. For *under certain conditions* (whose possible occurrence or importance we discuss in paragraph 11 *et seqq.*) the effect of the possibility of free exchange might be that a potential producer of a particular good would deem it unprofitable to produce it. Thus we can at all events *imagine* an ideal co-operation in production which differs from that brought about by competitive forces.

6. But before proceeding to consider this possibility, let us remind ourselves of a more practical aspect of the question. It can be equally clearly

seen that the power of free exchange with its accompaniment of price uniformity, although not necessarily bringing about the ideal conceivable situation, will in almost every case tend to *enforce* a situation in which some freedom of choice between alternatives (to individuals as consumers) will exist. It is this freedom of choice which will ensure the subordination of individual interests to an expression (albeit imperfect) of the interest of society.[6] Moreover, the uniform prices of competition will, it seems probable, in themselves facilitate the co-operative process as a result of their obvious definiteness. Our practical judgment on this point must rest, therefore, upon the importance of the cases in which consumers might benefit from the frustration of free exchange. Now Edgeworth could show clearly enough in *isolated hypothetical* cases how circumstances might arise in which discrimination would lead to some or more investment where any system of uniform prices would lead to none or less; but the cases which he considered in the abstract seem to have no relevance in relation to the actual economic world. Regarded in the light of the practical problem of devising an economic system which will enable the most efficient distribution of the community's resources according to some ideal derived from consumers' will, his examples appear to have importance in few fields.

7. Given human institutions as they are, and means of practical reform of those institutions which are within our powers of conception, the determination of values under free exchange may still have to be regarded as the one which maximises the sensitiveness of social response to individual preference, irrespective of any benefits which abstract analysis may show are attainable through discrimination. It is the co-operative aspect of the productive process under consumers' direction which brings out most strongly the benefits of competitive uniformity. The manufacture of many physical commodities is arranged by means of a long series of contracts between different co-operant producers; and the more perfect the arrangements for allowing social forces (i.e., market) as opposed to private (i.e., expressed through monopoly or the State) interests to control the planning of production, the more numerous and complex are such contracts likely to be. Practical arbitrariness of price is likely to defeat complexity in organisation. The efficiency of the modern productive process rests upon its "round-aboutness." All rational economic intitiative is taken in the light of a whole chain of values attaching to the services of the different productive resources which work together to produce the final product; and the determinateness of such values under ideal discrimination is nothing more

than a theoretical abstraction. Even under actual discrimination the optimum prices which producers would charge to each class of customer would be very vague indeed. Such prices can be fixed in any instance only by the most hazy estimation. Free exchange prices, on the other hand, have a much greater degree of actual determinateness. The focusing of all demand through the channel of the market eliminates many elements of *practical* arbitrariness, for the hire price of any productive agent is, in general, determined by a whole range of alternative uses open to it. There is, it follows, a greater likelihood of accurate judgment as to the relative profitableness of different lines of productive activity under conditions of free exchange than under discrimination[7] (quite apart from the absence of aggressive selling or development selling).[8]

8. The point can be illustrated by an example from the opposite extreme. There are occasions on which the solution produced by individual choice between alternatives cannot be tolerated because of the lack of uniformity produced. In the case of the determination of the hours of labour in an industry or factory, the arranging of separate contracts with each worker would obviously involve large sacrifices of efficiency in a co-operative economic régime. Competition tends to enforce a collectively agreed uniformity here because its mutual benefits greatly outweigh its disadvantages to the parties concerned taken as a whole. Yet we have no reasons for supposing that the relative desires for leisure on the one hand and income satisfactions on the other are at all uniform in different individuals. The practical advantages of the collective determination of the amount of leisure overshadow the social gains to be obtained from personal choice, in the same way that the collective provision of street-lighting and sewers is more efficient than arrangements made by individual contract.[9] The case for discrimination, however, disparages the results of individual contract on exactly the opposite grounds. Edgeworth, discussing its possible benefits, allowed the dictum to fall from his pen and that a "regulated discrimination of prices, such as might conceivably be practised by a Socialist Directory, but is not possible in a régime of competition, tends to increase the sum-total of utility."[10] And Mrs. Robinson sees the problem in exactly the same light when she says: "An all-wise dictator, to whom every utility function was known, could increase the social benefit derived from given resources by revising the constitution of the set of commodities produced under perfectly *laissez-faire* conditions." But the defence of the authoritarian State which carries weight is absolutely the reverse of this: it rests on the desirability of

standardising consumption—of eliminating the "wastes" that are alleged to arise in the application of productive resources in response to an *unduly diversified* social demand. We must, then, set the *conceivable* advantages from the *ideal* co-operation in which prices to different individuals are not necessarily uniform, against the very definite benefits of the *compulsory* subordination of each individual to the will of the group (even under economic inequality); and we must remember that the uniformity and determinateness of competitive prices themselves enable the better practical arrangements for co-operation.

9. To the student of actual society such a balancing might appear superfluous, for it would be impossible in any large community to organise things in a like manner to that of a small group in the case of which the proposition might be imagined to have *some* validity.[11] How, for example, could the mass of consumers make known the relative urgencies of their *individual* needs or aspirations? There is no devisable mechanism either for broadcasting the facts of individual scales of preference or for organising a co-operative response to them. Even if the "ideal discrimination" described by Professor Pigou as "discriminating monopoly of the first degree" does not lose all its theoretical realism when the notion of utility is regarded with scepticism, it remains the purely abstract conception which he has made it; and equally chimerical must any system be which envisages universal knowledge of the scales of preference of all individuals being somehow embodied in an index to which the co-operative use and disposal of productive resources could be enabled to respond. The ideal is one towards whose attainment it seems impossible to take any steps.

10. We may have to admit that in the world of reality, even if competitive institutions were the most perfect imaginable, certain consumers' needs would, under imaginable circumstances, receive less satisfaction than they might. Provided that we are prepared to make an abstraction wholly divorced from reality, we can conceive of a "Socialist Directory," such as Edgeworth thought of in this connection, or "the all-wise dictator" of Mrs. Robinson's imagination, focusing the separate scales of preference of each consumer and, with complete knowledge of the economies achievable from economic co-operation, ordering production in accordance with the diversified situation of which it has in some mysterious way become aware. "Scarcities" would then be different from what they would be under free exchange—how much so would depend upon the likelihood of the occurrence of those conditions in which discriminatory prices can enable

improved co-operation in consumers' interests. And in response to a different complex of scarcities, the method of distributing productive resources and hence of determining the constituents of the flow of satisfactions would be different. Free exchange, in other words, may lead to an expression of "scarcities" that hides an individual's true nature behind an arbitrary uniformity.[12] In the ensuing discussion we shall not again refer to the practical fact that a régime permitting discrimination must be inefficient from the point of view of complex co-operation based on contractual relations.

11. Unfortunately, Edgeworth's discussion of this topic was thoroughly confused because, in spite of pertinent criticism by Mr. C. F. Bickerdike, he never grasped the true significance of the costs situation in relation to this question.[13] To-day, however, it is agreed that there can be no question of the beneficence of monopoly which enables discrimination unless the condition of decreasing average costs exists. Accordingly, let us now consider the meaning of this term. Decreasing average costs are a phenomenon which, in most cases, cannot be realistically represented in schedules. The condition rests upon the fact of the physical indivisibility of the first or subsequent increments of supply of productive equipment and resources, and it is connected with their most efficient disposal. It is especially likely to be important when, owing to technical considerations, the economic size of the increment of supply of co-operative equipment is large. The condition is more complexly determined when, for the same reasons, increase of scale enables more efficient specialisation. Now this problem should properly be considered as concerned with the effectiveness of co-operation in the whole of the productive system of a community;[14] and what constitutes a small increment in this relation may be a very big one from the point of view of a particular enterprise. But most of the discussions of this topic have envisaged the conditions of expansion of a single enterprise.

12. Let us first consider the question in the traditional way, however; that is, from the point of view of an individual undertaking. Cost schedules have usually been handled very much as though they represented phenomena of the utmost definiteness. Yet it is quite clear that very few actual productive undertakings would be able to realise big economies in the way of specialisation as a result of a moderate increase of demand; and after all, that is the most that can really be expected to result from discrimination in the case of products which experience shows us are already demanded under uniform price conditions.[15] In general, the occurrence of conditions in which dis-

crimination will lead to an increase of potential demand, becoming effective through the achievement of economies, seems to be absolutely improbable. And it is on this possibility that the theory of the beneficence of discrimination rests. Professor Pigou seems, indeed, to be putting the case against it unduly mildly when he says: "It appears, on the whole, exceedingly improbable that, in an industry selected at random, monopoly *plus* discrimination of the third degree will yield an output as large as would be yielded by simple competition."[16]

13. However, our discussion so far has not given us grounds for denying that circumstances might arise in which the possibility of discrimination would be a necessary condition for the provision of a certain indivisible increment of supply of productive resources.[17] We must, therefore, consider this possibility. It can be regarded simply as a special aspect of the general fact that the decreasing average costs condition depends upon a certain minimum scale being necessary for a certain degree of economic specialisation to take place. The case in which no output would be forthcoming except under discrimination does not fall into a special class: it is nothing more than an extreme example of the general rule. Thus, the provision of a railway where none previously existed must not be classified logically into a different category from the case of the addition of an extra siding to an existing railway system.

14. The difficulty of considering this problem arises largely from the fact that all the examples in the books are concerned with undertakings which have possessed some measure of "natural monopoly." We do not propose to consider here what institutions could enable social forces to compel such monopolies to conform to policies comparable to competition. Needless to say, the result would be an amount of investment determined in the same way as investment in non-monopolised fields, and there would also be price uniformity. Now in the enforcement of such a policy, if it were thought expedient to refrain scrupulously from any policy which might deter an increment of investment, temporary exemption from circumstances preventing discrimination might be extended to new enterprises setting up for the first time, provided that the true nature of the intended discrimination were made public and there were no serious protests from the parties to be discriminated against.[18]

15. The question of giving subsequent expansions protection of this kind does not involve any new principle. As demand increases, a certain position of the demand schedule will be reached which will cause a sudden jump

(through "internal" or "external" economies) in the schedule of costs. Improved specialisation will, in other words, then become possible. Now when the conditions exist in which discrimination will cause an effective demand for more units than will be demanded under competitive uniformity, it follows that this position (or series of positions) will be approached earlier. The whole effect lies in the hastening of the process. For a reduction of the uniform price charged by a productive enterprise (whether uniformity is due to the pressure of free exchange of products or to anti-monopoly enactment) will have the same effect of making new demand effective as such a position is approached. Hence, the relevance of discrimination to decreasing costs will simply depend upon how near to one of these positions the demand schedule happens to be at any time; for until the distance from such a position is equal to the difference between competitive and discriminatory demand there can be no social justification for any divergence from uniform prices. It will be, however, a matter of chance in any specific case as to how much nearer to one of them the maximisation of effective demand due to discriminatory price policy will bring the aggregate demand schedule. The case for permitting discrimination does not seem very strong, therefore, but permission to depart from uniform prices might nevertheless be extended to expanding concerns, provided that they were allowed a relatively limited power in this respect. As far as possible, the right to discriminate in those circumstances would have to be confined only to the specific dealings (or traffic) affected by the additional equipment; but for convenience the right of general discrimination within a limited range of charges might have to be temporarily permitted. Exemption of this type from the requirement of uniform charging could only be contemplated when the existing equipment was so fully employed under uniform charging that there would be obvious economies from expansion.

16. It is *possible* that whilst a full employment of existing immobilised resources may be achievable through discrimination, demand under uniform charging at competitive prices may be insufficient to enable this; and it might be feared that, whilst uniform charging is being practised, to insist upon the presence of conditions suggesting full employment before permitting temporary discrimination might restrain development. But there must have been some considerable increase of demand to have made expansion profitable, even under discrimination. For to satisfy the conditions which justify discrimination the increment of expansion must be large. Hence the growth of demand would have been likely to have brought about a heavy

utilisation of existing equipment. The insistence upon this condition would, therefore, be unlikely to check progress. Moreover, there is the further consideration (of conceivable importance under the restricted competition of actual practice) that a general increase of demand is likely to cause a smaller dispersion of prices to be profitable to a monopolist until the point at which expansion becomes profitable for him. For increasing prime costs are probable as fuller employment of equipment leads to relative congestion. In these circumstances it is more likely to pay a monopolist to encourage high-grade trade or traffic by lowering the tariff for it, and discourage low-grade trade or traffic by raising the tariff for it.

17. But the nature of the problem as a *practical* question (*i.e.*, as opposed to the abstract question) changes as an enterprise expands in response to developing demand. A large *additional* indivisible increment of investment has then to be regarded as relatively small in relation to the enterprise as a whole. With each successive expansion, the relative importance of discrimination as an inducement to *further* desirable investment decreases rapidly. To ask for the power to depart (temporarily) from the uniform price system, a developed corporation would have to produce a plan showing that the increasing effective demand resulting would enable some revolutionary re-disposal of equipment so as to produce startling economies. Such a position would be rare. If claims that it were present became common, that would be evidence of abuse and on grounds of administrative convenience the prohibition of all discrimination might be justified.

18. The important point is that if discrimination were authorised, it would be temporary only. We have no principles for determining what the period should be. But as the problem is one which can be shown to concern, in the main, development only (*i.e.*, the right original application of productive resources), we may assume that most invested resources worth preserving intact are confronted with increasing demand as time passes, and hence that most economies from improved specialisation will ultimately be realisable under competitive uniformity. Nevertheless, the main justification for insisting that discrimination shall be temporary is expediency—the avoidance of its worst evils. We have not denied that there might be some occasions on which, firstly, owing to the large size of the minimum initial unit of investment, and secondly (but to a rapidly diminishing extent), owing to the large size of subsequent units of expansion, the greater relative profitableness of discrimination would lead to some original investment or

some development where none would eventuate under competitive institutions (i.e., conditions equivalent in their effect to free exchange).

19. But even in the case of the first increment of investment, and even under the hypothetical conditions that we have postulated, the *a priori* improbability of such occasions arising might be argued. This conclusion may perhaps be regarded as the culmination of Professor Pigou's extension and application of the theories that Edgeworth brought into discussion. He assumes that "the law of decreasing supply price acts strongly." Then after some intricate analysis, he states the fundamental problem in simple terms. Referring specifically to the case of a railway, he says: "Clearly, if the demand price for a small quantity is greater than the supply price, some output will be evolved under simple competition, and, therefore, the conditions we have in view do not arise. Clearly, again, if the demand price for a small quantity is very much less than the supply price, it is unlikely that any output will be evolved either under simple competition or under discriminating monopoly, and, therefore, again these conditions do not arise. In order that they may arise a sort of intermediate position must, it would seem, be established."[19] Now it is obvious, as Professor Pigou points out, that this intermediate position is not likely to be operative in any railway selected at random. But on the other hand, in a progressive community a potential railway route must pass through a period in which the conditions of the "intermediate position" (that is, under which discrimination alone will lead to a railway being supplied) will rule. If the practice is forbidden, its provision will be delayed until further development of potential demand has taken place. Professor Pigou has given us no clue as to the sort of indications which might tell us when these conditions are present, and it seems likely that it would be almost impossible to determine this in practice. Interested parties could easily make out a plausible case for such a contention; but we know that they can do this at any time, and we know, indeed, that railway experts have generally argued that the necessary conditions are typical of railways at all stages of their development.

20. However, it may be unnecessary for us to rely upon the possibility of devising methods for discovering whether these conditions are or are not present in order to discuss policy. We may assume that the "intermediate position" in the development of a potential route in a progressive community will occur at an unknown time and will be unrecognisable. In so far as it exists there will be incurred a loss which will be borne by the ultimate

consumers of the products carried by railways—not by owners of railways, it must be remembered. The loss will in general occur through *delay* in the provision of equipment for transport services. The conclusion to which we may be forced, when we take into account the multitude of risks of misjudgment and the absolutely unpredictable factors that bear on all productive development, is that any such losses should be classified with those other losses due to inevitable imperfections of knowledge and foresight to which the consumer is subject. A sudden change in a district served by a railway, such as the opening of a new factory, may quite conceivably cause conditions to jump completely over the "intermediate position." Professor Pigou has suggested, on the assumption that the "intermediate position" is recognisable and definable, that in the case of a new railway, discrimination might be permitted until development has carried it beyond that stage. Accepting the proposition that in the provision of an extra track for a railway there is justification for discriminating rates "to be applied to the traffic carried on the new track only," Professor Pigou adds that in practice it would have to be applied to all the traffic which is not justified.[20] In view of the fact that we have been given no criteria for determining this "intermediate position," all suggestions for actually allowing discrimination at a certain stage may seem somewhat "academic."[21] Our suggestions do not entirely get over this dilemma. They are based on common-sense compromise. As we have suggested, there would seldom be justification for resort to temporary discrimination. If visible development is thought likely to cause a railway or new branch line ultimately to be profitable under uniform charging, a probable small "loss" in the interim will not deter the speculation involved in the undertaking or an expansion of it.

21. But Mrs. Robinson's case for the beneficence of discrimination has been made, in her article of last September, to rest on the fact that "every commodity must have falling average costs for small outputs." "There must therefore be," she continues, "a large number of non-existent commodities which would be introduced under an ideal distribution of social resources, and it does not follow, because the ideal output of each would be small, that in the aggregate they would be unimportant. The service of a doctor is only one example of innumerable commodities which, in an ideal economy, would be introduced, each to a small extent, wherever population is sparse, or incomes, tastes and habits are diversified." We have no quarrel with Mrs. Robinson's assertion that such cases are theoretically conceivable. But her inference that there are "innumerable" commodities which would be

produced under an "ideal" economy, but whose production would be frustrated owing to the price uniformity due to free exchange is quite unjustifiable. Let us try to conceive of these "non-existent commodities." Mrs. Robinson's only actual example is that of a doctor in a sparsely populated district. This is at any rate a superficially plausible illustration, but it can be misleading for two reasons.[22] In the first place, as we suggested in paragraph 11, from the point of view of the whole community, the fact of the indivisibility of an increment of resources will seldom have the importance that it will have to any locality; and in choosing an example based on the assumption of districts of sparse population she has introduced a case in which this consideration is relevant. Such sparseness will in itself be in part the product of whatever system of price policy is permitted or chosen. Let us suppose that medical services by a doctor were as *essential* as food for every individual. Then, in the absence of discrimination, there would not be any districts so sparsely populated that it would pay no doctor to serve them. Sparse population might exist, but wage-rates would have to be so high in such districts as to make it profitable for doctors to serve them. (We can imagine some co-operative or health insurance scheme having to be adopted.) If, on the other hand, medical services were not essential, but only desirable, the same considerations would apply. The absence of "qualified" medical services in one district owing to discrimination not being permitted would simply contribute to the disadvantage of living or working in that area. Now, whilst it is true that such a *local* community might be worse off in the sense of its attracting less resources than under a régime allowing discrimination, we cannot assume that the community as a whole would suffer detriment. The conception of social advantage envisages the whole area. It is the efficiency of specialisation and co-ordination within the community, not the economies achievable within a particular section of it, which is relevant to the problem of maximum social benefit. Doctors are trained (produced) for the community as a whole, and the desirable application of resources in the way of population distribution must take account of the fact that doctors are indivisible and can serve a limited geographical area. Increments of supply of resources have to be considered in relation to a huge volume of co-operant and physically mobile resources. The emphasis of this factor does not, however, dispose of Mrs. Robinson's point. It merely draws attention to what is almost certainly a more important consideration.

22. In the second place, the example is misleading because the idea of indivisibility is given too rigid a meaning. It is an easy mistake to assume

that reasoning developed in considering, say, bridges and railways, can apply to a wide range of other types of resources. But even in these specific cases it is possible to place too much stress on indivisibility. For instance, in the classic case of the toll-bridge, one should really take into account the possibility of different grades of bridge, from a cheap rope-structure (carrying a few foot-passengers) at one extreme, to a solid steel bridge (to carry heavy traffic) at the other extreme. The first step from the ferry to the bridge would probably involve a very primitive structure indeed, and that might be all that was justified. And when we come to a doctor's services, we must recognise that he is only one means of providing medical services. There are grades of doctors and substitutes for doctors: district nurses (equivalent, say, to 25 per cent of a doctor), patent medicines (bought through the mail-order system), and so forth. When substitutes (available in smaller increments, or provided in response to a plurality of demands) are possible, the indivisibility of increments of productive resources ceases to be important. A less expensive form of plant will then be the most economic response to a smaller demand. And in these circumstances the original apparent significance of decreasing average costs must be greatly whittled down.

23. In practice, substitutes have very wide significance. All channels of expenditure are competing with one another, and the transition from one substitute to the next is usually very close. This is often true of productive resources, but very nearly universally true of consumers' goods. And to the extent that consumers' goods are substitutes for one another, the plants that manufacture them are substitutes for one another and the hypothetical condition of decreasing average costs ceases to be important. We cannot here enter into a discussion of the nature and implications of the consumer's indifference in respect of slightly or even greatly different products. We must point out, however, that there are "almost as good" substitutes for practically everything. All the conceivable consumers' products that human beings can want may be arranged in schedules according to their affinities. In recognising this, we find the main refutation of Mrs. Robinson's objection to *laissez-faire*. Her "non-existent commodities" will almost certainly be found to lie in certain narrow gaps. The fact that "small output" commodities are not produced when (owing to the large size of the first increment of supply of a particular productive resource) falling average costs are experienced as an initial condition, does not imply a frustration of consumers' preference but an exercise of their preference for cheapness. What happens is that a voluntary standardisation takes place, and cheapness

is preferred to the special qualities of the nearest product in the schedule of affinities. The plant which supplies the larger output commodity actually demanded is the substitute which makes the indivisibility of the hypothetical small output irrelevant in problems of practical policy; and this being so, the phenomenon of decreasing average costs can no longer be realistically regarded as a determining factor.

24. In earlier paragraphs we saw that the conceivable advantages of ideal discrimination had to be set against the actual benefits of the compulsory subordination of individuals to the social will which is achievable under competitive uniformity. Now it is obvious that actual discrimination must diverge widely from ideal discrimination, even when arranged by the most enlightened "Socialist Directory" conceivable. That being so, any conceivable advantages derivable from it tend to be wiped out. It is not easy to define the circumstances in which actual discrimination will approximate to the ideal in such a way as to make its tolerance desirable. Practical policy might, we have rather hesitatingly suggested, validly permit temporary discrimination where the initial and subsequent units of investment are large. In this sort of case there is some plausibility in the suggestion that consumers' demand in relation to the cost situation is such that differential charging will be beneficial.[23] But in other fields in which discrimination is practised these circumstances are definitely not present; the practice is almost completely unrelated to the ultimate scales of preference on the part of consumers; or in Edgeworthian terms, there is practically no likelihood that the practice will lead to "total utility" or the sum-total of "consumers' surplus" being maximised.

25. Of the private profitableness of discrimination there can be no question, but it is productive circumstances having no constant relations with consumers' preferences which make it so useful to monopolists. For instance, there might be two producers incurring roughly the same immediate costs, but one employing a great deal of fixed equipment that cannot be diverted to any other uses, and the other using productive resources that can easily be diverted to some other fields of employment. Now the former would tend to be discriminated against by a co-operant monopolist seeking his maximum advantage whilst the latter would not be easily exploitable.

26. The existence of most of the differential charging that we find is based either (in the short run) on the exploitation of co-operant producers possessing immobile resources; or else (in the long run) at the consumers' expense through bringing about an unfavourable distribution of investment of

productive resources. It is an arbitrary private benefit that is obtained from discrimination in the majority of cases. There are no grounds for assuming that it produces an ideal distribution of investment adjusted to the existence of different scales of preferences on the part of consumers. It represents a pricing system developed in the interests of private profit and based mainly on chance facts arising out of the relations of many co-operating agents in the productive process. Thus, the discrimination that may be practised under the "basing point" system by American steel companies is not to be accounted for because it was a necessary condition of the original investment which somehow took account of idiosyncrasies in the tastes and preferences of the consumers of the ultimate products (that contain the steel, or are the result of the employment of capital goods containing it). Its explanation is that past circumstances have led to a certain geographical distribution of demand; and those producers using steel who happen to be distant from alternative sources of supply are therefore exploitable. The "past circumstances" referred to are best regarded as determined by chance factors. In addition, the threat or actuality of "aggresssive selling" on the one hand, and the use of "development prices" by monopolists (to reduce investment in immobile forms that can later be exploited) on the other hand, might affect the situation. But whatever view we take of this, there seems to be no reason for assuming that consumers' preferences for the products of steel are distributed locally in such a way that this form of discrimination has even the slightest tendency to maximise the totality of "consumers' surplus" or to render the response to consumers' preferences most effective.

27. Finally, we may, perhaps, clarify the position by classifying discrimination (excluding differential charging based on "joint supply") in a fourfold manner: (*a*) with a view to inducing investment in co-operant immobile resources in order that they might later on be exploited (that is, what is commonly called charging "development prices" or rates); (*b*) with a view to repelling investment in or driving away existing competitive resources (that is, what is best called "aggressive selling"); (*c*) with a view to obtaining maximum net return given the existing amount and distribution of productive resources (and, whatever the *motive*, this has the same *effect* as (*b*) when productive circumstances and not consumers' preferences make the practice profitable); (*d*) as the fulfilment of an expected condition essential for the specific investment to take place. (*a*) has the object of deliberately encouraging a change in the existing situation or trend of development favourable to the monopolist by misleading investors. (*b*) has

in part somewhat similar object—the aim of preventing a change in the existing situation unfavourable to the monopolist, or the enforcement of a favourable change by means of the actual or threatened use of aggressive selling. Actual development in the form of immobilisation of resources will be influenced by the possibility of (*a*) and (*b*) being used even if they are seldom actually put into effect; for possible exploitation or aggression will be anticipated. (*c*) concerns the maximisation of private advantage. (*d*) represents the possibly legitimate case; and we have shown this to be unimportant except in rare and clearly recognisable circumstances in which the tolerance of temporary interference with free exchange might be in the social interest.

Notes

1. J. Robinson, "A Fundamental Objection to Laissez-Faire," *The Economic Journal* 46, (September 1936), pp. 580-2.

2. The comparison is between the last but one increment purchased by A and the last but one purchased by B; the last but two purchased by A and the last but two purchased by B, and so on. Conventional terminology would express this position by saying that different individuals purchasing quantities of a certain commodity in a free market would have consumers' surpluses of different magnitudes.

3. The implication sometimes appears to be that the "loss" is in terms of consumers' satisfactions. At other times a loss in quantity of production seems intended.

4. F. Edgeworth, *Papers Relating to Political Economy* (London: Macmillan, 1925), Vol. I, p. 173.

5. The author believes that the most appropriate conception is that of "consumers' sovereignty," the acceptance of which as an economic ideal would not only bring greater realism into many studies in the logic of economic relations, but would enable the elimination of a whole host of common confusions. But we cannot employ the conception in this essay.

6. Assuming, of course, that competitively determined values are not indefensible on other grounds.

7. The power which monopolistic owners of co-operant resources have under a discriminating regime to exploit the owners of immobile productive equipment whilst retaining the custom of those whose capital is mobile is a different aspect of the problem which is referred to later.

8. By development selling we mean selling cheap with a view to enticing exploitable investment in immobile forms.

9. Another principle is also involved here, of course. Individuals who might refuse to contribute towards the provision of these things would nevertheless obtain the benefits arising from them, or contribute to the social detriment which they seek to avoid.

10. F. Edgeworth, *Papers Relating to Political Economy*, Vol. 2, p. 425.

11. E.g., as in the activities of a small tribe.

12. The writer believes that this point can be most clearly expressed in terms of "consumers' sovereignty." *Equilibrium* under natural scarcities reflecting simple consumers' sovereignty might in some conditions leave consumers less well served than under a system that can be imagined in the abstract. The productive scheme which could produce that equilibrium may perhaps be regarded as (over a field of indeterminate size) ignoring the idiosyncrasies of individual preference.

13. It is rather remarkable that Edgeworth's errors on this point, although avoided by subsequent theorists, have never been specifically criticised by those most competent to do so, with the result that students of his work are involved in quite unnecessary difficulties.

14. The notion of "external economics" achievable by a firm gives only partial recognition to this idea.

15. The fact that things like tariff protection have been followed in *some* cases by improved specialisation in an industry can be admitted, but it is quite impossible to know whether this has been a response to the increased demand secured for the industry; for in countless concrete cases it can be seen to have had no effect of this nature. Experience of industries under tariff protection makes us doubt whether there is any practical validity at all in typical arguments based on the decreasing cost hypothesis.

16. A. Pigou, *Economics of Welfare* (London: Macmillan, 1928), p. 287.

17. We are assuming here that the "indivisibility" prevents an accurate response of supply to demand. In practice there may be little in this. Thus even in the clearest case, that of a pioneer railway, or a toll-bridge, the standard and costs of construction may vary within a wide range according to estimates of present and potential demand. Insofar as this is possible, it will weaken the case in favour of discrimination. We refer to this point again in paragraph 22.

18. Under defensible discrimination all purchasers must gain; for if any of them are worse off, we have no valid grounds for assuming that their aggregate losses are not greater than the others' aggregate advantages.

19. Pigou, *Economics of Welfare*, p. 311.

20. Ibid., p. 312.

21. Furthermore, unless consumers of the railway's services could be warned of an impending change, temporary discrimination would be liable to stimulate "exploitable" development. We refer to this point again later on.

22. Two additional reasons make the example of doctors difficult to consider: (a)

we are bound to be affected by our irrelevant conviction that it is right that all individuals should have medical services; (b) we are apt to accept rather uncritically the necessary persistence of the present organisation of medical professions for the purpose of extortion from the sick whom the public opinion holds are "able to pay."

23. We find, appropriately, that with transport undertakings, in the case of which our suggestion is that temporary discrimination might be permitted, there may be some connection between freight classification and consumers' preference. As a rule the practice is, in a broad way, to charge higher freight rates on commodities that are expensive in relation to their bulk or weight. Such differential charging will bring fewer protests, for the freight item in costs will seem small. But *that* does not enable us to assume that it is defensible on standards of social advantage. There are, however, grounds for believing that in general there is some connection between the weight-price ration (or volume-price ratio) and consumers' scales of preference. The movement of a ton of copper, for instance, will presumably contribute more towards the "total utility" of Edgeworth's conception than the same service rendered in connection with a ton of coal.

12 • *The Nature of Aggressive Selling*

It is a common implication of contemporary economic discussions in the Press, and in the speeches of chairmen of companies and politicians, that the modern economic system tends naturally to generate a sort of competitive tornado, to liberate certain ruthlessly ruinous forces which must be controlled or resisted lest we all perish economically. Such beliefs are not easy to criticise, for they are usually imported as assumptions which are supposed to be obvious to all. Most difficult to answer are those writers who appear not to condemn the whole principle of competition but to argue that some amount of it only is good. In addition we often find the same people arguing that it is bad at one time because we never get it in its "perfect" form, and at another because in its complete form it would be ruinous. But inconsistent contentions in an argument do not prove that one of them cannot be true, and the demonstration of inconsistency does not convince. We are seldom given, however, anything resembling general principles to tell us just *what sorts* of competition are good or bad or just *how much* of it is good or bad. Popular assumptions on the point really present no argument to attack. But some writers of standing seem to have wavered. We do not propose to show in this article how apparent misconceptions among reputable economists seem to have arisen. The present writer has dealt with certain confused notions concerning the conception of competition in recent articles in the *South African Journal of Economics*.[1] To some extent the present discussion builds on those, and the ensuing argument may, perhaps, be more clearly un-

Reprinted with permission from *Economica* 12 (1935).

derstood if read in conjunction with them. In those articles, values under "natural scarcity" are distinguished from values under "contrived scarcity"; contrived scarcities are shown to exist whenever any hindrance is placed in the way of the completely free disposal and utilisation of all natural sources according to the dictates of "consumers' sovereignty"; natural scarcity being regarded as a reflection of consumers' sovereignty and the latter being regarded as a more realistic criterion of social economy than the traditional notion of utility. The institutions which are effective in bringing about values under natural scarcity are called "competitive institutions." The notion of equilibrium under such institutions is shown, in the article mentioned, to involve difficulties, owing to no value attaching to various desirable services such as inventing and certain kinds of risk-bearing. In the present essay we propose to ignore these difficulties. The confusions concerning the essentially ruinous nature of competition do not arise out of them.

There *is* a sense in which competition may be regarded as ruinous. Given the survival of aristocratic or "leisure" class traditions in society, and the monopolistic and authoritarian character of modern communities, any sudden increase in the effectiveness of competition might have a disastrous effect. It is an irrational world that we are studying, and we must face the facts that perfect competitive institutions are unattainable, and that their fanatical acceptance as the goal of practicable reform in the short run is likely to be disastrous. The existing distributive system depends upon the diversion of productive effort through deliberate and customary restrictions in a hundred different forms. Not only is the division of the value of the flow of productivity between social classes fundamentally influenced thereby, but between various groups within the same income-level strata similar tendencies assert themselves. The stark equalitarianism and impartiality of competitive institutions, their callous disregard for private interests, would conflict radically with the present social order. They would bring dismay and desperation to those whose income-rights were violently reduced. As the present writer has argued in another article, "the psychology of modern communities has become adapted to a situation in which restraint of competition is the normal thing. Social habits, ideals, beliefs, aspirations, and sometimes morals, are adjusted to its existence. Human nature as we know it has been reared and fashioned in a system in which privately contrived restriction and coercive intervention by the State in the determination of values are operative on all sides. Even our leaders in commerce and industry and government are profoundly influenced by this economic tradition. They would be bewildered by far-reaching changes in the economic framework within which they are accustomed to work. To attempt to arrange things so that competition suddenly has a much more unrestricted sway might be disastrous to many conspicuous classes, and the repercussions from their losses might be felt over the whole economic field. A perfect competitive system can still be accepted as a democratic and equalitarian ideal, but there are circumstances in which it ought to be subordinated to gradualness in any policy which has the effect of dissolving protected income rights.''[2] In studies such as the present we must ignore the difficulties of readjustment and detriment to human happiness which revolutionary redistribution would involve.

But among other problems we still have the question to answer: Is it true, as Proudhon alleged, that ''competition kills competition''? Can it be employed aggressively (either through price-cutting or some other expression) so as to bring about monopoly? If so, what laws or institutions will frustrate those who endeavour so to employ it? Adam Smith recognised the power of ''a combination of strong men to eradicate weak ones by low or unremunerative prices, and having secured a monopoly to commence a legal pillage of the public.'' In conformity with his faith in the disintegrating force of self-interest, he thought, however, that monopoly would, ''sooner or later'' disappear. Other writers in these days hold diametrically different convictions. Robert Liefmann has told us, for instance, that ''competition pushed to the extreme becomes monopoly. The climax of competition is monopoly, and all competition is but a striving for monopoly.''[3] This view seems to rest (a) upon the naïve assumption of unlimited and progressive economies as the scale of operations expands, or (b) upon a failure to grasp the significance of what it is best to call ''aggressive selling,'' the use of a price policy as a coercive device. We shall here be concerned only with the latter.[4]

In practice, the use of this sort of aggressive power appears most obvious when it is employed by large amalgamations or under deliberate collusion within a ring or cartel (as in the employment secretly of subsidised ''fighting ships'' by shipping conferences). But it may also exist even when open collusion or amalgamation between competitors is forbidden. We propose, therefore, to consider its nature in circumstances in which there is no collusion or amalgamation. We shall take the simplest cases and consider under varying assumptions the position (1), under what has been called "duopoly" (that is, competition expressed between the owners of two sets of resources, either of whom, alone, would have had complete monopoly); and (2), under what Professor Chamberlin has called "oligopoly" (the situation which exists where there are a few producers only). We shall consider duopoly and oligopoly in the cases of ownership (*a*) of naturally supplied commodities which, in the absence of restriction, would be so plentiful as to have an infinitesimally small or no exchange value; (*b*) of naturally supplied commodities which have value through the natural supply being limited and incapable of expansion by human agency; and (*c*) of commodities supplied through the use of productive equipment and effort.

The classic example of duopoly is one used by Cournot which involves the relations between the owners of two mineral-water springs. It is convenient for us to make use of a similar illustration but to express the problem somewhat differently. Let us consider an isolated community served by a few *ordinary* drinking-water springs,[5] competing sources of water supply for drinking, e.g., rain or deep wells, being costly. Consider each one of these springs to be owned by one person, and no person to own more than one spring. Let us assume (i), that each spring is capable of supplying such quantities of water that, in the absence of restriction of the amount sold, its value will be nil, even if it is the only source of supply; (ii), that each owner incurs no expenses in preparing the water for sale: in other words, that he has no costs of production; (iii), that the water is provided by Nature at an absolutely regular rate; (iv), that it cannot be accumulated except for a few days (or we may assume as an alternative that its qualities are perishable); (v), that the demand schedule for drinking water as a whole is determinate and has some elasticity; (vi), that consumers have immediate and full knowledge of prices asked; (vii), that they are indifferent as to what source to patronise, so that in the event of their awareness of any divergence in price they will immediately transfer their demand to the cheaper source; (viii), that each duopolist or oligopolist is aware of what the others are doing; (ix), that each of the owners wishes to maximise his receipts; (x), that there is no collusion between them and no control of one by the others, and (xi), that price discrimination on the part of any single owner is forbidden.

By making these assumptions, especially by considering *all* receipts to be derived from restriction of supply, we are really considering a case capable of alternative illustration. We can imagine instead an unrestricted power of taxation being accorded to a certain body of men in the form of a complete monopoly of a commodity of no natural value, but no stipulation being laid down concerning the division of the proceeds of the tax among them and each of them being allowed to sell unlimited quantities. It is clear that we can say nothing about what distributive scheme is likely to eventuate, and it is also clear that it will be to the advantage of each of them that the price shall conform to that which maximises their receipts. We may expect, therefore, "reasonableness" or tacit collusion among them, if not deliberate collusion embodying their ideas of reasonableness in something like contract form. Indeed, the absence of all collusion is unthinkable. Hence we have in this illustration a plain exposure, firstly, of the indeterminacy of "the quota"; secondly, of the futility and hence unlikelihood of aggressive selling among rational oligopolists in respect of the sharing of purely monopoly revenues; and thirdly, of the determinate nature of the optimum price, irrespective of how many oligopolists there are to share in the proceeds. This approach does not form, however, the most convenient basis of exposition for our present purpose, although it forecasts the nature of subsequent conclusions. In considering separately the position of each spring owner, we may at first appear to be stressing the obvious or unnecessarily repeating what is already plain. But the purpose of seemingly superfluous detail will, it is hoped, become apparent as the essay proceeds.

Let us us consider duopoly. The output will tend to approximate to the optimum output for a single monopoly of the sources of supply. For each duopolist will know that if he allows a larger amount on the market or asks a lower price the other will immediately do likewise; and as such competition can clearly benefit neither of them but must, on the contrary, work to their detriment, they will refrain from it. There will be no object in their practising price-cutting as there will be nothing for either to gain. And if the price should for any reason be below the optimum, it will pay them both to return simultaneously to it. The same conditions will rule under oligopoly. Other things being equal, the number of owners practising tacit collusion will make no difference to the problem. Output will still tend to approach the optimum price for a perfect collusive monopoly. It may be that the more producers there are, the more unrealistic will be some of the assumptions listed in the previous paragraph; but that is the only way in which an increase in the number of springs will affect our argument. Under the unreal conditions of our hypothesis the optimum price for the output as a whole will still be approached.

Let us now consider the implications of our assumption (x), namely, that there is no collusion between the parties and no control of any one by others.

Returning to the case of duopoly we see that any increase of price demanded by A would have to be followed by so instantaneous an imitation from B that the collusion might be regarded as virtually deliberate. And if A cuts price B's imitation must be so immediate as to suggest virtual control. Under "oligopoly" this will still be true. A gradual rise of price to which all conform together will be the only conceivable condition for a rise, and a market-wide fall of price the only condition for a fall; and yet the attainment of the optimum price will be likely to be brought about. Hence, it is doubtful whether we can really think of independence attaching to the separate owners in these conditions. For instance, under oligopoly, if A acted irrationally or (relaxing our assumption (ix)) altruistically, by reducing price, B would be forced immediately to follow his price policy. But B might conceivably respond to A's price-cut by forcing the price still lower, perhaps even to nil, in order to coerce A into conforming to a price at or near what he judged was the optimum.[6] B's aggression in that case must be regarded either as in the nature of a demonstration of the folly of competition; or else it must be thought of as preliminary (*a*) to an offer to purchase the other's property in the spring, or (*b*) to deliberate negotiations for formal collusion. From our point of view, a useful way of regarding this phenomenon is to think of aggression as being actually undertaken only when a threat (of which rational duopolists must be permanently aware) is ignored. It is the continuous consciousness of this threat that makes our hypothesis of independence (assumption (x)) lose much of its meaning. Even in the absence of specific action which might be considered to be a communication or a command from one party to the other, neither individual can be thought of as autonomous. This is clearly equally true under oligopoly and in the actual society that we know. The nature of private income rights (in a society in which there exist "contrived scarcities") are such that the individual who might be prompted (for whatever reasons) to give the community more complete access to the gifts of Nature is faced with personal loss or sometimes even ruin.[7] Hence, under the assumptions here postulated, there is no possibility of initiative being devoted towards the achievement of conditions in which values will reflect natural scarcities, except in the case of quarrels over the division of the spoils. And in these latter circumstances, the benefit to consumers is, as we shall see, likely to be temporary only. Certain other circumstances, certain "external factors" not so far considered, must bear on the situation in order that forces leading to the realisation of the consumers' sovereignty ideal may be released.

When we consider the division of the market between the various owners of the water supply, we are again reminded of the unreality of our assumptions. Under duopoly, as A and B are by our hypothesis equally advantageously situated, there is no reason why, under the influence of chance, they should not halve the custom. Indeed, we must assume the equal sharing of the market, for if consumers are truly indifferent as to what sources of supply to patronise, that will clearly be the result.[8] But let us relax for a moment our assumption (vii) as to consumers' indifference. There may be a very slight measure of habit or inertia among them which, in the absence of differential prices, will keep the majority "loyal" to one supplier. There may be a sort of "goodwill" of an admittedly most flimsy nature. In these circumstances if, as a matter of history, one party A has supplied water to one quarter, and the other B to three-quarters of the consumers, this situation may come to be regarded as "reasonable" (especially if the income-rights attaching to the two springs have been bid for and capitalised according to market interest rates). Where existing relations are believed to be "reasonable" they will not be likely to be upset under duopoly. They will form a sort of dominant initial state from which future relations will be ordered. Thus, let us suppose A and B to sell out on the basis of their present sales and the result to be that ten persons acquire A's property (supplying one quarter of the consumers), and thirty persons B's property (supplying three-quarters of the consumers), the shares of each person being of the same value. In these circumstances, such a division of the proceeds will probably be accepted as obviously "fair." We are likely to find, therefore, the practice of tacit collusion or "reasonableness," and the effect of this will be to preserve the income-rights of each of them. On the other hand, where A is the sole owner of one spring and B the sole owner of the other, A may suddenly come to the conclusion that the position is "unfair" and set about price-cutting in order to break down the slight element of consumers' inertia, and in the hope that it will later be to B's interest to allow "reasonableness" once more to rule their relations. For we must conceive of him reckoning on the new distribution of custom, when tacit collusion is again being practised, being determined by chance. Patronage will be likely to be divided on an equal basis; and the benefits derived from the price war by the consumer will have been temporary only. There will, of course, always be much in-determinacy in the division of the gains from restriction whether due to tacit or deliberate collusion. Indeed, it is difficult to expect anything else under the principle of "live and let live." That principle rests on a kind of altruism akin to "honour among thieves." We see, however, that tacit monopoly in all its forms tends to preserve the *status quo*, no matter how unstable or precarious it may be from other causes, simply because the *status quo* is likely to be accepted as essentially reasonable and just. We find exactly the same tendency under formal collusive monopoly, where the allocation of quotas always tends to preserve the *status quo*, however arbitrary it may be.

The omission of assumptions (vi) and (vii), namely, that all consumers have full knowledge and, being indifferent, immediately transfer their demand when they can profit from price discrepancy, does not alter the situation fundamentally. For the greater the consumers' inertia, the smaller the immediate gain or the greater the immediate loss to the price-cutter, and the smaller the immediate loss to the owner who refrains from cutting. Hence, whilst considerable inertia decreases the probability of retaliation, it reduces the profitableness of an initial price-cut. In the case of duopoly, A will not be obliged to follow *immediately* a price-cut initiated by B, for he may at first lose only a small margin of his customers, and may hope that B will soon "come to his senses." But ultimately the same motives will influence him as would determine his actions under perfect mobility among customers. Indeed, the existence of consumers' inertia may necessitate his cutting below the price at which B has been selling in order to get back his original proportion of the market. A's retaliation can be regarded as an attempt to recapture "goodwill." But the inevitableness of A's reaction will almost certainly deter an initial price-cut by B. If, for any reason, a price below the long-run optimum for the two owners exists at any time, the possibility of either of them initiating independently an *increase* of price is rendered more likely; for if A should advance his charges slightly, he might, in the short run, lose insufficient orders to cause a serious diminution in his aggregate receipts, and he might possibly even reap a short-run gain from that policy. On the other hand, B might achieve a greater profit temporarily by not responding to A's tacit suggestion through example that prices should be raised; but he will realise clearly enough his long-run interest in the higher price; and their joint motive for silent co-operation in working towards the optimum price will be at least as strong as under conditions of perfect mobility among customers. It is possible that B will not follow because he thinks that the optimum price for the whole output is being exceeded. He will, however, have much to gain and little to lose in that event from the practice of trial and error; and although price and output will be dictated by the more pessimistic party there will still be this definite tendency towards an equilibrium near the private optimum.

Our assumption (viii), that each party knows what the others are doing, cannot be omitted in the presence of assumptions (vi) and (vii) that consumers have perfect knowledge and are perfectly mobile. For as any price-cut by A will mean that B loses *all* his customers until he responds, he can hardly be unaware of A's action. We can, however, eliminate assumptions (vi), (vii) and (viii) together. Let us consider, then, the case in which all owners are not immediately aware of what the others are doing and in which consumers lack complete knowledge of the market, and are therefore unable to transfer their demand immediately to meet price discrepancies. Under duopoly, should A become aware of demand falling off, he may assume that aggregate demand is falling and not notice that *some* of his customers are being attracted to the patronage of B who is deliberately charging a slightly lower price. He may nevertheless cut prices slightly to meet the decline in demand, and eventually get back a measure of custom nearer the original proportion of the (presumably larger) quantity demanded. B (whose cut may not necessarily be due to a wrongly estimated change in demand) may be afraid to go farther for fear of a price war. A sort of arbitrary equilibrium may be established in this way. B will then have achieved the whole of his special return; and for the future the two of them will be permanently worse off at that equilibrium unless the former price had exceeded the optimum. Thus, B's motive to cut with a view to increasing his share of the trade will not be very strong unless he can rely upon his temporary differential prosperity enabling him to dispose of the whole or part of his property at an inflated price. There will be but meagre chances of private gains from a price war in quest of a larger quota. Moreover, the price having once been brought down, it will still pay far-sighted duopolists to follow each other's lead in attempting to re-attain their optimum price, which is the tendency, as we have seen, both in the presence and absence of the inertia which now forms part of our assumptions. In this case B's temporary power to cut prices profitably in the first place depends not only upon the existence of considerable mobility among some of A's customers, but also upon that mobility not being so large as to cause A to become aware of the *transfer* of custom (as opposed to the apparent decline in demand). On the other hand, when consumers' inertia is strong, when, over the short run, the degree of mobility among A's customers is small, there may be no motive for B to cut at all, for inelasticity of demand in the short run will have brought sacrifices, and by the time that sufficient custom has been attracted to him to compensate for the lower price per unit sold, A will be likely to have realised the situation and to have retaliated. Where consumers' inertia is strong and where, for any reason (such as a fight for quotas), the price is below the long-run optimum for both of them, an independent *increase* in price, as we have already seen, is likely. A, relying on the inertia of a large number of his customers, might raise his price and lose insufficient orders to cause a diminution in his aggregate receipts and, in fact, possibly experience a greater aggregate return. Then B, finding a slight increase in the demand for his supplies, will also be likely to consider raising his price even if he has not noticed that A's policy has driven certain customers to him. Under duopoly in these circumstances, then, the tendency for price to approach again the private optimum will still be present.

Where numbers are greater, i.e., under oligopoly, there are no grounds for modifying this conclusion. Let us consider the case in which mobility among certain customers of each owner is great enough to bring short-run gains to price-cutters but not large enough to stimulate an immediate price response on the part of other suppliers. A single individual, for instance, may count on cutting price in the hope of greatly increasing the amount supplied by him—perhaps doubling or even trebling it—without exercising sufficient influence on the market as a whole for the other owners to become aware of a noticeable falling off in their own sales for a considerable time; or if several individuals pursue the same policy of allowing more on the market, and a general falling off in price is the *ultimate reaction*, this might still not be felt to be serious or its cause recognised by those individuals who allow only their customary supply to be placed on the market. When the price has fallen, the fact of inertia may have brought about a redistribution of demand among the different owners. This redistribution may be of various degrees of permanence. If inertia is fairly small, the proportions of total output left to each owner may soon be the same as they were at the outset. In that case, the original price-cutters will soon have reaped to the full their private gains; and to obtain a further differential return it will be necessary for them to start price-cutting once more. Where there is considerable inertia among consumers, however, the factor of numbers makes the position somewhat different from what it is under duopoly. Although it may take much time and entail short-run sacrifices for one owner to attract customers, the other sellers are likely to be even more slow in realising what he is doing.[9] Through the delay in their retaliation, he may be allowed to retain permanently any increased proportion of the total market so secured. For when the others *do* notice his successful manoeuvres, they may think it worth while tolerating his gains and treating bygones as bygones, in order that prices shall at any rate be maintained for the future by a "reasonable" attitude among sellers.[10] They may feel the folly of aggression or punitive competition. If they do not, and seek to win back stolen goodwill, the consumers are likely to experience the temporary benefits of a price war. Forbearance in the future will, however, tend to preserve an existing distribution of "goodwill," accepted as "reasonable," which different owners may have acquired in the past. As we have seen, the tacit monopoly relationship between sellers works to protect the *status quo*. Thus, under the conditions postulated, whilst economic inertia enables the employment of skilful tactics which may add to the custom and hence the wealth of individual owners, it does not destroy the profitableness and inevitableness of tacit collusion. And where those with control of the sources of supply are completely rational, the existence of this inertia does not weaken the tendency for maximum receipts to be obtained by them. The continuous impending threat to price-cutters will still remain, and although some owners may dare to show defiance, and in so doing actually benefit themselves by capturing "goodwill," the threat will, in general, it seems, be effective.

So far we have been considering the case of tacit monopolisation of commodities with no (or infinitesimal) natural scarcity. We must now consider the supply of commodities which *are* naturally scarce. In the following discussion our assumption (i) is, then, omitted and assumptions (ii) to (xi) restored. The burden on our imagination is least, in view of our assumption of *natural* scarcity, if we now choose the example of mineral-water springs of rare medicinal qualities rather than ordinary drinking water. We must imagine these springs giving a limited but absolutely regular supply which is incapable of being added to by means of human effort or expenditure. Let us now add the further assumption, (xii), that exactly the same quantities are provided by each spring. In these circumstances, the value of the mineral water under natural scarcities will be expressed in that price which just enables the whole supply to be taken off the market. To charge a price lower than this will necessitate rationing, or some would-be consumers going short. To charge a higher price will necessitate allowing some part of the supply to run to waste. We may expect the latter actually to take place. It will still be to the interests of owners to contrive scarcities in this way if the elasticity of demand is less than unity in the region of the price determined by natural scarcity; and the motives leading to the attainment of the price which is expected to produce the maximum receipts will still be operative.

Under duopoly, the smallest price-cut by A, assuming B's passivity, will lead to the whole of that part of the demand being transferred to him which is satisfied by the natural supply that he controls. If the initial actual supply is less than half the natural supply, A will obtain the whole of the custom but still, on the assumption of a very small cut, not dispose of the whole of the output of his spring. But B's passivity is inconceivable, no matter what the relationship of actual to natural supply. Retaliation or conformance to the lower price will still be the rule. B's power of retaliation will be as great but no greater than in the case of the duopolisation of commodities of no natural value. For even if he sells at below the price determined by natural scarcities, he will not be able to steal any more of A's custom. On the contrary, such a policy on his part will be likely to increase the demand for A's supply, because consumers who will not normally demand will absorb part of B's supply. It follows that others will have to go short, and some of those disappointed can be expected to look elsewhere for the supplies they need and so enhance the value of A's supply. In these conditions (which are, of course, hardly conceivable), price discrepancy will exist together with the rationing of half the supplies and the bidding up of the value of the other half. The implications of this are of the utmost importance. Whilst the continuous impending threat to price-cutters is equally present in the case of goods which are naturally scarce, a general outbreak of price-cutting such as is commonly called a "price war" will have no tendency (under our assumptions) to cause the ruin of owners of natural resources, or even severe losses to them. Indeed, the "ruinous" competition that is likely to be precipitated either by quarrels about the division of the market or from the external factors which we have yet to discuss may be regarded as the very force which will ensure the most complete availability to the community of Nature's gifts; and it will be the voluntary acquiescence of spring owners when confronted with such competition that will lead to this. The omission of our assumption (xii) that each spring provides the same natural quantity does not alter this conclusion. If A's spring provides only one-tenth and B's nine-tenths of the aggregate natural supply, once A is selling his full output for the highest sum it will fetch, and no part of B's supply has been allowed for some time to run to waste (and under assumption (iv), it cannot be held off the market), B will have no power to force *further* losses on A with a view to compelling him to practise tacit or deliberate collusion. Under oligopoly the same position can be seen to rule.

Let us now drop our assumption (iv) that the commodity cannot be accumulated or has perishable qualities and consider the case of the duopoly in which, instead of allowing the surplus to run to waste as output is restricted, B accumulates a large supply in a reservoir. The existence of an accumulated stock complicates but does not destroy the idea of natural value. The retained supply, being available for consumers if the owners are prepared to release it, must be brought into the reckoning. It is wrong to think of the price necessary to absorb the existing rate of *new* supply only as reflecting value under natural scarcity. We must think of any stocks being continuously added to the existing rate of output at that rate which, given the costs of storage and the rate of interest, will be most profitable to its owners[11] (assuming that they are not hoping to obtain benefits from aggression). The accumulation may be used, however, not in this way, but deliberately placed on the market at a more rapid rate in order to force a low price with retaliatory or punitive intention. It may be used by B, for example, to compel A to abandon his "ruinous competition." But A will know, under our assumptions, that the supplies that B is putting on the market cannot last for ever, and the attempt at his coercion by that policy is bound to fail. For A will accumulate until B's supplies are exhausted at the unnecessarily low price, and then dispose of his own stock in accordance with an estimate of his long-run interest.[12] The more drastic B's price-cut, the better for A, in the given circumstances, for the sooner will the "surplus" be absorbed. As soon as stocks have been disposed of, further accumulations by B will be possible only by a process which is to A's temporary advantage, and which may be regarded as a source of gain likely to countervail subsequent losses during the off-loading of B's accumulation. Thus, starting from an initial position of competition between owners placing the whole of their regular supplies on the market, and rationally liquidating any accumulation, we see that aggressive selling to force one or more of them into a tacit or deliberate monopoly is bound to fail. The motive to restrict in order to obtain a higher return will still be there, of course, but competition starting from this plane cannot be "ruinous." Under oligopoly, the power to use accumulations in order to ruin individual owners is even less conceivable than with duopoly, for under our assumption (xi) (the absence of discrimination), any price-cut would have to extend over the whole market, and the recalcitrant individual would receive no more damage than the others. The exclusion of assumptions (vi), (vii) and (viii) (consumers' knowledge and indifference, and suppliers' awareness) does not complicate the position to any extent. Under duopoly, B's attempt to capture A's goodwill (with a view to his coercion) by a secretly accumulated surplus will probably cause A, on becoming aware of the nature of these activities, to pursue a similar policy to that which we have seen he would be likely to follow if he possessed perfect knowledge from the start and consumers were completely mobile. We must expect A to follow with price-cuts whilst he is unaware of what B is doing. For we are assuming that he must get rid of the whole of his output and that he is not allowed to discriminate by charging lower prices to those of his customers who are tending to move. In the light of our assumption (xi), (of the proscription of discrimination), therefore, the values which cause marginal consumers to move will still determine price, in spite of consumers' immobility. When A does recognise B's aggressive policy, he may start accumulating the whole or part of his supply; but in view of consumers' immobility (assumptions (vi) and (vii) being omitted) we may assume that through his refusal to cut he will retain a gradually declining proportion of his former customers. B's accumulation having been spent, A will recommence selling and liquidating rationally his own reserves. But B, with his reservoir exhausted, will find that he has failed to capture any goodwill, unless two sets of prices rule in the market. If the price charged by both duopolists is the same at the margin, then, in view of assumption (xi), this margin will determine the price for the whole. There may remain, however, a price interval which marginal consumers at any moment may have failed to cross. But we must imagine them gradually to bridge the gulf; for we attribute some mobility to them when we consider the possibility of goodwill being captured. Thus B will cut continuously to avoid further accumulation of his supply and the price of A's supply will tend to be bid up as the range of potential purchasers expands. The tendency for the two prices to meet will be immensely strong even if there should be a definite personal preference for or prejudice against dealing with one or other of the owners. Hence, given some degree of consumers' immobility, the fact of accumulated stocks does not create conditions which make it possible for competition to become "ruinous" through the "theft" of goodwill. That is, it will not make possible a condition in which, say, half the supply, controlled by A, will sell for less than the other half, controlled by B, to an extent which can be regarded as likely to ruin either party.

So far we have assumed throughout (assumption (xi)) that price discrimination must not take place. But when discrimination is practised, under conditions in which goodwill can be a determining influence (i.e., in which assumptions (vi), (vii) and (viii) are absent), the imposition by certain owners, with or without accumulated stocks, of considerable losses on recalcitrant suppliers is conceivable. For instance, under duopoly, B may attempt to dissuade A from price-cutting by retaliating in those parts of the market only in which A's goodwill is strong. In these circumstances, the relative supplies of the two parties are of importance. If A's spring provides only one-tenth and B's nine-tenths of the aggregate natural supply, the fact of inertia in the market may enable B to undersell drastically to A's customers alone. That will result in the value per unit of A's supply being less than what the average value per unit of B's supply would be if the whole output were allowed on the market at a uniform price just low enough for its absorption. Such a process can clearly be used with coercive or punitive effect, either with a view to forcing A to follow a particular selling policy (or to force him to sell out), or else for some ulterior purpose, such as private spite. There will, however, be definite limits to the power of aggression in these circumstances. It is not very probable that the price of the supply selling in the area previously satisfied by the owner with the small supply will be for long much below the price determined by the natural scarcity of the whole. Heavy price-cuts in one section of the market are in practice likely to be infectious and gradually to spread their influence over the great bulk of transactions. The power to discriminate is more likely to work as a deterrent force making price-cutting by a small supplier trying to steal goodwill obviously unprofitable to him. A will know, for example, that if he cuts, B will follow by local or particular discrimination to prevent any filching of his customers. B will have little need to act aggressively because of the very strength of the tacit threat in his possession, for in any case A's natural supplies being only one-tenth of the whole, A's *relative* sacrifices are likely to be nine times as great as those of B. Under oligopoly similar conclusions are reached. *We must remember, however, that in all the above discussion we have noticed no reason why there should be a desire to initiate price-cuts.* If we exclude the case of the scramble for quotas, then only misjudgment, or the relaxation of assumption (ix) (that each owner wishes to maximise his receipts), seems likely to cause the breakdown of tacit monopoly under the assumptions that we have made. *The "external conditions" which may precipitate competition have not yet been noticed.*

Our conclusion that in the absence of discrimination aggressive selling cannot be "ruinous" to individuals, in the sense of destroying the value of natural productive resources that are scarce, clearly applies also to the value of productive equipment that happens to exist. No difference of principle arises in considering a natural spring providing a certain quantity of mineral water and a well sunk at a considerable expense which provides an identical supply.[13] Hence an investor in such a well, intervening in a situation in which the whole present output is being sold, will have nothing to fear from aggression on the part of the owners of the existing natural supply. It follows that desirable investment in immobile equipment will not be deterred. The investor will know, of course, that his own addition to the flow of the product will reduce the price; and it will be the expected *ultimate situation* that will determine his action.

We have now reached the stage at which those "external forces" that have already been referred to as precipitating competition in a field of tacit monopoly are being considered. Let us restore assumption (xi) under which discrimination is forbidden. It is then potential or actual interlopers who ruin the quiet restrictive activities of oligopolists seeking to maximise their receipts.[14] The willingness of interlopers to invade any such field will obviously depend upon how they expect existing sellers to react. Unlike the vested interest of present suppliers, the desire of the newcomers to share in the fruits of restriction cannot be regarded as a time-honoured fact. The quantity that they attempt to *insert in (we avoid the words "add to")* the aggregate supply will not appear to the others to be "reasonable," so that the likelihood of hostility against them, and a consequent "scramble for quotas" is certainly not small. If their intervention has been so gradual or tactful, however, as to attract no particular notice, we may find that in the interests of the preservation of "reasonable" prices, their profitable disposal of an output at the optimum price will be tolerated provided they show no disposition to expand. We may expect to find this often, in spite of there being no reason to suppose that the aggregate actual output will be greater[15] and in spite of the interlopers contributing to that output having pushed out part of the supplies of others. Indeed, the interlopers might be allowed to sell the whole of their supply if that amounted only to a very small proportion of the whole. But if the supply of a single interloper happened to constitute a large proportion of the whole we can hardly imagine the acceptance of his full output as "reasonable"; and for that reason it is not very likely that he would intervene with the idea of selling all that his well provides. So low might value fall if the whole supply were sold that, in some conditions, a rational interloper must be regarded as having intervened only in the expectation of being able to share in the benefits of restriction, in being able to capture by a species of respectable (and given probable reactions, *desirable*) blackmail, part of the proceeds of a tax on consumers which the oligopolists have levied. For this, he will need to have some reserve supply (or "capacity") in hand. He will require a greater flow to enable his retaliation in the event of the non-conformance or "unreasonableness" of the others. He will know (in practice vaguely realise) that his success will depend upon the acquiescence of others, in their own interests, in his invasion. He will count on pacifism paying the attacked party, or that situation existing in which it will pay to let bygones be bygones.

On the other hand, every imminent invasion of their sphere will have an important effect upon the original oligopolists' motives. They may realise (*a*) that if they sell continuously the whole of their supplies it will not pay any interloper to bore a well; (*b*) that if they continue their present policy of tacit restriction such an intervention will be inevitable; and (*c*) that in that event their receipts under tacit collusion with the interloper will be no greater than if the whole of their present supplies were put on the market. Thus, in view of the probability that reasonableness will be less likely with an increase of numbers, and that one successful interloper will encourage others, we can imagine oligopolists voluntarily selling a quantity greater than their private optimum, and in the extreme case, selling the full flow for what it will fetch. For the effect of the addition of a well to the source of supply will be greatly to reduce the value of the increased full supply (i.e., when none of it is allowed to run to waste). Hence the owners may believe their best policy to be to sell all that nature or their equipment provides; and once they are doing this, there will be no hindrance to the determination of values under natural scarcity, for subsequent interlopers will be completely protected. Moreover, given the absence of the right to discriminate, in view of the implications of our earlier discussion, it is improbable that aggression after the event (i.e., subsequent to the interloper's investment) will pay, especially against a small interloper. Hence the degree of restriction is likely to be reduced through potentially competing investment.

In the case in which the supplies of natural springs are inadequate from the point of view of popular demand and the cost of boring is low, then, even with the whole output being disposed of, further expenditure on boreholes will still be a profitable investment. The investor in these circumstances is absolutely protected against any deleterious effects from aggressive selling. It is when the existing price is above the level required to dispose of the present flow from springs plus the flow from existing wells, i.e., when part is running to waste or being accumulated, that a would-be interloper will hesitate, and his hesitation will be due to his realisation that if, following his entry, all the available supplies are thrown on the market, the price will then be too low to justify his contemplated investment.[16] Nevertheless, he may feel that for reasons that we have noticed, he can still count on the continuance of the ruling price, or some price not far short of that; and in those circumstances the prospective investment might be regarded as a legitimate speculation. Whilst fear of aggression among potential interlopers will therefore be greatest where tacit monopoly has produced a contrived scarcity by reducing the aggregate flow of a commodity, an entrepreneur may still see the probability of a small investment in the tacitly monopolised field being a good proposition; for he may rely, as we have seen, on existing suppliers not cutting their own throats in order to cut his. In this case the monopolists, duopolists, or oligopolists are likely to fix a price lower than the optimum but higher than the natural price in order to dissuade possible interlopers. This will result in a kind of equilibrium at a price above the natural, for there will be no tendency for independent investment to bring an equilibrium reflecting natural scarcities. Where this condition exists there must be present elements of "advantage of site and size," usually called "natural monopoly."

One case of this arises when the efficient scale of operations is so large that a particular area can be most cheaply served by one plant only. There will then be no obligation on its owner to sell the product or service at the price determined (under its efficient arrangements) by natural scarcity. Both the amount of fixed investment and the degree of utilisation of plant (i.e., the investment of mobile or "circulating" capital) will be determined by private, not social interest. To illustrate this with the simplest conceivable example, let us imagine our isolated community to be served, not by natural springs, but by a single well, constructed at a cost, which gives a certain supply. The owner knows that a further relatively small expenditure—say on pumps, will greatly add to its output; but judging the present flow to approximate to the optimum (from his point of view), he does not make this investment. Obviously no interloper knowing this to be the situation will intervene, for he will realise that the consequence will be that the former monopolist *will* make the further investment. The latter will then be in a position to produce a supply the sale of which will bring about a ruling price at which the available productive resources of society will be more profitably employable in other pursuits. Or, with a view to combating immediately any signs of interloping enterprise, the monopolist may purposely retain a reserve capacity. Thus the ability under these conditions to cut prices temporarily provides the power to deter competing investment and so protect existing monopoly. It is true that such a "natural monopolist" might be successfully "blackmailed" or "bluffed" along the lines suggested in the three previous paragraphs; and we may find him protecting himself against such a possibility by asking less than his optimum price as a permanent policy. But in his ability to *scare* off investment we have, nevertheless, the explanation of a form of threatened aggressive price-cutting which no type of anti-trust control resting upon the simple forbidding of discrimination can prevent.

The method of creating competitive institutions, and eliminating monopolistic institutions when natural monopolies or similar arrangements exist, is a difficult problem which we cannot now examine. The present writer has suggested elsewhere[17] that the aim must be to remove autonomy from the individual firm in respect of the amount of investment and the degree of utilisation of equipment and other resources, and to subject the entrepreneur more effectively to social (i.e., market) forces. That is only one part of the field of anti-trust control, however, and to deal with it adequately we should have to consider the whole field. A careful analysis of the principles of competitive institutions would, it is thought, lead to the conclusion that diffusion of initiative in respect of the power to take advantage of non-equilibrium in relation to natural scarcity is the fundamental principle. But we cannot now dwell on the prohibition of deliberate collusion or amalgamation. What our discussion has made clear is that *the prevention of "unfair competition" is a perfectly straightforward function of anti-trust tribunals.* The simple and effective proscription of price discrimination, either in its obvious or hidden forms, would have prevented, it seems to the writer, the greater part of the monopolistic abuses which have so curbed the colossal natural and technological resources of the United States.[18] That is the impression gathered by an observer viewing American experience through the printed word and from the detachment of a far-off country. What has confused popular and some instructed opinion has been the focusing of attention upon the rights of producers, a defect which the conscious acceptance of consumers' sovereignty as an ideal instead of a vague conception of the maximisation of social utility or welfare might have removed. Unfair competition has been thought of as unjustly deleterious to certain producers. But the producer as such does not need protection.[19] He has voluntarily taken the risk of meeting with retaliation in a régime which permits it.[20] He cannot plead that he has acted altruistically for it is impossible to plan economic institutions on the assumption that individuals will be motivated by altruism. The object of a law passed at any time to forbid "unfair competition" (i.e., price discrimination) must be regarded as that of protecting *subsequent* not *past* investors. Its purpose is to stimulate the *right distribution* of investment between different channels in the future; and the right distribution must be the decision of consumers' sovereignty. In the present writer's opinion, "injustice" to the producer can only be said to arise when he is "exploited" in the sense of being faced with a new or enhanced contrived scarcity of some co-operant resources subsequent to the immobilisation of his productive resources.[21] But that is a different point.

If the above analysis is valid, then it is plain that the implications, had they been understood by the framers and interpreters of anti-trust legislation, would have cleared away a whole mass of economic and juridical controversy. To some economists the central principle, namely the prohibition of discriminatory charging,[22] seems to have been obvious from subtle insight or sensitive intuition. This article has sought to demonstrate the truth of their views by an examination of the problem under the simplest conditions. There must be many a student in other countries who has viewed with as much dismay as disinterested American economists the results of judicial incompetence and political pressure which have frustrated the effective administration of the Sherman Act and its successors. If the present submergence of anti-trust legislation under "National Recovery" is to be permanent, the world may have lost one of America's greatest contributions to it, namely, experience in the art of creating competitive institutions.

Notes

1. W. Hutt, "Economic Method and the Concept of Competition," *South African Journal of Economics* 2 (March 1934), pp. 3-23.

2. W. Hutt, "Logical Issues in the Study of Industrial Legislation," *South African Journal of Economics* 3 (March 1935), pp. 30-1.

3. R. Liefmann, "Monopoly or Competition As the Basis of a Government Trust Policy," *Quarterly Journal of Economics* 29 (February 1915), pp. 308-25.

4. The power to buy or sell or otherwise compete aggressively may, of course, constitute the principal private advantage of large-scale operation in many cases, in that it enables the large concerns to preserve the power to buy and sell monopolistically.

5. It is useful to take *ordinary* water springs for the first stage of the discussion, because we are most of us used to considering ordinary drinking water as having an infinitesimally small exchange value. Cournot's example, in referring specifically to mineral water, reflects the fallacy that utility is independent of quantity. As, under competition, the mineral water would have had no value in his example, Cournot's argument would have been equally applicable to ordinary water.

6. Of course, the duopolist practicing this aggression will voluntarily suffer losses, but losses which, from the private standpoint, might be regarded as capital expenditure, for they will bring their return later.

7. This applies whether these contrived scarcities are based on the advantages of site and size (as under "natural monopoly"), conscious collusion, or the tacit collusion which we are now considering. In the case of a benevolent "natural monopolist," whose plant (or other resources) enjoys the advantages of site and size, there is no question of a threat, of course, to deter him from price-cutting. But for values determined by natural scarcities to rule for his product he would have to sacrifice income-rights for which he may have bid at a previous stage.

8. As a matter of fact, to say that consumers are indifferent is the same thing as saying that the most probable division of custom between the two sources will be equal. The idea is highly notional, being based, for instance, on a complete abstraction of the factor of situation (or distance). But we can imagine the two springs happening to be situated close together.

9. This appears to constitute the sole significance of the distinction between monopoly and duopoly on the one hand, and oligopoly (with any number of competitors, provided that no interlopers can intervene) on the other hand.

10. Here also we have an enlightening parallel with the case of collusive monopoly under actual conditions. Many a small producer who has exceeded his quota is allowed to remain in the cartel or is allotted a larger proportion of output as a bribe to retain his cooperation.

11. If we omit assumption (iii) that the water is provided at a regular rate, we must imagine fluctuating price tempered by the deliberate accumulation and depletion of stocks which are released so as to produce, as nearly as possible, the maximum aggregate return.

12. A's possible inability "to wait" is irrelevant as we have assumed that no expenditure is required to obtain the commodity that he sells. His private commitments are also practically irrelevant. The postponement of his receipts from sales

does not entail the cessation of his income, for *his* stocks will be mounting as B's stocks are dispersing. A may have to borrow on his stock at current valuations and pay interest; and B might threaten to force this burden on A.

13. It is convenient to make assumptions concerning such an investment which are in harmony with our earlier assumptions, namely, that the supply provided by a given borehole is fixed and cannot be added to except by further investment which produces a permanent expansion in natural supply. Part of the flow can still, of course, be allowed to run to waste. We assume also that each well is owned by one person and that no person owns more than one well. These assumptions enable us to avoid defining the "full utilization" of a piece of productive equipment, a task which would complicate exposition without affecting principles or conclusions. The idea of "full utilization" must obviously come in when we consider the *services* of plant, especially if it is not operated every day and for the whole twenty-four hours.

14. The interlopers may, of course, be some of the original suppliers who wish to sink new wells, but we are here assuming that no person owns or invests in more than one well. In practice the "external forces" are often expressed not through new interlopers, but through expansion of the plant of existing producers. Our assumption is made for simplicity of exposition. It does not affect the principle.

15. For the optimum price maximising aggregate receipts will be no different. We shall notice later the conditions in which a price intermediate between the optimum and the natural will rule.

16. In practice this circumstance is most often met with in the form of idleness, generally called "excess capacity" of plant, and not in the concrete form of the flow of a commodity partly running to waste.

17. W. Hutt, "Economic Method and the Concept of Competition."

18. Natural monopolies would still possess the power (although diminished) to control the amount of investment in them and the degree of utilization of their plant, even in the absence of discrimination. We must admit that our failure to discuss the question of the desirability or the reverse of price discrimination on other grounds must be regarded as a serious omission. But the circumstances in which it is defensible appear to be capable of definition, they are clearly recognizable, and, we believe, they are extremely rare.

19. There is a case for special protection through the courts of individuals or corporations when the prohibition of price discrimination is incapable of simple or common sense interpretation. A story is told of a wealthy American who was annoyed by a hairdresser and took his revenge by subsidizing a rival who followed him throughout the country and undercut him at "cut-throat" prices wherever he went until his ruin had been accomplished.

20. His interests may happen to coincide with those of the consumer, of course, in that laws which protect him in the short run may ultimately lead to the consumer's advantage.

206 • INDIVIDUAL FREEDOM

21. We can include in this category what may be called "development selling," namely, the temporary supply of co-operant resources at below the price determined by natural scarcity with a view to enticing exploitable investment in immobile form.

22. What constitutes discriminatory charging in certain cases (e.g., in the case of plants rendering *services* at different times, or in the case of "return journeys") may not be immediately obvious. The present article is, however, merely concerned to make clear the principle.

13 • *The Yield from Money Held*

My aim in this essay is to attempt to carry the tenor of Mises' teaching a step further in the field of monetary theory. A feature of his great contribution, *Human Action*, is its insistence that all goods and services have the same *scarcity* significance, i.e., that they all stand in an identical relation to human choice and exchange. It seems to me that money and monetary services ought to be included under this principle, in a manner in which Mises himself has not argued. In this field all economists have shared, I feel, in a hindering tradition which, had the logic of his approach been extended, Mises would have thrown off. I refer to the notion that money is "barren," "sterile," "unproductive," "offering a yield of *nil.*" This view is held today by economists of all schools. Yet practically without exception they talk of the "services" rendered by money or the "utilities" derived from money. It is in this respect that we find the clearest justification for Wicksell's confession that in the field of monetary theory, "diametrically opposed and sometimes self-contradictory views are defended by the most famous writers."[1] To the best of my knowledge the doctrine of the sterility of money has so far been subject to *explicit* challenge only by T. Greidanus.[2] The latter has, however, not yet explained the full significance of his "yield theory."[3]

In three articles published since 1952,[4] I have discussed an ambiguity in the concept of the "volume of money." We have to distinguish, I have

Reprinted with permission from *Freedom and Free Enterprise*, edited by Hans Sennholz. © 1954 by D. Van Nostrand, New York.

suggested, between the idea of *the aggregate amount of money measured in actual money units,* like pounds, dollars, francs, etc., and *the aggregate amount of money assets measured in "real terms,"* i.e., measured in units of constant value in terms of "things in general."[5] The former I regard as "containers" of varying amounts of the latter.[6]

The notion that money has a "yield of *nil*," i.e., that it differs from other assets in that it is "dead stock," persists, I think *in part* owing to the above-mentioned ambiguity. For one of the usual explanations of this supposed peculiarity of money relies on the fact that an increase in its "quantity" does not mean that there is any increase in "wealth" or "welfare" or "total utility." But this is true only of the number of money units or "containers" and not of what is contained in them. It is not true of the aggregate amount of money assets measured in real terms. Money so conceived is as productive as all other assets, and *productive in exactly the same sense.* And the fact that the number of "containers" (units) may be varied whilst *the aggregate amount* of what is contained in them may remain constant (or *vice versa*) in no way affects the truth that money assets offer prospective yields just as the rest of the assets possessed by individuals, firms, banks or governments. As objects of investment, they are chosen for the same reason that other objects are chosen. Thus, if their marginal prospective yield at any time is *below* that of other assets, it will pay to part with some of them, and if it is *above*, it will pay to acquire money assets up to the point at which the marginal prospective yield has fallen to the rate of interest. Now Mises himself, and several other economists, maintain explicitly that the amount of money which individuals and firms decide to hold is determined by the marginal utility of its services.[7] Yet for some reason they have not made the next small step needed to recognize this prospective yield (of "utilities"), which invites the holding of money, as the normal return to investment.

The prospective yield from investment in money assets consists, I suggest, (a) of a prospective *pecuniary yield*, in which case the money assets are producers' goods;[8] or (b) of a prospective *non-pecuniary yield* in personal convenience, in which case the money assets are consumers' capital goods;[9] or (c) of a prospective "real," i.e., *non-pecuniary*, speculative yield, in which case the assets are producers' goods, whether held privately or in the course of business. In the case of (a) and (b), the yield is derived in the form of technical monetary services of various kinds, which permit the most economic acquisition of other factors of production or goods for consumption. In the case of (c), the yield is derived in the form of the greater command over non-money assets which a *unit* of money is expected to have at some later period. As we shall see, these statements are all *implied* by Mises' teaching, but never expressed by him in terms of prospective yield. In the following pages, I shall try to support my thesis that it is logically correct, and appropriate from the standpoint of exposition, to refer to the prospective yield or return from the holding of money assets, just as one does from the holding of non-money assets. I shall do so through an examination of the principal arguments which have been used by economists since the earliest times to explain why money has *no* yield, pecuniary or otherwise.

I am inclined to think that the tradition which I am questioning arose originally through the influence of Locke upon Adam Smith. The latter's description of "ready money . . . which a dealer is obliged to keep by him unemployed," as so much "dead stock, which . . . *produces nothing* either to him or to his country,"[10] gave influential emphasis to a bad precedent. Locke had three times used the very same words of money, "produces nothing." Unlike land, which produces something valuable to mankind, said Locke, "money is a barren thing"; and yet it was, he argued, subject to the same laws of value as other commodities.[11]

But the idea is ancient. Several writers have attributed it to Aristotle,[12] for he condemned usury on the grounds that "the birth of money from money" was "the most unnatural" mode of making money.

Edwin Cannon insisted that it is by no means certain that Aristotle thought money *was* barren, but merely that he thought it *ought to be*.[13] Wicksteed pointed out that Dante, following Aristotle, emphasized the unnaturalness of money breeding money, by expressly associating usurers with sodomites![14] Bacon (who argued for the toleration of usury) said, "They say that it is against nature for money to beget money,"[15] but did not explain whether "they" meant that it was immoral or impossible. Shakespeare, in the same context of the controversy over usury, made Antonio, in *The Merchant of Venice*, refer to "a breed of barren metal."[16] We can hardly blame Shakespeare for what he made one of his characters say; yet through this passage, Bonar agreed, "a wrong twist" was probably given to Aristotle's meaning.[17] And Bentham, facetiously[18] ridiculing what Aristotle was supposed to have held, alleged that the "celebrated heathen" philosopher described money as barren because he "had never been able to discover, in any one piece of money, any organs for generating any other such piece."[19]

Now although this discussion of the legitimacy of usury continued to be clouded by the confusion of the concept of money with that of capital (all money is capital, but not all capital is money), it appears to have been responsible for the continuing and still current fallacy that "money does not multiply itself," as do other forms of productive capital. And we must, I fear, blame either Locke, whose failure to throw off the ancient and barren notion of "barren metal" thereby perpetuated it, or else Adam Smith, who was too uncritically indebted to Locke (or Aristotle directly) and propagated the insidious fallacy.

Locke's influence was all the greater by reason of the impressive rational treatment which he devoted to the role and functions of money. He had a remarkably modern grasp of the tasks which money has to perform.[20] Indeed, he perceived clearly what we call today the "institutional" factors determining the demand for money."[21] And most interesting of all, he saw that money had "the nature of land," the interest on land being but the rent.[22] In using these words, he seemed to come very near to stating the very truth for the recognition of which I am now pleading; for, he said, the *"income"* of land is called "rent" and that of money, "use" (see page 221). A little later on, however, he apparently remembered Aristotle (or Antonio!) and wrote: "Land produces something new and profitable, and of value to mankind; but money is a barren thing and produces nothing."[23] In part, the confusion here seems to be due to the narrow view of what constitutes productiveness; although, as I have said, the old confusion between the concepts of money and capital seems mainly to blame. He thought of money *lent* as productive to the lender, but presumably not productive to the borrower. Yet there is similarly no *direct* pecuniary return from land unless it is hired out to someone else. Does that mean, then, that our land brings us no return, pecuniary or real, when it is not lent? Obviously not. Of course, if one finds that *the whole of* one's cash balance is unnecessary (i.e., if some part of the balance offers no speculative or convenience yield valued at above the rate of interest), and one then fails to make other use of the redundant sum, or to lend it to someone who can, the surplus *will* remain "barren," just like unutilized land. A trader's stocks of *anything* may be wastefully large. There is nothing unique about money in this respect. It was owing to Locke's failure to make the small further jump necessary, and to state that the productiveness of money does not differ in any material manner from that of land, that we may have the origin of the root fallacy which has confused monetary theory ever since. The subsequent tradition has been to regard money as having "resource value" or capital value, but no "service value."

Between Locke and Adam Smith, various writers perceived the *usefulness* of money, e.g., Cantillon and Hume, but they failed to see that "usefulness" is a mere synonym for "productiveness" or "yield."[24]

Adam Smith's contribution on the point, although obviously inspired by that of Locke, differed slightly from it. At times, he regarded money as "the instrument of commerce,"[25] but at other times he *denied* that it was "a tool to work with."[26] "Gold and silver," he wrote elsewhere, "whether in the form of coin or of plate, are utensils . . . as much as the furniture of the kitchen."[27] But he would not have described furniture as "productive." This "dead stock," he said of money, "is a very valuable part of the capital of the country, which produces nothing to the country."[28] His acceptance of such a paradox can probably be explained, as with Locke, by the narrow conception of "productivity" of his day. "The gold and silver money which circulates in any country may," he said, "very properly be compared to a highway, which, while it circulates and carries to market all the grass and corn of the country, produces itself not a single pile of either."[29] To some extent he was, I think, misled through his desire to refute the fallacies of the Mercantilists. He wanted to show the folly of accumulating money in the belief that it represented "wealth," and was accordingly led to the assertion that, whilst it "no doubt, makes always a part of the national capital, . . ." it is "always the most unprofitable part of it."[30]

It is surprising that, as the eighteenth-century view of productivity was abandoned, the essential yield from money assets did not come to receive explicit recognition. But as Greidanus has pointed out, Ricardo failed to recognize that money is needed, not only for payments but to be kept on hand.[31] Senior recognized that money was "of the highest utility"[32] but contended that its use gave "no pleasure whatever." He added, "Its abundance is a mere inconvenience" because we should have to carry more of it.[33] Obviously, he was here thinking of what I have called "money units."

J. S. Mill's insight was not very much deeper. He recognized that money assets had a task, he referred to "the quantity of work done" by them, he even spoke of their "efficiency," and he fully understood that the demand for such assets was a function of the amount of traffic which they facilitated.[34] But he confused the notion of "rapidity of circulation" with that of "efficiency." He did not realize that, *certis paribus*, if units of money circulated more slowly, that would be due to there being more work, not less work, for them to do.

Cairnes (like Adam Smith) was led astray through an attempt at easy refutation of mercantilist ideas.[35] He wanted to answer Tooke, who had discussed *metallic money* as though it were, in itself, a source of productive energy, and who had argued that "an addition to the quantity of money" was "the same thing as an addition to the Fixed Capital of a country"—as equivalent in its effects to "improved harbours, roads and manufactories."[36] But to deny that the acquisition of specie is necessarily a wise form of investment is not to deny that money is instrumental capital. Nor does the fact that it may take a wasteful form (e.g., gold coin, when convertible paper would serve equally well) imply that money assets as such do not provide a flow of valuable services.[37]

Böhm-Bawerk was surprisingly contented with the naïvety of Aristotle, whose argument he summed up as follows: "Money is by nature incapable of bearing fruit."[38] And yet he recognized that interest "may be obtained from any capital, . . . from goods that are barren as well as from those that are naturally fruitful."[39] The explanation of the paradox again appears to lie in the dogged persistence of the crude notion of productiveness, a notion which was responsible for Böhm-Bawerk's rejection of the "use theories" of interest. He twice quoted the same trenchant passage from Hermann in which it was pointed out that "land, dwellings, tools, books, *money*, have a durable use value. Their use . . . can be conceived of as *a good in itself*, and may obtain for itself an exchange value which we call interest."[40] But this repeated quotation was merely for the purpose of refutation. To Böhm-Bawerk, "use" meant "physical" or "material" services only.[41] "For any 'use of goods' . . . other than their natural material services," he said, "there is no room, either in the world of fact, or in the world of logical ideas."[42] It is "theoretically inadmissible to recognise relations as real goods."[43]

Von Wieser mentioned various reasons why holdings of ready money were indispensable or speculatively profitable;[44] but he thought that the "advantage in value" is only *realized* by such holdings when the object is ultimately acquired for which the money was accumulated.[45] And although he used phrases which at first suggest that he had perceived that money units are useful or necessary for reasons of the same economic nature as other productive assets or durable consumption assets,[46] and although he clearly regarded money as part of circulating capital,[47] he used his chief concepts in a far from rigorous manner. One can hardly feel that he was visualizing, even dimly, the prospective yield which induces the acquisition of money assets.[48]

Wicksell accepted explicitly Aristotle's contention that money is "sterile."[49] It "does not itself enter into the processes of production," he said.[50] Yet, in discussing the various functions of money (e.g., as resources to meet unforeseen disbursements), he discussed also the factors determining its average period of "rest" or "idleness," notions which suggest that it must have periods of work or activity. He held that money was held "not to be consumed . . . *or to be employed in technical production*, but to be exchanged for something else. . . ."[51] He did not explain why the fact that money is not consumed, or intended to be exchanged for something else, should prevent it from providing continuous services in production.[52] But in criticizing Menger for his false distinction between "money on the wing" and "money in hand," he wrote, "Some money may often lie untouched for years in the till, though it has not, on that account, ceased to serve as a means of circulation."[53] Here, surely, is an admission that money in the till is *providing continuous services*, that it is *not economically idle*, or "resting," and that its usefulness is not concentrated into the moment at which it is spent.[54]

Marshall referred to the services (without using this word) rendered by holdings of currency, in making business "easy and smooth,"[55] and discussed the balancing of the "advantages" of holding resources in this form with the "disadvantages" of putting more of a person's resources into a form "in which they yield him no *direct* income *or other benefit*."[56] But somehow he did not see that he was comparing one "advantage" with another "advantage," i.e., one end or means with another end or means. It certainly seems that he also was in some measure misled by the realization that a mere increase in the number of *money units* (pounds, francs, dollars, etc.) does not, in itself, result in an increase in the flow of monetary services. He said, "Currency differs from other things in that an increase in its quantity exerts no direct influence on the amount of services it renders."[57] That view, combined with the influence of the "barren money" tradition, appears to account for his insistence that the holding of resources in the form of currency "locks up *in a barren form* resources that might yield an income of gratification if invested, say, in extra furniture; or a money income if invested in extra machinery or cattle."[58] *This contrast* of furniture and money (as opposed to Adam Smith's *identification* of furniture with money) curiously failed to suggest to him, or his critics and disciples, that he was making a false distinction. Money assets (held as consumers' capital goods) render non-pecuniary gratifications just like those rendered by furniture.

How much wiser was Edwin Cannan's insight, in his *Modern Currency:* "Our need for currency is analogous to our need for houses," he said.[59] And he was, I feel, ahead of his contemporaries in his recognition, from the beginning, that the demand for money is essentially *a demand to hold.*[60] Nevertheless, the passage quoted seems to be inconsistent with what he wrote elsewhere. Thus, in his *Money,* he wrote at one point in the traditional way, that "people only want money in order to buy other things with it. . . ."[61] In reality, people want money so as to be in a position to acquire other things *at the most profitable time, or at the most convenient time.* Had it been put this way to him, Cannan, like anyone else, would have agreed at once.[62] As things are, after having recognized that the services of money are analogous to those of a house, he wrote that holdings of money "are not *directly* productive."[63] People would not diminish their holdings "without reason," he continued, "because it would, they believe, be inconvenient to have less in hand." But cash in hand and at the bank does not differ in this respect from any type of stock in trade. The main difference is that, in the case of money stocks, it is easier to rectify any mistaken judgment which has led to surplus stocks (but less easy to rectify any deficiency).

Wicksteed (agreeing with his interpretation of Aristotle) illustrated what he thought was "the exact nature of a circulating medium" as "something which X, when he has given Y something that Y wants, is willing to receive in exchange *though he has no use for it himself,* because he knows that he can, in his turn, get something that he does want in exchange for it."[64] No article, he contended, which is accepted as a medium of exchange, occupies "on its own merits . . . such a place on (people's) relative scale as would justify the exchange."[65] But if we had "no use for" money, would we not always part with it immediately we got it, so that the velocity of circulation would be infinite? The fact that we hold money assets for any period at all indicates that, although we do not want to use these assets *in any other way,* their services *do* occupy a place on our scale of preferences, just like the services of all the other capital resources which we refrain from exchanging.[66]

Cassel recognized that "an object in general demand" which develops "spontaneously into a general medium of exchange . . . naturally acquires a *new attraction,* in virtue of *its new property.*"[67] But he did not represent this "new attraction," or the "new property," as a new and additional *use* (personal or business); and on the next page he employed the words, "merely to be used later for exchange with another commodity."[68]

Robertson (Sir Denis H.), in spite of his highly independent and original approach to the question, has never torn himself away from the tradition which regards "idle money" as unproductive. The following passage from the 1947 edition of his delightful textbook is not one of the "little bits of specially dead wood" which he cut out of the 1928 version.

> . . . The value of money is (within limits) a measure of the usefulness of any one unit of money to its possessor, but not to society as a whole: while the value of bread is also a measure (within limits) of the *social* usefulness of any one loaf of bread. And the reason for this peculiarity about money is the fact that nobody generally speaking wants it except for the sake of the control which it gives over other things.[69]

Again I ask, then why is the velocity of circulation not infinite?

Pigou, in *The Veil of Money*, refers to the damage which would be inflicted on us if we lost the services of money. It would be just as if roads and railways were destroyed.[70] But he similarly insists that money is "only useful *because* it exchanges for other things," and he accepts the tradition that "a larger quantity does not, as with other things, carry more satisfaction on its back than a smaller quantity, but the same satisfaction." Nevertheless, he differs from previous writers (with the exception of Greidanus and the possible exception of Cannan)[71] because he makes it clear that by "quantity of money" he means "the *number of units of money* embodied" in the "instrument" or "institution" of money (Pigou's italics.) The mere fact, however, that a particular economic good is capable of being diluted is no proof that it is not useful or productive. Milk does not cease to be useful because its adulteration does not increase its gross usefulness.[72]

Pigou has recourse also to a metaphor which previous writers have used, namely, that of comparing money to the oil in a machine. He refers to it as a "lubricant."[73] Now a lubricant is always *consumed*, whereas money assets are economically durable. If we use this metaphor, then, we must regard money assets as the resources which supply a continuous flow of lubrication. The comparison then succeeds in suggesting the continuous yield which money assets offer. But it may still leave the wrong impression that the services of money consist in "circulation."[74]

Keynes adopted the Marshallian view of money being resources, but barren resources (although Marshall seems to have been nearer than Keynes to a perception of the essential productiveness of money assets). Yet the terminology of *The General Theory* suggests, in itself, an awareness of the continuous services of money assets; for it appears at first to be conferring a definite name upon the yield which is expected to flow from an investment in such assets, namely, "liquidity."[75] Certainly, liquidity is regarded as (a) something valuable and (b) something continuously received or enjoyed. This is implicit in the contention that we *want* a "reward" for parting with it for any given length of time, and that we *shall be* "rewarded" for so doing. "The power of disposal" over money assets, said Keynes, although it offers "a potential convenience or security," and although people are "ready to pay something" (a "liquidity premium") for this advantage, brings forth, "so to speak, nothing . . . in the shape of output."[76] But if the capital value of my till is £ 100 and the average amount of cash in the till is also £ 100, may they not be expected to make an equal contribution to my output? However, Keynes contended that the liquidity which is provided continuously by *money held*, and for which people are prepared to pay a premium, represents a yield of *nil*. The holders of money are envisaged as refusing to part with this yield of *nil* unless they are paid the rate of interest.[77]

Keynes built a heavy structure on this thesis that money assets are absolutely sterile. So much is this so, that Greidanus actually contrasts him with Marshall. Greidanus contends that Keynes' view—first expressed in his *Tract*—that money has no utility apart from its exchange value, although supported by quotations from Marshall,[78] completely overlooked "the advantages of holding currency" which Marshall stressed.[79] "The place Marshall would have assigned to the 'advantages,' Keynes in his equation allots to the number of consumption units we wish to buy in a certain period."[80] But the fact that Keynes did not realize that his views about the services of money diverged so fundamentally from those of his great teacher is surely due to Marshall's own exposition reflecting some conceptual confusion.[81]

Keynes' acknowledged followers have, as far as I am aware, failed to examine or test this crucial stone in his foundations. Apart from the false impressions created through his having excluded the acquisition of assets which provide liquidity from the concept of "investment," there remains this notion that money assets differ from other assets in that they do not multiply. For instance, L. Tarshis, in a 1948 exposition of Keynesianism, contends that, against the advantages of liquidity, "the holder of money must set the disadvantage that it does not multiply, that his wealth held in that form does not grow."[82] Of course, it does multiply in the sense that any agent of production provides valuable services which may be embodied into cumulable resources. The services of consumers' capital goods (including cash balances) *are* always consumed; but those of producers' goods (including cash balances) are incorporated into wanted things with exchange value. That is why they are acquired or retained.

Even Mises, who has so clearly perceived and emphasized the essential homogeneity of the scarcity concept, has not yet rejected the traditional view. Money, he says, is "an economic good,"[83] but neither a producer's nor a consumer's good.[84] It is not acquired by people "for employment in their own production activities,"[85] and it is "not a part of capital; it produces no fruit."[86] Although "indispensable in our economic order . . . [money] is not a physical component of the social distributive apparatus in the way that account books, prisons, or fire-arms are."[87] Adam Smith said that money was unproductive because it was like a highway.[88] But Mises would insist that a highway *is* productive. Money, he says a little later, does not derive its value from that of its products, like other products, "for no increase in the welfare of the members of a society can result from the availability of an additional quantity of money."[89] Now it is true (as he puts it in his *Human Action*) that "*the services money renders* can be neither improved nor impaired by changing the supply of money,"[90] for he is here referring to *the number of money units*. But it is not true that the aggregate stock of all commodities, securities or tokens which can serve the purposes of a medium of exchange and which are demanded for that purpose, does not contribute to "welfare" in proportion to its value. When society decides to use assets to a greater extent for the monetary services which they can perform, that *does* result in a preferred use of all scarce resources and an increase in "welfare" in that sense. Money assets held provide valuable services (utilities), and they do derive their value from their power to render these services. The fact that some assets held for medium of exchange purposes may have value because they can be used for other purposes also (e.g., a gold coin) does not affect this truth.

It may be objected that, when the assets held are mere tokens, as with currency notes and demand deposits, their value is derived, not from the value of their services, but (a) from their market convertibility into goods in general or (b) from their contractual or legal convertibility into a monetary metal or other currencies. But in the absence of *faith* in convertibility in some such sense, the assets would be incapable of rendering a medium of exchange services. They could not constitute money. It remains true, then, that we part with non-money goods and services in order to acquire money because we judge that money can render us services; and we hold so much of it as renders services which we value more highly than those rendered by non-money assets.

Far from denying the productiveness of money assets held, however, Mises constantly stresses their "services." And in a most lucid passage he describes the nature of their *productiveness*[91] (although without using this word). He insists that "what is called storing money is a way of *using* wealth."[92] One's holdings of money do not represent "an unintentional remainder," he says. Their amount "is determined by deliberate demand."[93] Money is "appraised on its own merits, i.e., the *services* which each man expects from holding cash."[94] And it does not perform its task by circulating, but by being held. Thus, he says: "Money is an element of change, not because it circulates but because it is kept in cash holdings."[95] Indeed "there is no fraction of time in between in which the money is not a part of an individual's or a firm's cash holding, but just in 'circulation'."[96] And although it is true that people are continuously acquiring money in order continuously to part with it, they accumulate it in the first place "in order to be ready for the moment in which a purchase may be accomplished."[97] For this reason, he *denies* that there is a difference between money and vendible goods.

I get the impression therefore that, in his *Human Action*, Mises is on the point of saying that it is merely the *pecuniary* yield which is missing from the *private* holding of money assets.

H. S. Ellis, in an early work on *German Monetary Theory* (1934), also comes remarkably near to stating the correct principle—so near, indeed, that it looks almost as though, having prepared for combat, he is unwilling actually to clash with the great weight of authority against him. He certainly appears to be trying to escape the conclusions of his own analysis. Thus, he recognizes the "flow of utilities" from money holdings and says that this flow "appears to the producer indirectly as a *plus* in quantity of product ascribable to his possessing a perfectly liquid asset and to the consumer as a *plus* in satisfactions in the form of convenience. . . ."[98] Moreover, he realizes that the circulation of money "*terminates* the flow of services. . . ."[99] On all these points, he is well ahead of most writers. Yet at the same time he wants to "preserve the undeniably separate character of monetary *services*,"[100] partly for reasons which I do not follow, but partly because he feels that money assets as such, although providing services or utilities, cannot be properly regarded as part of the aggregate assets of the community. This is so, he says, because it would be double counting, such as would result if one included mortgages or stocks and shares as well as the assets they represent as part of society's aggregate capital.[101]

But to obtain the goods which money is said to "represent," one must *exchange* money assets for non-money assets, whereas, if a company is liquidated, the shareholders do not *exchange* assets, i.e., they do not *buy* the capital resources of the firm: they receive them without any exchange taking place (in practice after the assets are realized for money). Similarly, if a mortgage is foreclosed, there is no *exchange* of assets. Money assets do not, then, "represent" *in the same sense* the assets for which they can be exchanged. They are themselves assets which are just as productive (although in a different way) as those for which they are exchanged.[102] To appreciate this, one must try for a moment to forget about the number of units into which these assets are divided and to think of their aggregate amount in real terms.

As far as I know, only one economist has come at all close to *an actual enunciation* of what I regard as the true theory of the yield of money assets, namely, Greidanus, who has significantly described his theory, "the yield theory."[103] But his contributions on this subject appear to have had little influence upon other economists, whilst his treatment has not brought out explicitly what I conceive to be the full basic truth—the fact that money assets are not only subject to the same laws of value as other scarce things, but are equally productive in all intelligible senses.

Surely the reality is that, although money is always held (except perhaps by misers) with a view to its being ultimately passed on to others, the act of passing it on is merely the *culmination* of a service (technical or speculative) which it has been rendering to the possessor. Indeed, the transfer itself occupies a mere moment whilst the services which flow from the possession of money are continuous over time. The essence of all these services is *availability*. In the terminology which I suggested in my *Theory of Idle Resources*,[104] money assets are not unemployed or resting when they are in our pockets, or in our tills, or in our banking accounts, but in *pseudo-*idleness, like a piano when it is not being played, or a fireman or a fire engine when there are no fires. If it could be shown that there exist various forms of wasteful idleness in money which could be classed as *withheld capacity*, or which correspond, say, to a trader's redundant stocks (which, through mismanagement, he fails to realize), we could rightly talk of "idle money," but not otherwise. And the fact that money units may be held speculatively does not mean that they are not being *used*. Stocks of goods retained because their sale now would, it is anticipated, realize less than their sale later on, including all such goods[105] in warehouses and shops, are normally *being used*, in the course of the production of "time utilities." The same applies to money units. When speculatively held, they represent money *in use*.[106]

Hence money does not do its work by circulating. The common analogies of "the circulation of the blood," or "the oil of a machine" are both bad analogies. Because money units are exchange media, they just happen to change ownership more than other types of assets. If we imagine that the work of money is circulation, then we must conclude that money is always idle; for the transfer of money must be regarded as instantaneous![107] It has been suggested that, if people generally were paid quarterly instead of weekly, the demand for money would increase because more money would "be kept idling about at any one time."[108] That is quite the wrong way of putting it. There would be more work for money units to do,[109] more *monetary services* would be required, and more *money* would therefore be required. Changes in the average interval between purchases (i.e., changes in the velocity of circulation of money units) do not mean changes in the average period of *idleness* of those units, but changes in their average period of *service* to each holder, which is a very different thing.

During an inflation there might *appear* to be an enormous demand for money assets in the sense that people want them *for periods of time which they intend to keep as short as possible*. In such circumstances, in spite of a multiplication of transactions, and in spite of increased circulation, the amount of work actually needed from money assets falls off. Each money unit becomes less productive because the real yield in convenience, etc., is *diminished* by a real loss. Certainly, people still want money units "for what they will buy," but they value them less than ever.[110]

It may be objected that the nature of money is such that it *does* do all its work in instantaneous skips from buyer to seller, or from debtor to creditor, or from giver to receiver. The objection may be answered by means of a comparison with a climber's rope. Can it be said that the rope on which the climber is belayed is of service to him only when he actually loses his grip and dangles on it? Obviously not, for without the security it provides, he would almost certainly not have been attempting that particular climb.[111]

Some may feel that I am stressing a point which is of verbal rather than of substantial importance. But as Greidanus has pointed out, in the minds of the Keynesians, the failure to recognize the real but non-pecuniary yield enjoyed has led to material fallacies. Once the productiveness of money assets is recognized, the notion that the rate of interest is determined by the demand for and supply of *money assets*, or the demand for and supply of the *services of money assets* ("liquidity"), ceases to have meaning. And the modifications of that theory, like the various compromise revisions of Keynes' theory of interest by his disciples, become equally untenable. For if money assets are demanded, like all other assets, up to the point at which their marginal prospective yield has fallen to the rate of interest, it becomes obvious that the demand for and supply of merely one category of capital assets cannot be held to be the determinants of the ratio between the value of the pure services of assets in general and their capital value, which is the best way of conceiving of the rate of interest. If interest is envisaged (as Keynes regarded it) as the "reward" for not hoarding, it has to be accepted equally as the "reward" for not investing in each and every other productive field. Or, more generally, the "reward" for not investing in any productive field (including that of money assets) is the "average" or "general" return which can be expected from all other fields of investment—allowance made for entrepreneurial remuneration.[112]

It might be argued that there *is* one respect in which money assets are different, namely, that their *real* volume or stock is not determined by their being produced and consumed. That is, whereas services may be embodied into non-money assets for replacement or net accumulation purposes, this is impossible with money (although the number of *money units* could be affected by the production of any commodity into which such units are contractually or legally convertible—e.g., gold, under the gold standard). The truth is, however, that money is in exactly the same position as certain other non-money assets in this respect. Thus, consider the case of land, in the sense of site. With the growth of population and the expansion of the productive purposes to which land can be put, its aggregate value in real terms will increase. Similarly (and *ceteris paribus*) the real value of money assets will increase to the same extent under such circumstances.[113] But the *services* of money assets *are* produced and, like all other services, they are either consumed or embodied into products.

In conclusion, I suggest that if we understand that the demand for money assets is a demand for *productive resources*, we are in a better position to grasp the nature of the difficult problems which arise owing to (a) *uncertainties about* the future value of the money *unit* (in practice, uncertainties about what governments or monetary authorities will do) or (b) (less important and rather less difficult) realized changes in the value of the money unit.

Notes

1. Wicksell, *Lectures on Political Economy* (London: Routledge and Sons, 1934), II, p. 190.

2. T. Greidanus, *The Value of Money* (London: Staple Press, 1950).

3. Mises has criticized Greidanus' work on the grounds that an analysis of the motives which lead people to keep money on hand cannot explain purchasing power without bringing in the notions of cash holding and the demand for and supply of money. But I have interpreted Greidanus as meaning that the "yield" he stresses *is* the return to the *holding* of money.

4. In *The South African Journal of Economics* as follows: *The Nature of Money*, 20 (September 1952), pp. 56-60; *The Notion of the Volume of Money*, 20 (September 1952), pp. 231-41; *The Notion of Money of Constant Value*, 21 (September 1953), pp. 215-26, and (December 1953), pp. 341-53.

5. The definitions which I have found useful differ from those which Mises employs, in that the term *money assets* as I use it covers all assets (tokens or commodities) the value of which is affected by reason of their being demanded for their "liquidity," i.e., for the *medium of exchange* services which they can perform. Commodities and securities which perform monetary services and other functions as well are included in the proportion to which they are money. On this point, see Hutt, *The Nature of Money*, p. 61.

6. Some of the difficulties arising from the concept of real terms are discussed in Hutt, *The Notion of Money of Constant Value*.

7. E.g., L. Von Mises, *Human Action* (New Haven: Yale University Press, 1949).

8. E.g., cash in the till, which offers prospective *pecuniary* yields in exactly the same way that the site, or the buildings, or the materials, or the labor necessary in business offer pecuniary yields.

9. E.g., the notes or cash in one's purse or the balance in one's personal current account, the yield from which is in terms of "gratifications," just as with one's furniture or house.

10. A. Smith, *The Wealth of Nations* (New York: P. F. Collier, 1902).

11. J. Locke "Some Considerations of the Consequences of the Lowering of Interest . . . , 1691." In Locke, *Works* (London: Th. Tegg, 1801), pp. 36-7. Locke discussed payment for the use of money, but then became caught in the persistent confusion between capital and money which was so common before Mill's time.

12. Aristotle, *Politics*, I (10), 1258b, Jewett translation. Undoubtedly, Adam Smith was also directly influenced by Aristotle's remarkable insight into the nature of money. Senior pointed out that Adam Smith used a phrase which would serve as a translation of a phrase in Aristotle's *Ethics*.

13. See the delightful symposium, "Who Said 'Barren Metal?'," by Cannan, Ross, Bonar, and Wicksteed, in *Economica* 2 (June 1922), pp. 105-11. This paragraph is based on that symposium.

14. Ibid., p. 109.

15. Ibid., p. 107.

16. Ibid., p. 105.

17. Ibid., p. 107. Bonar also pointed out that Aristotle's ideas on the subject had come down *via* the canonists.

18. Böhm-Bawerk described it as "witty," Cannan as "coarse."

19. Cannan et al., "Who Said 'Barren Metal?'," p. 105.

20. Thus, he recognised "the necessity of a certain proportion of money to trade" (Locke, "Some Considerations . . . ," p. 21); he saw that the necessary proportion "depends not barely on the quantity of money, but the quickness of its circulation" (ibid., p. 23); he explained that a coin could "rest in the same hand one hundred days together," which would make it "impossible exactly to estimate the quantity of money needful in trade" (ibid., p. 23); and he gave a surprisingly complete treatment of the indispensability of money as an instrument in the hands of different classes of the community (laborers, farmers, tradesmen, landholders, brokers, consumers, etc.) (ibid., pp. 24, et seq.).

21. For example, he wrote: "It were better for trade, and consequently for everybody, (for money would be stirring, and *less would do the business*) if rents were paid by shorter intervals . . . A great deal less money would serve for the trade of a country" (ibid., p. 27, my italics). If he had said, instead, that there would have been *less work for money to do*, he would have been much nearer to enunciating a really satisfactory theory.

22. Ibid., p. 33.

23. Ibid., p. 36. On other occasions he appeared to waver. Thus, at another place he actually *implied* that money is productive, although *less frequently* than land. He referred to "the many and sometimes long *intervals of barrenness*, which happen to money more than land. Money at use, when returned to the hands of the owner, usually lies dead there, till he gets a new tenant for it" (ibid., p. 65, my italics). But as we shall see, money does not work by circulating.

24. See Greidanus, *The Value of Money*, pp. 21-31.

25. Adam Smith, *The Wealth of Nations*, Vol. I, p. 396. Hume also used the word "instrument" for money.

26. Ibid., Vol. I, p. 279.

27. Ibid., Vol. I, p. 304.

28. Ibid., Vol. I, p. 304. (He repeated these words—"dead stock," "produces nothing"—in the same paragraph.)

29. Ibid., Vol. I, p. 304.

30. Ibid., Vol. I, p. 404.

31. Greidanus, *The Value of Money*, p. 39.

32. Senior, *Industrial Efficiency and Social Economy*.

33. Ibid., p. 41.

34. J. Mill, *Principles* (New York: Appleton and Co., 1892).

35. T. Cairnes, *Political Essays* (New York: A. M. Kelley, 1967).

36. Tooke, *History of Prices* (London: Longman, Orme, Brown, Green, and Longmans, 1838-57), Vol. 6, p. 216. He elaborated on Adam Smith's comparison of money to a highway, and argued that more money was equivalent to broader, smoother, and longer roads.

37. Cairnes argued (assuming a metallic currency) that if a merchant "can safely dispense with a portion of his ready cash, he is enabled, with the money thus liberated . . . to add to his productive capital. . . . On the other hand, if he finds it necessary to increase his reserve of cash, his productive capital must be proportionally encroached upon . . ." (Cairnes, *Essays*, p. 92.) And "precisely the same may be said of the currency of a nation"; for "the chief advantage of a good banking system consists . . . in enabling a nation to reduce within the narrowest limits this unproductive portion of its stock" (meaning metallic stock) (ibid., pp. 92-3). Unfortunately, he was not led to face the paradox that, even under such a banking system, the metallic backing, reduced to these "narrowest limits," must have had some productive function or it could have been dispensed with entirely. Still less was he led to perceive that credit was performing a productive function of an identical nature at a much smaller social cost (i.e., at a much smaller sacrifice of other things). This was in spite of his recognition that credit will "affect prices in precisely the same way as if it were actually the coin which it represents" (ibid., p. 95).

38. Böhm-Bawerk, *Capital and Interest*.

39. Ibid., p. I.

40. Ibid., pp. 194 and 233 (my italics).

41. He admitted some fears about the "employment of this physical conception in regard to a certain limited class of material goods . . . e.g., a dwelling house, a volume of poems, or a picture . . ." But, he argued, the fact that a "house shelters and warms is nothing else than a result of the forces of gravity, cohesion, and resistance, or impenetrability, of the non-conducting quality of building materials";

and "the thoughts and feelings of the poet reproduce themselves . . . in a direct physical way, by light, colour, and form of written characters; and it is this physical part of the mediation which is the office of the book" (ibid., p. 222). He would evidently have regarded the books in a library as wholly without use except when a reader's book was brought "into the necessary relation with his eye for the image, which is continually being formed by reflection, to fall on the retina" (ibid., p. 221).

42. Ibid., p. 231. The argument which occurred to him, and should have shaken him, that "the possession of good machines might assist the maker to secure, say, a good credit, a good name, good customs," etc., he dismissed as "hairsplitting" (ibid., p. 230, footnote).

43. Ibid., p. 261.

44. F. Von Wieser, *Social Economics* (New York: Greenberg, 1927).

45. Ibid., p. 169. (For a refutation of this view, see below, pp. 219-21.)

46. E.g., ". . . in order to cover the same marginal use, more or less money has to be expended" (ibid., p. 263). "The theory of the value of money must start from the service of money, just as that of the value of wares starts from their serviceability" (ibid., p. 265). ". . . The need of money is nearly akin to the need of commodities. In the monetary economy, everyone meets his personal need of goods by first covering the need of money. The latter, like the former, is also influenced in the final analysis by the magnitude of the needs and the law of satiety" (ibid., p. 285).

47. Ibid., pp. 294-9.

48. The omission of references to important writers on money like Jevons, Menger, and Irving Fisher is due to their having followed the tradition I am criticizing without having contributed any new slant on the point at issue. ·

49. Wicksell, *Lectures.*

50. Ibid., p. 190.

51. Ibid., p. 15 (my italics).

52. Wicksell seems to have had some misgivings on this point. He wrote: "Now this is also true of a merchant's goods." He says, however, that it is then "a question of *continued production* . . . or . . . an intermediate link in the process" (ibid., p. 15). But are not a merchant's stocks of money just as much a link in the productive process?

53. Ibid., p. 21.

54. Never quite happy on the subject, Wicksell argued also (a) that money assets are different from other assets because they always remain in the market, "though in different hands"; and (b) that "money itself has no marginal utility, since it is not intended for consumption" (ibid., pp. 19-20). Yet are money assets any different in this respect from other durable assets? They do not come into the market unless we put them in. And no durable goods have marginal utility "in themselves," unless they are consumed or "used up" in production. Only the services which they render

have marginal utility. He contended also that, whilst the supply of real capital is limited by physical conditions, "the supply of money is in theory unlimited" (*Interest and Prices*, p. 26). Here he obviously meant "money units."

55. A. Marshall, *Money, Credit and Commerce* (London: Macmillan and Co., 1923).

56. Ibid., p. 44 (my italics). Why did Marshall use the word "direct?" I feel that he was almost on the point of recognizing explicitly the "indirect" yield (pecuniary or non-pecuniary) from money assets. He may have meant "or other *direct* benefit."

57. Ibid., p. 49.

58. Ibid., p. 45 (my italics).

59. E. Cannan, *Modern Currency and the Regulation of Its Value*, p. 11. It is interesting to notice that Keynes *contrasted* houses and money (*The General Theory*, pp. 226-8).

60. See T. E. Gregory, *Professor Cannon and Contemporary Monetary Theory*, p. 37, in *London Essays in Economics*.

61. E. Cannon, *Money: Its Connexion with Rising and Falling Prices* (Westminster: P. S. King and Son, Ltd., 1923).

62. Had he consistently thought in this way, however, he would have made the point referred to in his passage quoted in my footnote 71 much more effectively.

63. E. Cannon, *Modern Currency*, p. 12 (my italics). It is interesting to compare Marshall's phrase "no direct income" with Cannan's "not directly productive." The word "direct" is not very helpful.

64. Cannan et al., "Who Said 'Barren Metal?'," p. 108 (my italics).

65. P. Wicksteed, *The Common Sense of Political Economy* (London: Routledge and Kegan Paul, 1948-1949).

66. Because I insist upon the continuity of services or yield from money assets, this does not mean that I deny the truism that such assets are demanded in order to be "exchanged for something else" *at the appropriate moment, i.e., when the services rendered have fully fulfilled their purpose.* But one eminent economist who read the typescript of this article assumed that I was denying this!

67. G. Cassel, *Theory of Social Economy*, Vol. 2, p. 350 (my italics).

68. Ibid., p. 351.

69. D. Robertson, *Money* (New York: Harcourt, Brace and Co., 1922), p. 31.

70. Pigou, *The Veil of Money* (London: Macmillan, 1962). The pertinent data are all on pp. 24-27.

71. Greidanus (in his tract, *The Development of Keynes' Economic Theories*, p. 36), has distinguished between the "nominal amount of money" and "the quantity of money in terms of goods," for which I would use the terms "the number of money units" and "the amount of money in real terms." In his earlier work, *The Value of Money*, p. 162, his exposition was less effective because he had not made this distinction clearly enough.

The germ of the distinction is also present in Cannan's article "The Application of the Theoretical Apparatus of Supply and Demand to Units of Currency," *Economic Journal* 31 (December 1921), pp. 453-61, in which he explained that the demand for money can only be said appropriately to have "increased" when more units *of the same value* would be demanded. At a lower value per unit there would have been, in my own terminology, a demand for the same amount of "money in real terms" (measurable only in abstract units of constant value but for more "actual money units," such units having been "diluted").

72. I feel that if Pigou had conceived of the total value of assets demanded for and used for monetary purposes being measured in "real terms," he would have stressed the term *instrument* rather than the term *institution* as a description of the aggregate collection of money assets. His comparison of this "institution" with the laws of property and contract does not seem to me to be appropriate or helpful.

73. Pigou, *The Veil of Money*, p. 25. (Compare Marshall, *Money, Credit and Commerce*, p. 38; Robertson, *Money*, p. 10.)

74. See below, pp. 219-21.

75. The term *liquidity* had not, I think, previously been used in the sense which Keynes gave it. It had been employed mainly in connection with the special case of the reserves of banks, insurance societies, etc. Discussing banks, Cassel defined "the *liquidity* of the assets as the ratio of the sum of the advances which falls due for repayment daily to the sum of the advances made." *Theory of Social Economy*, Vol. 2, pp. 403-4.

76. Keynes, *The General Theory*, p. 226.

77. Keynes' equation (*The General Theory*, top of p. 228) to illustrate the fact that, in equilibrium, "wealth owners" will have "nothing to choose in the way of advantage" between the holding or acquisition of houses, wheat and money, would, if it had stood alone, have given the impression that he was about to say: "The *liquidity premium* is, of course, simply another name for 'yield,' when we describe the services of money." But, in fact, he stressed the opposite, in deliberately *contrasting* the yield from a house with the *absence* of a yield from money.

78. In his *Tract on Monetary Reform* (pp. 78-9), Keynes quoted some of the very passages from Marshall which I have quoted above.

79. T. Greidanus, *The Development of Keynes' Economic Theories*, pp. 2-7.

80. Ibid., p. 6.

81. Marshall certainly failed to realize clearly enough that money assets, in providing "advantages" or "benefits," were as productive as all other instrumental capital or all durable consumers' goods. Like several writers before him and after him, he appears to have come very near to perceiving this truth, but for reasons which I find puzzling, he never managed to make the final jump.

82. L. Tarshis, "A Consideration of the Economic and Monetary Theories of J. M. Keynes," *American Economic Review* 38 (May 1948), pp. 261-71.

83. Mises, *Theory of Money and Credit*, p. 85; *Human Action*, p. 415.
84. Mises, *Theory of Money and Credit*, p. 79.
85. Mises, *Human Action*, p. 398.
86. Mises, *Theory of Money and Credit*, p. 90.
87. Ibid., p. 85.
88. See above.
89. Ibid., p. 86.
90. Mises, *Human Action*, p. 418 (my italics).
91. Ibid., p. 398.
92. Mises, *Theory of Money and Credit*, p. 147 (my italics).
93. Mises, *Human Action*, p. 399.
94. Ibid., pp. 414-5 (my italics).
95. Ibid., p. 415. See also p. 396, where Mises questions the assumption of the mathematical economists that services rendered by money "consist wholly or essentially in its turnover, in its circulation."
96. Mises, *Human Action*, p. 399.
97. Ibid., p. 400.
98. H. Ellis, *German Monetary Theory* (Cambridge, Mass.: Harvard University Press, 1937), p. 109.
99. Ibid., p. 109 (footnote).
100. Ibid., p. 109.
101. Ibid., p. 110.
102. Ellis uses another argument to justify the separate classification of money assets. He argues that "individuals hold money *only because* it has exchange value, whereas they would desire shoes even if shoes were free goods" (ibid., p. 113). But the point at issue is the similarity of money *assets* and non-money *assets*. Free goods would not be assets; and only assets can be used as media of exchange.
103. Greidanus, *The Value of Money*.
104. See my *Theory of Idle Resources* (London: Jonathan Cape, 1939), pp. 57-70, for the definition of *pseudo-idleness*, and pp. 146-173 for the definition of *withheld capacity*.
105. I use the word "normally" here because these stocks may represent not *pseudo-idleness* but *withheld capacity*, i.e., goods which are being withheld, not speculatively, but with a view to maintaining or forcing up prices.
106. This passage must not be taken to imply that I regard the speculative holding of money as part of a state of affairs which society can passively accept. My point is simply that such money cannot be described as "wastefully idle."
107. Cannan made this point in a reference to the "disastrous confusions" which can arise through the "common mistake" of dividing currency into that which is "actually circulating" and that which is "idle" (*Modern Currency*, p. 8). The demand for houses, he said, does not depend upon the number of transactions in

them, but comes from "those who want to *hold* houses: even the speculator wants to hold for a time" (*Money*, 4th ed., p. 72).

108. D. Robertson, *Money*, p. 37.

109. No diseconomy would necessarily be involved. There might be less work for other productive factors.

110. Cannan made this point in his *Money* (4th ed., p. 23). He said that "what every one wants the money for . . . is to buy commodities and services in the hopes of making a profit because 'things are going up'."

111. An eminent Keynesian economist who read the typescript of this article wrote: "You contrast the view that money has utility on its own account by performing a definite service with the view that money is valued only by reference to what it will buy. You take these views to be contradictory to one another and criticize some authors for holding both views simultaneously. You seem to feel that an author who recognizes the inherent serviceability of money ought to shake off this other view that money is wanted for what it would get. I suggest, on the contrary, there is nothing mutually contradictory about these two views . . . Thus, the two theories are not mutually exclusive but support each other." I ought to make it clear that I do not regard the truism (it is hardly a "theory") that "money is wanted for what it would get" as conflicting in any way with the theory that money assets are productive. Hence I do not criticize any authors for holding "both views simultaneously" but for denying the productiveness of money assets, which they usually do in simple, unambiguous language.

112. It is unnecessary to discuss here the qualifications which this assertion requires when the value of the money unit is rising or falling.

113. On the determinants of this real value, see my article "The Notion of the Value of Money."

Summary
and
Conclusions

What emerges most clearly from Professor Hutt's essays is his great concern with individual liberty and material welfare, and with the menace which the encroaching power of the federal government in alliance with Keynesian economics poses to both. The rapid growth of special interest legislation thwarts the operation of the price system and attenuates private property rights by income transfers from the productive to the nonproductive sector of the economy. As such this legislation threatens both freedom and living standards.

Although economic growth has effected little change in America's income inequality, it has clearly raised the living standards of all income groups—the poor at least as much as the rich in percentage terms. Two fundamental ways to eliminate poverty are to depend upon the long-run forces of economic growth and the short-run forces of income redistribution. Under income redistribution, the living standards of the poor can only be raised once-and-for-all. *Future* low-income groups will have to rely on economic growth. Income redistribution, in other words, is a zero-sum game. Hutt would like us to stop concentrating so much of our national energies on dividing up the pie and focus more on political and economic reforms which would increase its size. He concludes that our political and economic policies increasingly stymie economic growth, holding us within our "production possibilities boundaries." These same policies also keep us from achieving our "freedom possibilities frontier." Change certain political and economic policies, says Hutt, and you can achieve higher living standards as well as more individual freedom. Above all, Professor Hutt is a reformer whose concern is with the normative economic problems that affect us all.

Professor Hutt views the government as a group of people who can only partly be disciplined by the ballot box. They should be (but are not) disciplined by a constitution which prohibits the making of any laws that favor specific groups. The state should never utilize its power to achieve differential advantages through discriminatory taxing and expenditures according to race, sex, income, wealth, occupation, and so forth. Hutt favors a constitutional amendment that would outlaw all forms of special interest legislation except for aid to the poor and disabled. Constitutional restraints are needed to ensure that one group does not use the government as a vehicle to coerce another (except in the defense of the freedom of others). He sees a defect in collective decision-making that biases public versus private spending decisions in favor of the public sector. Public provision of goods such as health care may be voted for because a substantial number of lower and middle income voters believe that the rich can be stuck with the bill. Hence, even though they may believe that total costs under government provision would exceed the total costs under private provision, they will favor the public provision. This happens because through the political arena they can achieve a tax price which is less than the market price they would have to pay for equivalent goods in the private sector. Such behavior is always inefficient and wasteful of scarce resources. Hutt believes that it is also immoral.

Liberty is fostered, says Hutt, when governments are permitted to act solely for the *collective* benefit. The government should confine itself to national defense, police, and justice, and to the making and applying of a framework of nondiscriminatory rules under which market-disciplined entrepreneurs can plan and coordinate the economy. The concept of consumer sovereignity—a term which Professor Hutt believes he coined[1]—is the key to the application of restraints imposed through the market place. Consumer sovereignity is simply the power to choose to buy or not to buy at the prices asked. Only two forms of power are legitimate: democratic government power and free market power.

Professor Hutt stresses that civil rights inequalities are based mainly on man-made barriers to equality of opportunity. Minimum wage legislation denies low-productivity workers the opportunity to receive on-the-job training through the acceptance of initially low wage rates. Minimum wage floors thus diminish opportunities to improve productivity and thereby to eventually enhance worker employment opportunities. Similarly, Hutt criticizes the standard rate for the job (e.g., all carpenters on a job draw the same pay) because it prevents the hiring of low-skilled workers on jobs. He favors differential pay scales for the same kind of work based on differential abilities. In effect, the common practice of standard rates for the job acts as a minimum wage law that denies the low-productivity persons an opportunity for human capital development. Exclusionary practices by unions which deny blacks the opportunity to compete and to acquire apprenticeship training should also be prevented. Such reforms as these would be opposed by organized labor and by politicians who benefit from current racial troubles.

Under classic liberalism, says Hutt, the state has the duty to suppress all forms of coercive power. Price fixing, production restrictions, and strikes should be prohibited. His political platform, which he does not believe is politically impossible, would outlaw all private economic coercion and would require that all legislation and all private contracts be declared null and void if they could be shown to be discriminatory. For example, race discrimination in the Republic of South Africa has been perpetuated by state power and trade union collusion designed to preserve the status quo. The result has been to effectively stymie the growth of economic opportunity. (Since four-fifths of South Africa is black, Hutt thinks that only a weighted vote franchise would be acceptable to the whites who now wield the political and economic power.) For years, Hutt, with his characteristic emphasis on individual liberty, has been suggesting solutions to the racial problems of his homeland. For these attempts Hutt has been treated as a *persona non grata* by the government of South Africa.

Hutt believes that the immediate outcome of the one-man-one-vote system would be in the best interest of neither the blacks nor the whites. He feels that voting requirements besides age are not discriminatory *if* there is genuine opportunity to acquire such qualifications or *if* steps are being taken to create opportunities for equality. Hutt feels that the long-run interest of the country will be best served by limiting the voting franchise to persons who have attained some well-defined educational qualifications. Hutt would also deny the right to vote to anyone who is receiving public assistance, on the grounds that adults living on charity should not be in a position to vote in favor of extending benefits to themselves. At one point, Hutt raises the question of whether public employees should have the vote! He believes that the most vital nondiscriminatory principle for a democratic society is that majorities should have no power to enrich themselves through government at the expense of minorities.

II

It may be that Professor Hutt's role as a leading critic of Keynesian economics will be his most enduring achievement. His book *Keynesianism—Retrospect and Prospect* is a penetrating critique of much of present-day macroeconomic theory and policy. Hutt sees Keynesian economics as a major cause of two related problems: growing central government power and chronic inflation. He has steadfastly refused to follow Keynesian-type models, concepts, and jargon, even when they came to dominate the exposition of most non-Keynesians.

Only a few weeks after publication of Keynes' *General Theory*, Hutt wrote that Keynes' *magnum opus* may, through its "alluring and politically easy suggestions. . . prove to be the source of the most serious single blow that the authority of orthodox economics has yet suffered." Since that time, Hutt has continued to hold that his words of 1936, "politically easy," explain why governments are finding that they have (in Hayek's phrase) "a tiger by the tail"—their dilemma of inflation or unemployment. The phenomena of recession and depression are caused, Hutt has maintained throughout, neither by deficiencies of "demand" nor by defective monetary policy, but rather by defects in the pricing of inputs and outputs, though *unanticipated* inflation can certainly crudely mitigate the latter defects.

Professor Hutt believes that Keynes' *General Theory of Employment, Interest, and Money*, published in 1936, was a step backward for the economics profession, and probably for mankind. Keynes obfuscated more issues than he clarified, though much of what is good in Keynes' famous book was overlooked by English and American Keynesians who emphasized the liquidity trap and the inability of money wage cuts to result in real wage cuts. The demonstration of "underemployment equilibrium" was thus venerated as the great analytical achievement of Keynes. The thesis of "under-consumption" a la Alvin Hansen became the popular explanation of recession and depression. At full employment, saving exceeded business investment, so the government must "fill the gap" by deficit spending. Fiscal policy, often considered without reference to the money supply, became the *sine qua non* of macroeconomic stabilization policy. The economics textbooks filled up with Keynesian diagonal cross diagrams, and students were told that increases in government spending were the sure path out of recessions. While this policy might be useful as a prescription for *massive* unemployment, such as existed in the 1930s, it has been of little use in the period since World War II. During the past thirty years, mild and short recessions have been the order of the day, and attempts to stabilize aggregate demand through fiscal policy have not been very successful. In the first place, government deficit spending involves increased government borrowing which apparently crowds out an approximately equivalent amount of private spending, leaving aggregate demand unchanged. The principal net effect may simply be an increase in the size of the public sector relative to the private sector of the economy. If the deficit is financed by printing money (as when the Federal Reserve System cooperates by making open market purchases), the deficit can be very expansionary. Wealth and portfolio substitution effects stemming from an increased rate of monetary expansion reinforce the government deficit spending. When deficits are financed by money creation, little crowding out of private spending occurs because interest rates are not forced up by government borrowing. The long inside lags in fiscal policy due to the time-consuming political deliberations which are needed to cut taxes or implement new spending programs make fiscal policy a clumsy tool of economic stabilization. Keynesian economics has led to an overemphasis on problems originating on the demand side of the economy to the severe neglect of the supply, or cost, side of the economy.

Professor Hutt points out that unemployment occurs because, in some industries, money wage rates chronically grow faster than productivity. This situation results in higher unit costs—real wage rates go up—and firms cut back along their labor demand curves and reduce the quantity of man-hours hired. When the added cost of hiring labor exceeds the added value produced by labor, i.e., when the money wage rate exceeds the value of the marginal product, worker layoffs result. The basic problem is that real wage rates are above the *equilibrium* real wage rates—where the labor demand and supply curves intersect. Since the money wage rate is rigid downward due to collective bargaining agreements, it is impossible for the real wage rate to decline in the short run unless prices are raised. Firms attempt to pass the higher labor costs per unit of output through to buyers of their output, but the higher prices have the effect of reducing the quantity demanded. At the higher prices, buyers purchase less; firms need less labor, so the layoffs persist.

At this point, says Hutt, Keynesian demand management policies (largely deficit spending) come to the rescue. Deficit spending financed by money creation expands demand for most products, including the products of those firms and industries suffering unemployment. The increased money supply permits firms to mark up their prices *and still not lose sales*. In those industries where unemployment exists (as well as in other industries), product demand curves are shifted rightward, i.e., increased. In this way, the government eliminates or avoids the union-caused unemployment by expanding total demand and causing inflation which reduces above-equilibrium real wage rates. The upshot is that money wage rates have risen but so have prices. Hence, in the aggregate, real wages are only higher by the amount of the productivity increase. What we have is simply a wage-price spiral situation in which, due to political pressures, the government acts to validate excessive wage hikes by expanding aggregate demand. This cost-push inflation model has three necessary ingredients: union power to force up wages in excess of productivity; business power to mark up selling prices over costs; and government power to rescue the economy from unemployment by inflating the economy. In other words, says Hutt, price and wage relationships in *particular* industries are coordinated by the crude means of a *general* inflation.

Inflation gives short-lived employment creating effects, short-run Phillips curve tradeoffs, provided that the inflation is unanticipated. Hutt believes that, to a degree, inflations are unanticipated, but he has long realized that a policy of striving for short-run Phillips tradeoffs between inflation and unemployment could ultimately result in an accelerated inflation. In the long run, the unemployment rate cannot be reduced by a willingness to accept a higher inflation rate.

Hutt would experiment with deliberate price and wage cuts to cure unemployment in particular industries, e.g., the auto industry. He would prefer, however, to achieve competitive conditions in labor markets which would prevent labor monopolies from forcing up wages faster than productivity. Legislation which applies anti-trust laws to unions would make industry-wide bargaining illegal. Rigorous enforcement of existing laws against union intimidation and violence would also be needed. Hutt's rule of justice is that all man-made scarcities are wrong and reflect extortion. Strikes should be prevented because they involve settling disputes through "might is right," which is not conducive to equity and justice. Only free market determined prices have the ethical attribute of a "just" price, according to Hutt. The government should foster competitive resource and product markets by outlawing all forms of labor and product monopolies. If the courts are able and willing to halt coercion by enforcing laws against anti-competitive behavior, then all justification for private use of coercive power is eliminated. One wonders what would be the meaning of collective bargaining when the strike threat was absent. However, Hutt would give unions the power to initiate legal proceedings against any collusive behavior by management which may have monopsonistic effects on prospective wage rates.

III

Professor Hutt is a reformer who recommends the establishment of an economy which clearly resembles the textbook model of pure competition. In this model, no seller or buyer sets his own price—prices are determined in the larger market place with each buyer and seller exercising no power to influence price and output. This applies to products as well as to resources, e.g., labor services. Vigorous enforcement of anti-trust laws against monopoly in business and the passage of anti-trust laws applicable to labor monopolies would be required. Where scale economies make produce monopolies inevitable, e.g., utilities, regulation would be required. He speculates that to have a more competitive economy it may be necessary to reduce the costs of acquiring information by forcing private businesses to open their books to the public. Information about profitable opportunities needs to be as plentiful as possible. The concealment of profit opportunities for individual gain is anti-competitive and socially wasteful. He is concerned, however, that if we have perfect dissemination of private knowledge, the incentive for risk-bearing would be erased. As it is now, entrepreneurs obtain rewards by concealing, for a while at least, profit opportunities. By so doing, they gain enough remuneration to compensate them with a competitive rate of return on investment. If this system were changed to eliminate the concealment of profitable opportunities, it may be necessary for the state to pay entrepreneurs for adding to knowledge which immediately becomes available to all. This seems like an outlandish scheme, but it indicates Hutt's great concern with the problem of trying to invent competitive institutions to reform an economy distorted by high information costs and monopoly power.

His efforts to defend pure competition from attack led him in the early 1930s to challenge Joan Robinson's claim that under pure competition consumer preferences are not maximized. She had said that uniform prices over quantity under pure competition preclude the ideally discriminatory pricing that is necessary to ensure that small output goods are produced. Since all goods must have falling average unit costs over small output ranges, under a system of uniform prices some small output goods will not be produced. She believed there would be many instances where small output goods or services do not appear under pure competition because they cannot be priced at levels which cover average costs. However, under an ideally discriminatory monopoly they could be priced and made available so as to achieve an ideal distribution of social resources. In opposition, Hutt argued that market-determined prices do not result in consumer preferences being frustrated but are really an exercise of consumer preferences for cheapness. A low price is preferred to the special qualities of the small output substitute that is not supplied. The firm supplying the larger output under competition is the preferred substitute which makes the small output case irrelevant. Besides, says Hutt, discriminatory pricing would result in compulsory subordination of individuals to the social will.

Professor Hutt's piece on aggressive selling was motivated by the ill-conceived price fixing schemes of the National Recovery Act during the 1930s. Although he looked on oligopoly with disapproval, he pointed out that actual prices charged are both theoretically and in practice below those charged by a collusive oligopoly acting as a monopoly. His argument was that limit-pricing practices are resorted to in order to keep out potential competition. Hutt's refusal to use mathematics and geometry to add rigor to this analysis may have prevented him from garnering more credit for this early treatment of the theory of oligopoly. In particular, he seems to have anticipated some of the ''price-chiseling'' models of oligopoly behavior which others subsequently developed.

In the final essay included in this volume, Hutt provides a masterful, concise survey of the history of economic thought pertaining to money. His early idea that money is a factor of production to firms and a consumer capital good (yielding a nonpecuniary convenience yield) is insightful and ahead of the times. Hutt is also generous in his tribute to Tjardus Greidanus, a Dutch banker who has yet to receive the recognition he deserves from monetary theorists. The yield theory of the value of money espoused by Greidanus and Hutt deserves more attention than it has received. This seems especially true given that their work predates the famous "The Quantity Theory of Money—A Restatement," by Milton Friedman, in which he developed money demand in terms of a portfolio choice model that emphasized the importance of equating marginal yields among assets. The line of reasoning here is as follows:

People adjust their real cash balances so that the marginal subjective yield on those balances is equal to the going rate of return on other assets—the rate of interest, for example. If people do in fact adjust their real cash balances so that the marginal subjective yield is equated with the rate of return on assets in general, then there is a determinate theory of what the price level ought to be. Tjardus Greidanus and Hutt have pointed out that under such circumstances the purchasing power of the money unit must, in equilibrium, be such that the real quantity of money will have a precise size such that the marginal yield is equal to the rate of interest—using this last as a proxy for the rate of return on assets in general. In other words, the price level has to be such that given the nominal quantity of money in existence it will equate the marginal yield from money held to the marginal return on other assets in general. If there is an equilibrium real quantity of money, it is a matter of arithmetic as to what size the purchasing power of the money unit will be.

The yield theory of the value of money approach provides a convenient means for stating certain Keynesian conditions in quantity theory conditions. For example, in Keynesian terminology if new inventions increase the yield on capital goods, then the marginal efficiency of capital increases, the multiplier process magnifies the increase in investment, and income will rise. In terms of the yield theory, the increased yield on capital goods will raise the target yield to which the marginal yield on real cash balances is equated. The result will be that people will want to reduce their real cash balances by spending more on capital goods, and income will rise.

In another case, suppose that inflation has pushed the nominal interest rate to 12 percent, with the real interest rate being 6 percent and the excess being due to inflation. Now people must hold real cash balances sufficiently low to match the target yield of 12 percent—not the 6 percent real rate of interest. Cash balances will be pared down enough to provide a marginal subjective yield on those balances high enough to match the nominal rate of return. This is, of course, what appears to happen during an inflation expected to continue. Again, suppose that there is a rise in real cash balances caused by an increase in the nominal quantity of money. Now the subjective yield on cash balances falls below the yield on other assets in general. Real cash balances are reduced in order to raise their subjective yield. Prices will rise until the two yields are again equated.

The yield theory of the value of money leads to an undercutting of the Keynesian liquidity preference theory of interest. Now there is no given liquidity yield on money which pulls the interest rate into line. The liquidity yield is *itself* pulled into line at the margin with the rate of interest. Under these circumstances, one cannot explain the objective yield of the interest rate by the subjective yield on money. This important point was inititally made by W. H. Hutt in the essay included in this volume. One apparent weakness in the yield theory of the value of money is the assumption that money is the asset whose yield gets passively pulled into line with the interest rate (determined by wants, resources, and technology). Perhaps the amount of cash balances plays in principle the same role as the amount of any other asset in the economy. It may well be that tastes for cash balances count among the real factors which help determine the marginal rate of return on all assets. Thus if people's tastes change, the rate of interest could be affected.

IV

Those readers who would like to read more of W. H. Hutt's works should consult the bibliography that follows. In particular, the reader might want to examine his books, for a brief volume like this one can only sample his writings and cannot dwell on any topic in depth. A glance at the bibliography shows that Hutt has been a prolific writer—and he is still going strong at age 75! Few people have worked harder and longer for a cause they believed in than has Professor Hutt. The cause of individual freedom and the highest possible material welfare for all people are what he has been writing about for so many years. His scholarly production, we hope, will some day be recognized by economists and laymen as a valuable contribution to political economy.

Notes

1. William H. Hutt, "Economic Method and the Concept of Competition," *South African Journal of Economics* 2 (March 1934), p. 14.

Bibliography of William H. Hutt's Writings

Books

The Theory of Collective Bargaining (London: Staples, 1930).
Economists and the Public (London: Jonathan Cape, 1936).
The Theory of Idle Resources (London: Jonathan Cape, 1939).
Plan for Reconstruction (London: Kegan Paul, 1943).
Keynesianism—Retrospect & Prospect (Chicago: Regnery, 1963).
The Conditions for Economic Growth (Bombay: Forum of Free Enterprise, 1964).
The Economics of the Colour Bar (London: Deuthsch, 1964).
Neo-Keynesianism and Academic Freedom (Tokyo: Yoyo Keizai, 1966).
Politically Impossible . . . ? (London: Institute of Economic Affairs, 1971).
The Strike-Threat System (Arlington, Va.: Arlington House, 1973).
A Rehabilitation of Say's Law (Athens: Ohio University Press, 1975).

Articles

1. "The Factory System of the Early Nineteenth Century," *Economica* 6 (March 1926), pp. 78-93.
2. "Economic Aspects of the Report of the Poor White Commission," *South African Journal of Economics* 1 (September 1933), pp. 281-90.
3. "The Significance of State Interference With Interest Rates," *South African Journal of Economics* 1 (September 1933), pp. 365-68.
4. "Economic Method and the Concept of Competition," *South African Journal of Economics* 2 (March 1934), pp. 1-23.
5. "Co-ordination and the Size of the Firm," *South African Journal of Economics* 2 (December 1934), pp. 383-402.
6. "The Nature of Aggressive Selling," *Economica* 2 (August 1935), pp. 298-320.

241

7. "Logical Issues in the Study of Industrial Legislation," *South African Journal of Economics* 3 (March 1935), pp. 26-42.

8. "Natural and Contrived Scarcities," *South African Journal of Economics* 3 (September 1935), pp. 345-53.

9. "Discriminating Monopoly and the Consumer," *Economic Journal* 46 (March 1936), pp. 61-79.

10. "The Price Mechanism and Economic Immobility," *South African Journal of Economics* 4 (September 1936), pp. 319-30.

11. "Economic Aspects of the Report of the Cape Coloured Commission," *South African Journal of Economics* 6 (June 1938), pp. 117-33.

12. "Pressure Groups and Laissez-Faire," *South African Journal of Economics* 6 (March 1938), pp. 1-23.

13. "Privacy and Private Enterprise," *South African Journal of Economics* 7 (December 1939), pp. 375-88.

14. "Economic Lessons of the Allied Effort," *South African Journal of Economics* 8 (September 1940), pp. 205-13.

15. "The Concept of Consumers' Sovereignty," *Economic Journal* 50 (March 1940), pp. 66-77.

16. "The Economics of Democratic Socialism," *Economica* 7 (November 1940), pp. 419-34.

17. "War Demand, Entrepreneurship and the Distributive Problem," *Economica* 8 (November 1941), pp. 341-60.

18. "Distributive Justice," *South African Journal of Economics* 9 (September 1941), pp. 219-34.

19. "The Price Factor and Reconstruction" (with R. Leslie), *South African Journal of Economics* 9 (December 1941), pp. 441-44.

20. "The Sanctions for Privacy Under Private Enterprise," *Economica* 9 (August 1942), pp. 237-44.

21. "The Concept of Waste," *South African Journal of Economics* 11 (March 1943), pp. 1-10.

22. "Public Works and Reconstruction," *South African Journal of Economics* 11 (September 1943), pp. 198-209.

23. "A Critique of the First Report of the Social and Economic Planning Council," *South African Journal of Economics* 11 (March 1943), pp. 48-62.

24. "Plan for Economic Research in the Union," *South African Journal of Economics* 12 (June 1944), pp. 81-100.

25. "Full Employment and the Future of Industry," *South African Journal of Economics* 13 (September 1945), pp. 185-202.

26. "Two Studies in the Statistics of Russia," *South African Journal of Economics* 13 (March 1944), pp. 18-42.

27. "Further Aspects of Russian Statistics," *South African Journal of Economics* 13 (December 1945), pp. 344-63.

28. "The Development of the Soviet Economic System," *South African Journal of Economics* 14 (September 1946), pp. 215-19.

29. "The Yield on Money Held," in *Freedom and Free Enterprise,* ed. Sennholz, 1954.

30. *The Sterling Area: Financial Portion of the Union of South Africa*, University of London and Institute of Bankers, 1949.

31. "The Nature of Money," *South African Journal of Economics* 20 (March 1952), pp. 50-64.

32. "The Notion of the Volume of Money," *South African Journal of Economics* 20 (1952), pp. 231-41.

33. "The Notion of Money of Constant Value," *South African Journal of Economics* 21 (September 1953), pp. 215-26, and (December 1953), pp. 341-53.

34. "The Significance of Price Flexibility," *South African Journal of Economics* 22 (March 1954), pp. 727-30.

35. "New Light on Wicksell," *South African Journal of Economics* 27 (March 1959), pp. 38-42.

36. "A Question of Stereotypes," *Fortune Magazine*, 1963.

37. "The Critics of Classical Economics," *South African Journal of Economics* 32 (June 1964), pp. 81-94.

38. "Keynesian Revisions," *South African Journal of Economics* 33 (June 1965), pp. 101-13.

39. "South Africa's Salvation in Classic Liberalism," *Il Politico* 30, No. 4 (1965), pp. 782-95.

40. "Keynes: Obsolete But Influential," *Wall Street Journal* (September 1965).

41. "Unanimity Versus Non-Discrimination (as Criteria for Constitutional Validity," *South African Journal of Economics* 34 (June 1966), pp. 133-47.

42. "Twelve Thoughts on Inflation," *New Individualist Review* 3 (Winter 1967).

43. "Civil Rights and Young 'Conservatives'," *Modern Age* 10 (Summer 1966), pp. 231-38.

44. "Economic Position of the Bantu in South Africa," in *Western Civilization and the Natives of South Africa*, ed. I. Schapera (New York: Humanities Press, 1967).

45. "Misgivings and Casuistry on Strikes," *Modern Age* 12 (Fall 1968), pp. 350-60.

46. "Economics of Immigration," in *Symposium on Immigration*, ed. A. Plant (London: Institute of Economic Affairs, 1972), pp. 19-44.

47. "The Poor Who Were With Us," *Encounter* 39 (November 1972), pp. 84-90.

48. "South Africa's Solution in Classical Liberalism," in *Symposium: Essays on Economics and Economic History*, ed. M. Kouy (London: MacMillan, 1972).

INDEX